easy

Creating
CDs & DVDs

Tom Bunzel

W9-AVI-523

Contents

3 Completing Three Simple CD Projects .116

4 Starting to Capture with DVD MovieFactory 2.0 134

Easy Creating CDs & DVDs

Copyright © 2003 by Que Publishing

International Standard Book Number: 0-7897-2972-5

Library of Congress Catalog Card Number: 2003103650

Printed in the United States of America

First Printing: June 2003

06   05   04   03   4   3   2

Trademarks

All terms mentioned in this book that are known to be trademarks or service marks have been appropriately capitalized. Que Publishing cannot attest to the accuracy of this information. Use of a term in this book should not be regarded as affecting the validity of any trademark or service mark.

Warning and Disclaimer

Every effort has been made to make this book as complete and as accurate as possible, but no warranty or fitness is implied. The information provided is on an "as is" basis. The author and the publisher shall have neither liability nor responsibility to any person or entity with respect to any loss or damages arising from the information contained in this book or from the use of the CD or programs accompanying it.

Bulk Sales

Que offers excellent discounts on this book when ordered in quantity for bulk purchases or special sales. For more information, please contact:

U.S. Corporate and Government Sales
1-800-382-3419
corpsales@pearsontechgroup.com

For sales outside of the U.S., please contact:

International Sales
+1-317-581-3793
international@pearsontechgroup.com

Associate Publisher
Greg Wiegand

Acquisitions Editor
Angelina Ward

Development Editor
Kevin Howard

Managing Editor
Charlotte Clapp

Project Editor
Tonya Simpson

Copy Editor
Barbara Hacha

Indexer
Ken Johnson

Proofreader
Eileen Dennie

Technical Editor
Dallas Releford

Team Coordinator
Sharry Gregory

Multimedia Developer
Dan Scherf

Interior Designer
Anne Jones

Cover Designer
Anne Jones

Page Layout
Stacey Richwine-DeRome

Dedication

To my Mother and Father and Alan Shapero—may they have the peace they deserve.

Acknowledgments

I want to convey my appreciation to the very special friends—new and old—that I have in Los Angeles, particularly the group at Rancho Park, where I escape from technology to the tennis courts: Geoff, Darko, Mario, Gregg, Billy, Richard, Jay, Professor Bill, Attila, Mike and Ray(even though they left town), Abner, Pat, Dan, R. Pace. Without you I'd still be in therapy, or worse.

I would also be remiss if I did not acknowledge the efforts of my development editor Kevin Howard, project editor Tonya Simpson, technical editor Dallas Releford, and copy editor Barbara Hocha and the rest of the Que team. Thanks bigtime to my agent Danielle Jatlow and acquisitions editor Angelina Ward.

—Tom Bunzel

About the Author

Tom Bunzel's most recent book, *How to Use Ulead DVD Workshop*, was published by Que Publishing in 2002. He recently updated the *PowerPoint 2002/2001 Mac Visual Quickstart Guide* for Peachpit Press (2001) and also wrote *Digital Video on the PC* for Micro Publishing Press (1997). He has been contributing editor for *PC Graphics and Video*, *Laptop Buyers Guide*, *Computer Upgrade*, and *Micro Publishing News*.

He is a consultant and "technology coach" for the Neuroscience Education Institute, giving one-on-one instruction in PowerPoint to physicians. He also is an instructor for Learning Tree International, presenting courses on "Integrating Microsoft Office" and "Creating Interactive Websites—Hands On." Bunzel has lectured on PowerPoint, digital video, and business multimedia at the Teamplayers Networking Group of the Los Angeles Athletic Club, at Communicate, a multimedia facility in West L.A., and at the San Diego Computer Expo.

Tom Bunzel was one of the pioneers in digital media on the PC, creating multimedia presentations and animated video even before Windows 95. He has worked with speakers on their professional presentations, including Weatherman Gregg Ketter of KTTV-TV (Fox's L.A. affiliate), on his motivational, customer service, and sales speeches, and he trained the principals of MTA Films in Los Angeles and Todd Yamada, D.D.S., in PowerPoint and multimedia production.

Tom's Web site is http://www.professorpowerpoint.com.

Tell Us What You Think!

As the reader of this book, *you* are our most important critic and commentator. We value your opinion and want to know what we're doing right, what we could do better, what areas you'd like to see us publish in, and any other words of wisdom you're willing to pass our way.

As an associate publisher for Que, I welcome your comments. You can email or write me directly to let me know what you did or didn't like about this book—as well as what we can do to make our books better.

Please note that I cannot help you with technical problems related to the *topic* of this book. We do have a User Services group, however, where I will forward specific technical questions related to the book.

When you write, please be sure to include this book's title and author as well as your name, email address, and phone number. I will carefully review your comments and share them with the author and editors who worked on the book.

Email: feedback@quepublishing.com

Mail: Greg Wiegand
         Que Publishing
         800 E. 96th Street
         Indianapolis, IN 46240 USA

For more information about this book or another Que title, visit our Web site at www.quepublishing.com. Type the ISBN (excluding hyphens) or the title of a book in the Search field to find the page you're looking for.

1 Each step is fully illustrated to show you how it looks onscreen.

It's as Easy as 1-2-3
Each part of this book is made up of a series of short, instructional lessons, designed to help you understand basic information that you need to get the most out of your computer hardware and software.

2 Each task includes a series of quick, easy steps designed to guide you through the procedure.

3 Items that you select or click in menus, dialog boxes, tabs, and windows are shown in **bold**. Information you type is in a `special font`.

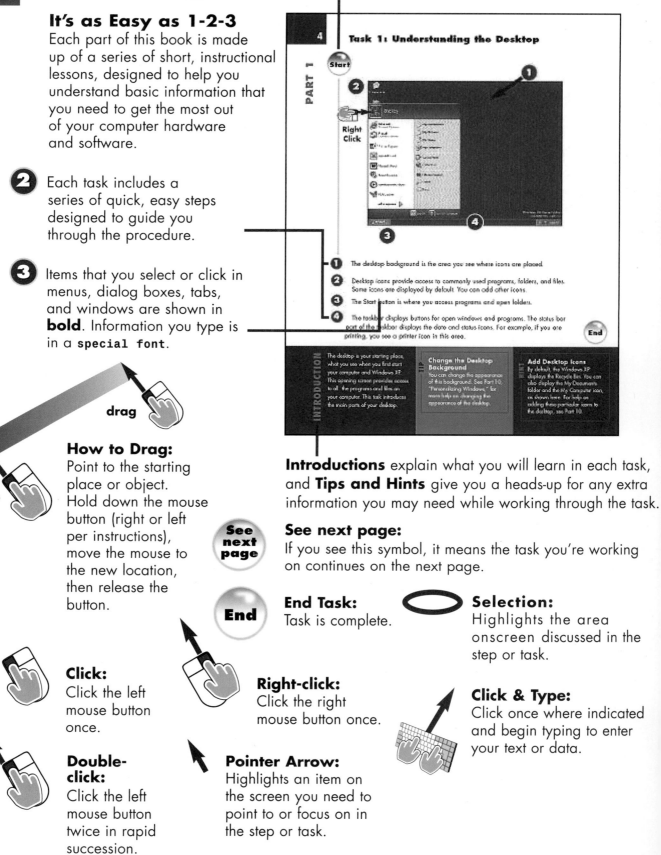

Introductions explain what you will learn in each task, and **Tips and Hints** give you a heads-up for any extra information you may need while working through the task.

How to Drag:
Point to the starting place or object. Hold down the mouse button (right or left per instructions), move the mouse to the new location, then release the button.

See next page:
If you see this symbol, it means the task you're working on continues on the next page.

End Task:
Task is complete.

Selection:
Highlights the area onscreen discussed in the step or task.

Click:
Click the left mouse button once.

Right-click:
Click the right mouse button once.

Click & Type:
Click once where indicated and begin typing to enter your text or data.

Double-click:
Click the left mouse button twice in rapid succession.

Pointer Arrow:
Highlights an item on the screen you need to point to or focus on in the step or task.

Introduction to *Easy CDs and DVDs*

You probably picked up this book in the computer department. But I bet that most of you are interested in it because you have also ventured into the consumer electronics area, looked at CD audio and stereo devices, or either rented or purchased movies on DVD. Or maybe you bought a DV camcorder or digital camera and you want to burn movies or images to CD or DVD.

The PC users among you, whether sophisticated or not, know that for things to work on a computer, they must follow many rules and principles.

Some of these concepts seem mysterious, and we like to keep things simple. We just want to point and click—like we do on a consumer electronic device such as a TV remote control or a stereo. But there's always more to it than that. For example, there are manuals for computers and then there are manuals for TVs. With a TV you connect a few wires, turn it on, and you're good to go. With a PC, you connect your keyboard, monitor, and mouse, turn it on and…wait a minute. You've just switched on the *hardware.*

Using a computer still requires a different level of knowledge and experience, which involves working with *software.*

Many of us have learned enough about PCs to write letters, surf the Web, and maybe even scan photos or do finances. But now we also know there's a lot more we can do. We know that we can *burn,* or record, a digital disc that can store most of our data, and what's more, the disc may also store music that plays on CD audio devices and movies that play on DVD!

In other words, we can escape the computer's rigid rules and regulations and sing and dance on dumb devices with simple manuals. And we also know that if we can do this, we can probably store (and safeguard) our most valuable "stuff" on the computer so that we can easily recover it if the computer happens to crash.

(Has that ever happened to you, or someone you know?)

But how do we do this magic? How do we create our own CDs and DVDs, and how do we know that they will play our music or our movies in the places we want and expect?

That's what this book is all about—making these tasks easy to follow and understand.

Although we will be going through three popular programs step by step, the concepts and projects we will cover are universal. Hopefully, you will benefit from this book whether you use the same programs, slightly different versions, or even entirely different tools to create your own CDs and DVDs.

Before we begin, we need to take matters just a bit further. I'm sure most of you "get" the difference between hardware and software, and many of you also understand some important distinctions within the world of software. What I am referring to is the difference between programs (or applications) and the files they create. (It will also help immeasurably to know where these files are stored.)

Understanding these concepts is critical to your success in doing the tasks in this book. Why?

Because the stuff that you eventually burn to an audio CD or a true DVD *is really none of these*. It is not a computer program, and it is not a "normal" file. It is simply a glob of digital goo that an audio CD player recognizes as music and that a DVD player recognizes as music or a movie. Geeks call this ISO 9660 or UDF 1.5.

But, back on your PC, where you're creating this stuff, before it's finally done, this digital material needs to adhere to very specific rules.

Just as Microsoft Word (a program) creates a very specific file (a "DOC" document file), and a Web browser reads a different kind of file (HTML), on the PC a music file (in order to play) must be either a WAV (Wave), an MP3, or perhaps a WMA (Windows Media) file. If it's a movie, it needs to be either an AVI or an MPG file— okay, or possibly a QuickTime (MOV) or *maybe* a Windows WMV (highly compressed for the Internet) file.

"Sure," you're saying, "but my PC plays audio CDs and DVD movies."

True, but when it plays them from a disc that can also be read by an audio CD or DVD player over in the stereo department, it's because the PC is really smart; but here's the thing to understand:

Your PC can't edit digital audio and DVD video in their native format because they're not files it understands—they're digital goo.

This is also true in terms of acquiring, or "capturing" digital music or video.

You've got video on a camcorder or music on a CD that you want to work with on the PC. What does it need to do? It needs to extract, capture, convert, or whatever you want to call it, that *digital goo* (be it video or audio) into the files that the PC programs understand. Again, if it's audio, that's Wave, WMA, or MP3. If it's video, that's AVI, MPG, MOV, or WMV. If it's not one of these animals, your PC will only play them, and you can't do any of the magic covered in this book.

I know, some of you smarty pants are saying, "but some video is *analog*." Then let's just call it *photographic goo*. It's still not stuff a PC understands until it's a file. In the case of audio, that's *.WAV, *.WMA, or *.MP3, for the most part, on the PC. If it's still digital audio, the PC is, for the most part, clueless about it. Until it's a file, most programs (except such things as your PC CD player or Windows Media Player) will spit it out like last week's meat loaf.

Because many of you have scanners or digital cameras, let's go back to photographic goo for a minute. When a picture is placed into a scanner, it's a piece of glossy paper that your computer has no clue about. What does the scanner do? It converts it into a file—JPG, BMP, or TIF most of the time—that you can crop and edit in a program such as Photoshop, PhotoDeluxe, Paintshop Pro 8 or PhotoImpact.

Many digital cameras are a bit smarter. They store their goo as JPGs right in the camera, the memory stick, or other media—and it can be downloaded as a file. (Some cameras already store video as MPG files, and if these movies are downloaded to the PC from these devices, you can do some simple editing.) But for the most part, we need to know that the stuff we are using on the PC—the material that the programs we cover in this book understand—has specific names and qualities.

Suppose you're a plumber, and your supplier gives you a bunch of rubber or plastic tubing to install in a house that specifically requires copper pipe. You can have all the skill and tools in the world (software), but if the products you use aren't copper pipe, they're not going to work. On the other hand, plastic or rubber tubing might be perfectly fine for moving water or air through an automobile engine or even a fire hose, but what you use in that house (or your PC) had better be copper or lead pipe.

And if you want to do really cool stuff (applications), such as take a shower or flush the toilet, you need to have the right stuff in the right file format (copper or lead). That's what learning these programs is all about.

We can take this "PC Plumber" (no, not politically correct) analogy a bit further. What else is critical to the success of the pipes you install? You need to know where stuff is located and where it belongs. You can't install the toilet in the kitchen and the dishwasher in the bathroom.

How many of you have downloaded files and forgotten where they went—or scanned images and couldn't load them into your image editing program because you didn't know where you scanned them? Well, guess what. Before you can make an audio CD or back up your critical files, you will need to know exactly what and where these files are.

Did my use of the words "back up" get your attention? It should, because maybe you lost something important once on a PC. Well these new files we're going to create will take some effort and knowledge, and after you edit a video or put together a music collection, you won't want to lose it. And the beauty of CDs and DVDs, the ones that can also play on your stereo or hi-fi system, is that they can cheaply safeguard the valuable stuff you have on your PC.

So, for those of you who don't know, let's review the key elements of what we need to understand to go on:

- We are going to use three very popular programs.

- Two of them (Roxio's CD Creator Platinum and Ahead's NERO) burn regular CD-ROMs (and even DVD) with music, data, and in some cases, video.

- We'll use Ulead's DVD MovieFactory to edit video and create a menu interface to successfully burn our own movies to a DVD disc that will play on a consumer DVD player.

Those are the tools of the PC Plumber.

NOTE: Some of these programs come bundled as "light" versions with CD-RWs, DVD recorders, and video capture hardware. We are using the full retail versions available in stores as this book is written; for the most part, many of the features and the basic interface will also resemble any bundled earlier versions of the software.

For the most part, these tools take a lot of the techie jargon out of the process. For example, instead of asking whether your DVD video needs to be NTSC or PAL (two different standards, one mainly American and the other mainly European), the programs we use will generally have you pick U.S.A. when you install, so you'll be okay. In PC Plumber terms, that means you won't be putting Belgian pipes into a house in New Rochelle.

Movies, pictures, and music will need to be in the proper format to be useful to the PC Plumber, and they may well be placed in folders called My Movies, My Music, and My Pictures—inside a larger folder called My Documents. These folders are like rooms (and closets or dressers) in a house. And in different houses (Windows 98, Windows 2000, and Windows XP) the My Documents folder might be in different rooms.

But in general, most houses share a common foundation—the main structure is called My Computer. The main room of the house, where most of the files (stuff) and programs (tools that make the stuff useful) reside, is called the C: drive.

Some houses have external spaces for moving files elsewhere—like a guest house, or a garage that holds a car or truck. On a computer, these are extra storage devices such as a floppy or a Zip drive, and they are assigned their own drive letters.

The floppy, as you might know, is known as the A: drive. The CD-ROMs or DVD-ROMs may be drives D through Z or even higher (God help you), and the removable drives, such as the Zips and the Jaz, also share these drive letters for reference, as do any additional hard drives. To see what drives you have, double-click My Computer. The drives are listed with the letters individually referencing them.

Somewhere under the C: drive is your My Documents folder. In newer PCs it is hidden in a folder called Documents and Settings, and there you can have different individual rooms for your house (like those belonging to your family), and each family member may have his or her own Internet settings and My Documents folder.

Confusing? A little. But once you get it, the rest of what we'll be doing together will be a lot easier.

Your helpful programs might decide where to put your stuff for you—and if you're not sharp enough to pay attention, this can make your task a lot harder. For example, instead of in My Movies, they might store some files in their own folders. Just be aware of these issues.

Now we can get started because we can begin to refer to and distinguish between programs, file types, and locations. You'll learn where the programs you're using store their stuff and the types of files you will create. Then, you can decide where to store your files for various projects, whether personal or business, and what types of files they should be.

And finally, you will understand what is best to burn to your CD or DVD disc so that they will restore any lost data on your PC, play wonderful music in your car, or show your wedding or vacation video to your friends and family.

Let's conclude by taking the PC Plumber analogy a step further.

Perhaps we can think of your hot water boiler as your CD-RW or DVD recordable drive. After all, it distributes water (like your data) to the various rooms in your house. Some of your programs (kitchen, bathroom) use the water in different ways and depend on its regular flow. You can also buy bottled water, and although it doesn't go into your boiler (or your toilet), in some ways that might be like buying a new CD or DVD.

When we burn a CD or DVD, we're making our own bottled water (or personal data source) using the programs we're going to learn. And when we boil the water a special way, we're burning audio CDs and DVDs that will supply us with music and movies for entertainment (a nice hot shower; a cup of coffee or tea).

Finally, when we connect to the main water source (the utility company) it's like the Internet—and we get either a strong flow or a weak flow according to our *band-width*; literally, the capacity of our pipes.

One last thing—before we begin burning CDs, let's talk about the discs themselves. CD media are generally CD-R, which means record *once*, or CD-RW, which means rewritable, so that you can record over them. You might think that the latter are preferable, but CD-R discs will play on more machines, and CD-RW discs will not play in many older audio CD players and in cars. With the incredibly low cost of this media, if you want to use your discs as widely as possible, go with CD-R media. If you mess up a disc, you've lost a quarter and gained a coaster.

So let's get started with Part 1, where we'll burn our own audio CDs for music and burn CDs for data.

Using Roxio Easy CD Creator

In this book we'll be using Easy CD Creator 5 Platinum and Nero 5—the full versions. You might have another version that came bundled with your CD-RW or DVD-recordable drive; in most cases you will be able to accomplish most, if not all, of the tasks covered here because the concepts are the same.

CD Creator begins with the Project Selector to get new users comfortable with the program and to quickly begin projects. Eventually, you can bypass it and just use the File, New project combination on the main menu to begin the task at hand.

Main Program Interface

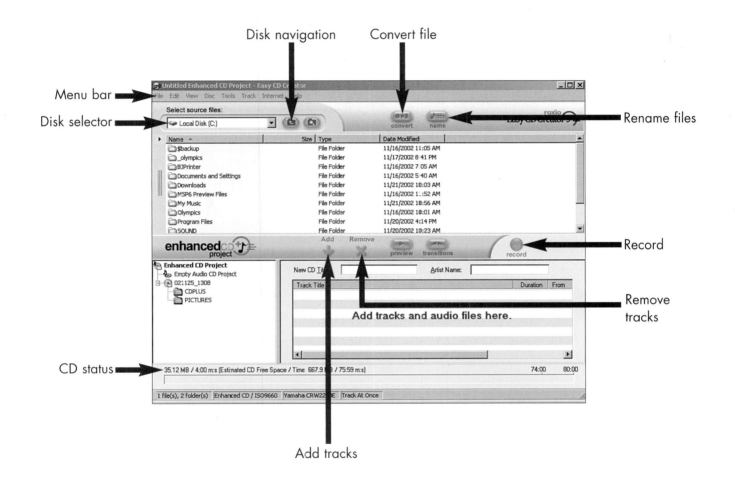

Disk navigation

Convert file

Menu bar

Disk selector

Rename files

Record

Remove tracks

CD status

Add tracks

Beginning a New Project in CD Creator

Start

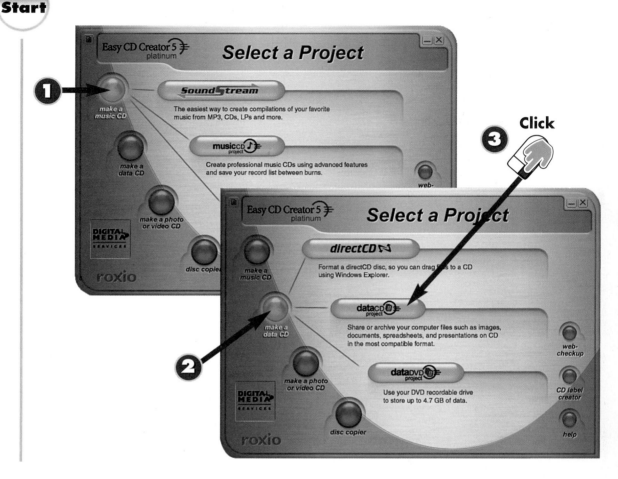

1 Open **Roxio CD Creator 5** and hover (don't click) your mouse over **Make a Music CD**. Three ways to create your own music CD pop up.

2 If you hover the mouse over the other buttons, the appropriate options appear. Hover over the **Make a Data CD** button to see three ways to create a data CD.

3 Click **Data CD Project**. (Don't worry, we'll do a music CD soon enough!)

INTRODUCTION

The easiest way to get acquainted with CD Creator for the first time is with the Project Selector. By going through it step by step, you can get a great idea of what you can accomplish, and you can get started quickly.

TIP

The DirectCD option turns your CD recorder into another disc drive to receive files that you drag and drop.

HINT

Using the Data DVD option in Roxio CD Creator might not create a "movie DVD" that will play on a standalone DVD player—or even on a computer DVD-ROM. It's used mainly to move data to the large-capacity DVD media.

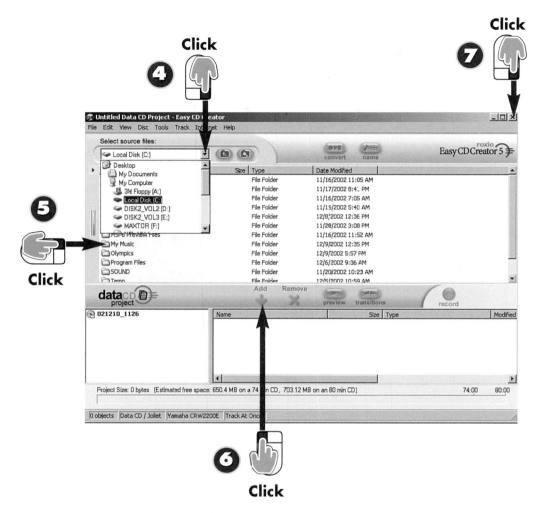

Click 4

Click 7

5 **Click**

6 **Click**

4 Take a minute to familiarize yourself with this screen; you'll see it's pretty intuitive. Click the **drop-down arrow** to see your available drives.

5 Select a folder that contains files. Select files or subfolders in the right panel. The Add button becomes active.

6 Click the **Add** button to add it to your CD project.

7 All you would have to do now to create your first CD is click the Record button, but for now, just close this window.

End

HINT Creating a data CD lets you burn your files to a disc for backup or to move them to another computer.

Creating a Data CD in CD Creator

Start

Click ①

② **Click**

Click ③

④ **Click**

① In the Project Selector, open a **Data CD Project**. The upper panel reveals the familiar Windows file structure.

② To locate your data, click the **drop-down arrow** at the top, and then "drill down" through the folders until you locate the folder with the files you want.

③ Select your folders and files.

④ Click **Add** or drag and drop the files to add them to the compilation. Repeat these steps until you're finished adding your files.

INTRODUCTION

A CD can hold much more information than a floppy disk (about 700 times more!), so they are ideal for backing up your important files. A data CD is a compilation with all kinds of folders and computer files—not just music files. Put a blank CD-R or CD-RW in your CD writer.

TIP

Although some of the data files we're burning are music files, they are being compiled and burned as *data files*.

HINT

The status bar shows how much data you will be able to fit on a CD. Keep an eye on it as you add files so you will know when you're close to your limit.

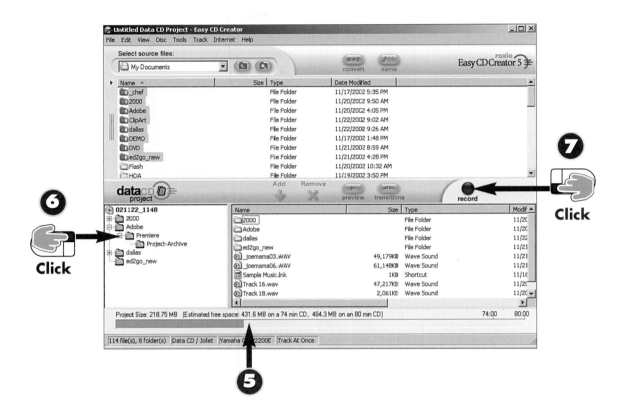

5 Look at the status bar to be sure you haven't gone over the disc capacity.

6 If you click your folders in the compilation window, you can make sure all the sub-folders and files were included.

7 Click the **Record** button to start the burn process.

End

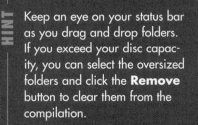
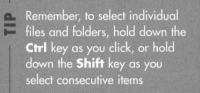

Setting Recording Options

Start

Click ①

Click ②

Click ③

Click ④

① With a compilation open, click the **Record** button.

② If you have multiple recording drives (not CD-ROM drives), pick the one you want.

③ Adjust the speed by clicking **Write Speed**.

④ Set buffer underrun, if available.

INTRODUCTION

Using the basic defaults will work most of the time, but it's good to understand your other recording options. Most of these options apply no matter what type of disc you are creating.

TIP

Although the Optimal setting in step 3 will generally work, and CD Creator will adjust down in speed automatically for disc media limitations, clicking the drop-down arrow to a lower recording speed will reduce errors.

HINT

Buffer underrun is a common feature that lets the program keep supplying data to the drive even if the hard drive hasn't quite kept up. Enable it if available.

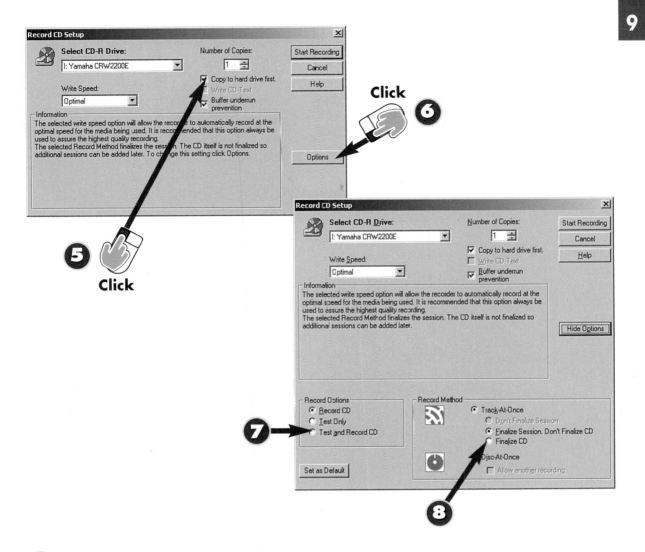

Click

5

Click

6

7

8

5 Click **Copy to Hard Drive First** to save a copy to your hard drive.

6 Click the **Options** button to open the Options panel.

7 Testing before you burn is a good way to avoid errors.

8 Finalizing the disc or closing the disc means no more data can be appended to it.

End

HINT
Saving a copy to your hard drive creates a disc image, which also reduces errors, and will enable you to make more copies later very easily. But a disc image cannot be edited in CD Creator.

Starting an Audio CD with SoundStream

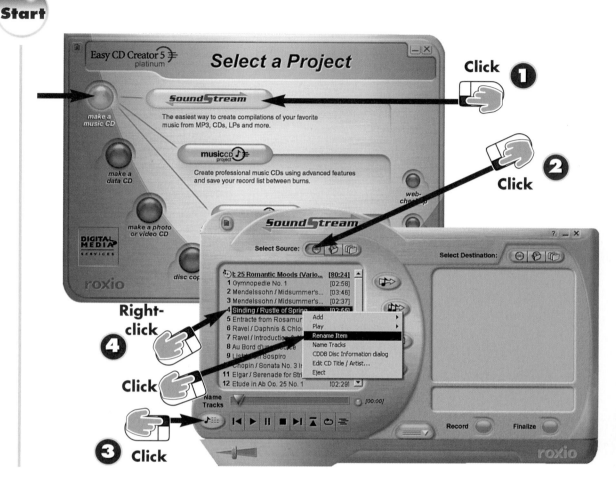

Start

1 Open the Project Selector again, hover on the **Make a Music CD** button, and select **SoundStream**.

2 Your audio tracks appear in the Source panel—or you might need to click the **CD** icon next to **Select Source**.

3 With an active Web connection, click the **Name Tracks** button, and the tracks will be named automatically from Roxio's online database!

4 You can manually rename your tracks by right-clicking each one and selecting **Rename Item**.

5 Click to select the tracks you want to include in your greatest hits collection.

6 After selecting the tracks you want, click the **Add Selected** button to move references to these tracks to the recording area. Your tracks will appear in the right panel.

7 Click the **Select Destination CD** icon.

8 Select your recording drive and click **Select**.

See next page

HINT You can always use the playback buttons at the bottom of the SoundStream program to play, rewind, and pause selected tracks; you also can drag the slider to adjust the volume.

HINT To add every track, click the Add All Tracks button.

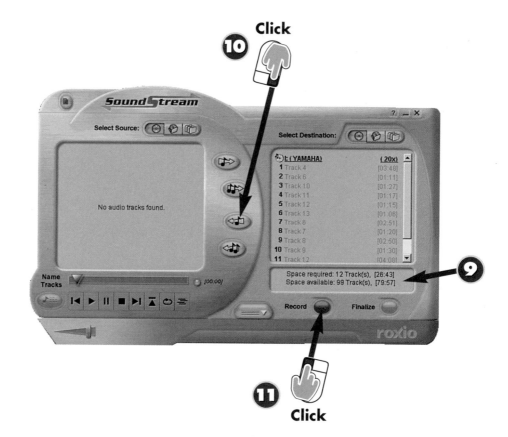

 9 Make sure you have enough available space on your disc.

10 If you don't have enough available space, you can highlight a song and click the remove button.

11 The **Record** button turns red, and you can click it to burn this disc (you will have to be ready to insert the source discs as prompted).

TIP

Windows XP will sometimes pop up and prompt you for action when you insert a new CD of any kind. Select **Take No Action** if you're in the middle of a project, and don't set any choices as the default. (Or just press the **Esc** key on your keyboard.)

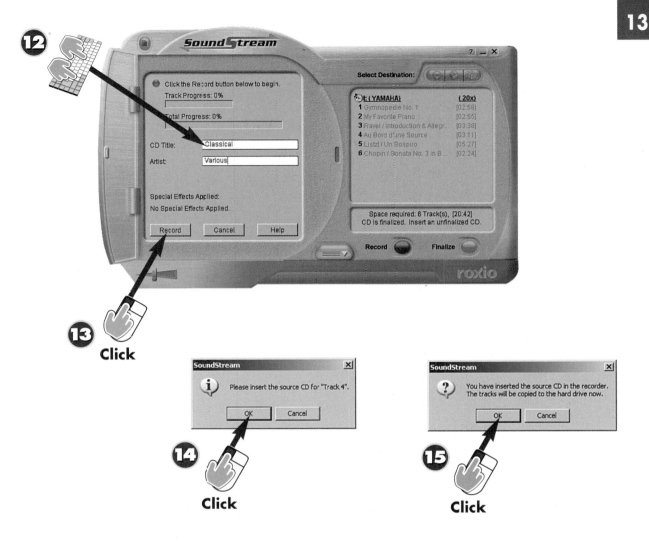

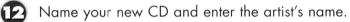

12 Name your new CD and enter the artist's name.

13 Click **Record** to begin.

14 If you don't have a second CD player, SoundStream will ask you to reinsert your first CD. Do so and click **OK**.

15 The compilation needs to be prepared. Click **OK**.

See next page

16 Click

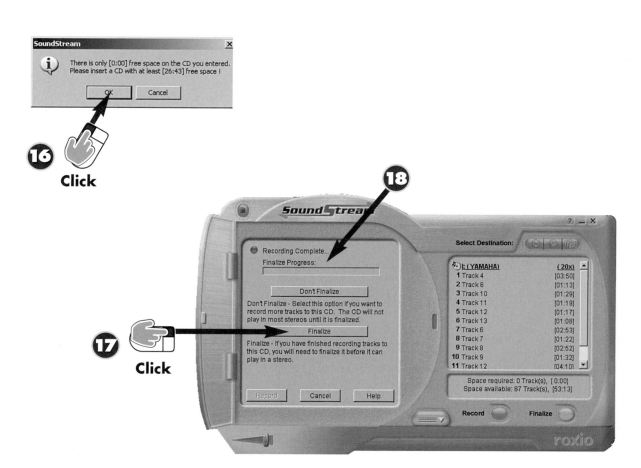

18

17 Click

The program prompts you for your blank CD. When you insert it and click **OK** to close the disc space information dialog box, a blinking red light will accompany the actual recording process.

16

17 Click **Finalize**.

18 Watch the Finalize progress bar.

End

Creating a Music Library

Start

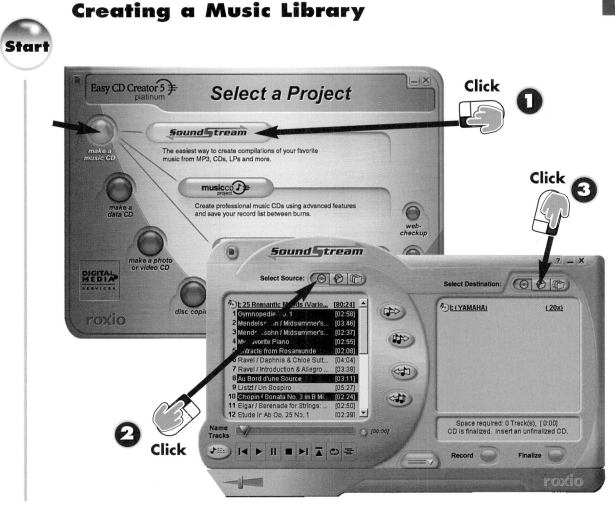

Click ❶

Click ❸

Click ❷

❶ In the Project Selector, hover your mouse over **Make a Music CD** and click **SoundStream**.

❷ Your tracks should appear in the left panel of SoundStream. If they don't, click the **CD** icon.

❸ For a destination, click the **Music Library** icon.

See next page

INTRODUCTION

What if you want to keep your tracks available to play or to burn again in different combinations, or even to play them locally directly from the hard drive? There are two ways to do this in SoundStream, each with pros and cons.

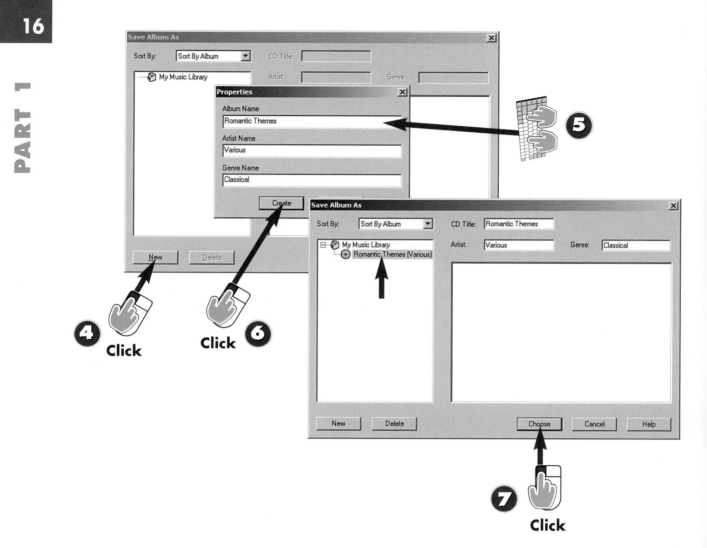

4 Click **New** to create a new album.

5 In the Properties dialog box, enter the information for your selection into **Album Name**, **Artist Name**, and **Genre Name**.

6 Click **Create**.

7 Click the newly created album so that it is highlighted, and then click **Choose**.

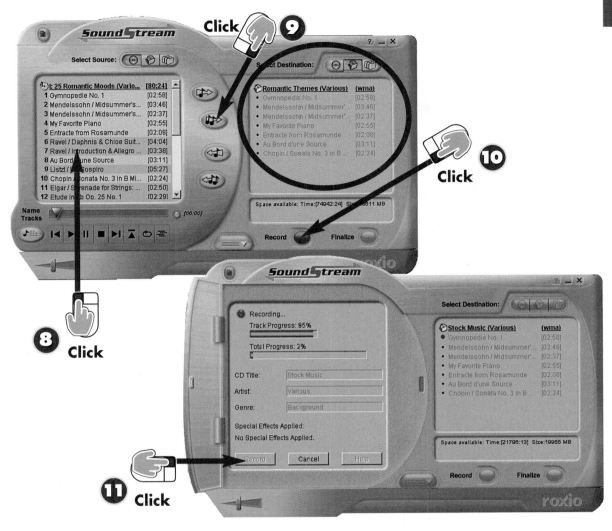

8 Your new album appears in the destination area with a Windows audio file extension—WMA. Click to select the tracks you want to add to the destination library.

9 Click **Add Selected** or **Add All**.

10 Click the red **Record** button—the Record panel, which you saw for burning a CD, opens, but you're now recording an album to your hard drive.

11 Click **Record** in the panel. When you're done, you can play your library files without the disc being in the computer!

End

HINT In SoundStream's Music Library, you can still remove or rename your tracks. Click to select the track you want to remove or rename, and then right-click it. Remove and rename options appear. To change the order of a destination track, click to select one or more tracks and drag them to a new location in your destination list.

TIP Remember to name your tracks manually, or use the online Roxio database with the **Name Tracks** button.

Making a Destination Music Folder

Start

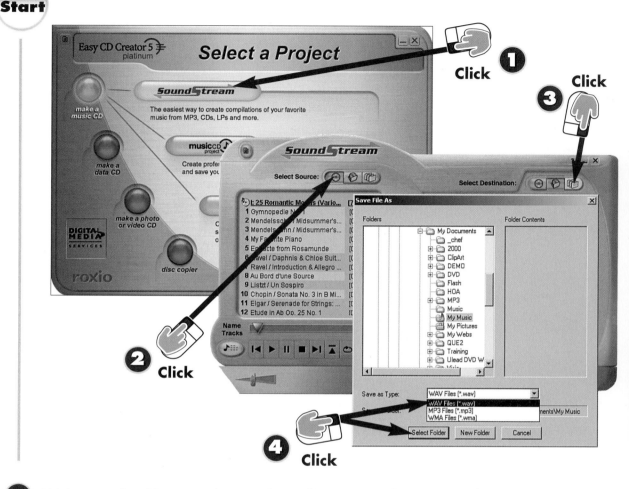

Click ❶

Click ❸

Click ❷

Click ❹

❶ With an audio CD inserted, open **SoundStream** in the Project Selector.

❷ If necessary, click the **Select Source CD** button to view your disk contents.

❸ Click the **Destination Music Folder** icon to select a destination.

❹ Select a file folder in the Destination panel to keep your files and click **Select Folder**.

INTRODUCTION

The best way to make an audio jukebox on your hard drive is to make a file folder your destination. This will make it possible to *extract* (save) digital-quality audio CD files as Windows WAV files. Saving them as WAV files will make them easier to use again later in CD Creator and in other Windows programs, such as PowerPoint, Media Player, or any application that uses audio.

TIP

Notice that the default file format is *.WAV. Leave it alone, but click the drop-down arrow to see the other choices: MP3 and WMA. For now, use the WAV file format unless you have very little hard drive space.

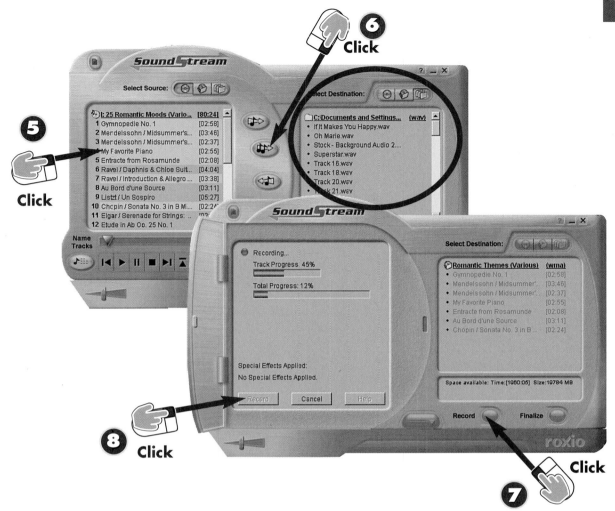

Click

Click

Click

Click

⑤ Your new destination folder appears in the destination area with a Windows audio file extension—WAV. Click to select the tracks you want to add to the destination folder.

⑥ Click the arrow with two music symbols to add them all.

⑦ Record the new selections. Click **Record**.

⑧ Click **Record** in the left panel. When you're done, you can play your library files without the disc in the computer!

End

TIP
When you created your music library, you created a WMA file format. These also went into a folder on your hard drive—the C:\My Music folder, with a subfolder with the name of the album you named.

HINT
Look at the sizes of those WMA files. They are much smaller, highly compressed files; they play nicely but they are no longer CD-quality audio files.

Adding Effects in SoundStream

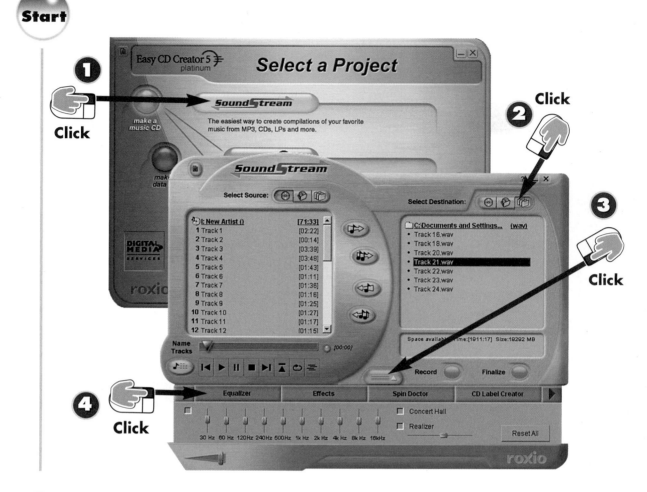

Start

Click

Click

Click

Click

1 Open **SoundStream** in the Project Selector.

2 Click to select a music library or folder destination.

3 Click **Show Options Drawer**.

4 Click **Equalizer**. The sliders let you alter the volume of various frequencies. Use trial and error and drag the sliders until you are pleased with the results. (Click **Play** to hear the results.)

INTRODUCTION

Now that you've gotten comfortable in SoundStream, let's take a little time to explore some extras, which include the capability to change the sound of your audio tracks.

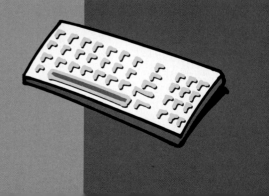

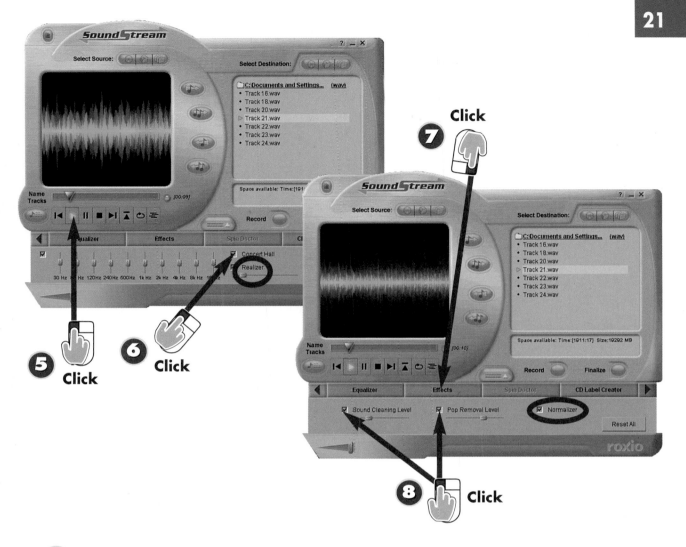

5 Select a destination track and click **Play** to hear the changes.

6 Click **Concert Hall** or click to activate and drag the **Realizer** for other effects.

7 Click **Effects** to activate the Effects panel.

8 Enhance its sound by adding and adjusting the **Sound Cleaning Level** and **Pop Removal Level** and checking **Normalizer**.

See next page

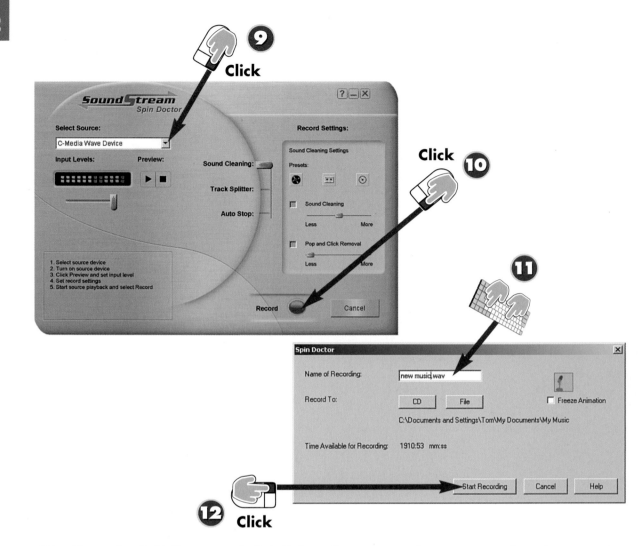

 Open the Spin Doctor and click **Select Source** to select your sound card to record analog audio. Begin playing your audio source into the sound card.

10 Click the **Record** button.

11 Create a filename.

12 Click **Start Recording**.

End

Creating a Digital Audio CD

Start

① **Click**

③ **Click**

④ **Click**

②

---

① Open **MusicCD Project** in the Project Selector.

② Review the main interface of CD Creator. Your source audio tracks are in the top panel. Under Music Project, type a name and the artist for your new album.

③ Manually rename the tracks by right-clicking or, with a Web connection, click **Name Tracks** to access the Roxio online database.

④ Select the tracks you want for your new greatest hits album.

See next page

INTRODUCTION

SoundStream is like the AOL of audio CD creation—it makes creating CDs more user friendly (but when you stop using it, it doesn't call you up at dinnertime). But now let's use the full power of CD Creator to make professional-style audio CDs—a new greatest hits album.

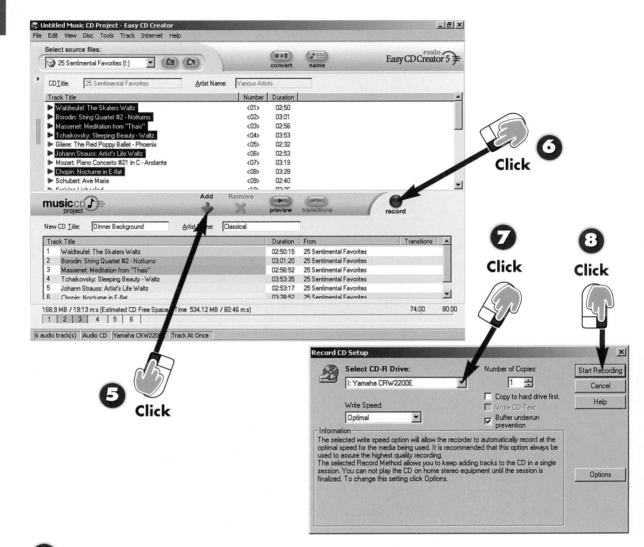

Click 6

Click 7

Click 8

Click 5

5️⃣ With the tracks selected, drag and drop them into the lower panel, or click **Add**.

6️⃣ Click the **Record** button.

7️⃣ Click to select your CD-R drive from the drop-down list.

8️⃣ Click the **Start Recording** button to begin the record process.

End

HINT You can replace the source audio CD with another if you like and continue to add tracks from the new CD.

TIP You can reorganize your tracks by dragging and dropping them into a different order. You can also click the **Remove** button to delete a track from the compilation.

HINT If you're using more than one CD for your source, and only one drive, you will need to insert your source discs as prompted. Watch the Record CD Progress dialog box. When prompted, insert a blank CD into your CD-RW drive.

Using Your Own Audio Files

Start

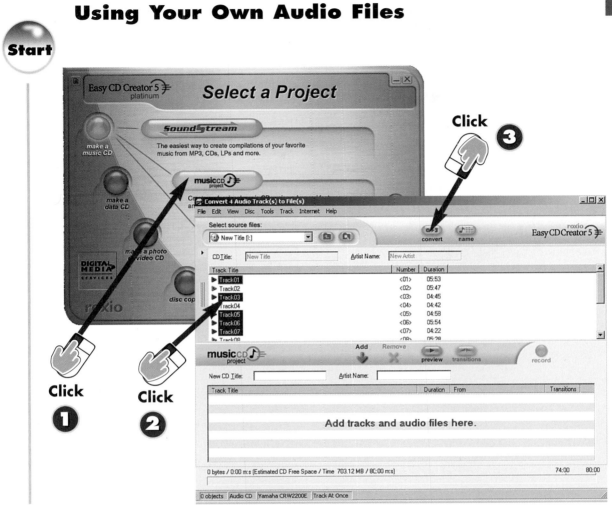

Click 3

Click 1

Click 2

1 Open **MusicCD Project** in the Project Selector.

2 Select tracks to convert.

3 Click **Convert**.

See next page

INTRODUCTION

Hopefully, you've grasped the difference between CD audio content (digital goo) and Windows WAV files that you've saved in a folder. If not, don't worry, be happy. We're going to convert files now.

4 Enter a filename and format.

5 Click **Save**. The files are extracted and named sequentially. (For you dentists, the extraction speed is also shown.)

6 Locate the folder with your music file collection and select your files.

7 Move your selected files to the CD and click **Record** to record your file collection to a CD.

End

Saving your compilations (projects) is a great idea so you can revise them later for new albums. Click **File**, **Save As** on the main menu, name the project, click to save it, and remember where you saved it. Double-click the project file anytime to reopen CD Creator to work with this project again.

Drag and drop your stored files and burn them directly from your hard drive. Click the **Record** button to start the burn process. Create any combination of albums from your stored audio files.

Don't confuse your project files with your new WAV audio files: One is a record of the choices you made; the others are the actual audio files on your hard drive.

Applying Transitions to Your Tracks

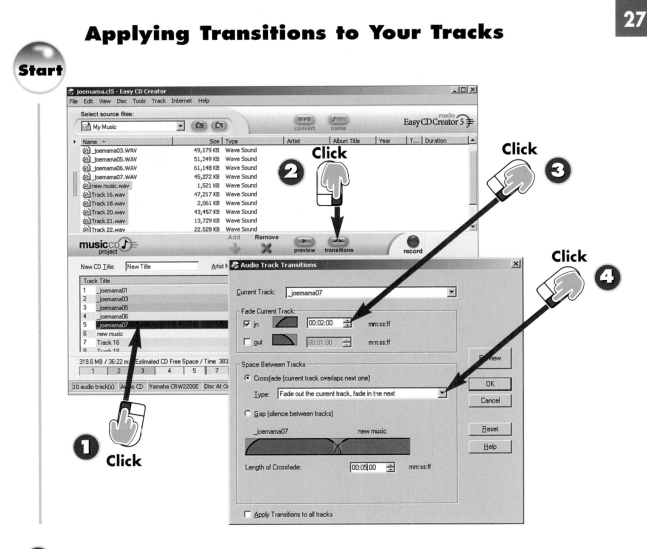

See next page

1. In the Project panel of CD Creator, click to select an audio track.

2. Click the **Transitions** button.

3. Set a duration (in seconds) for **Fade Current Track In** and **Fade Current Track Out**.

4. For a crossfade, click to set a duration for the time the current track will blend into the next.

See next page

INTRODUCTION

Nice touches that you can add to audio CDs are simple fade-in and fade-out effects between tracks. You can do this just before you burn the CD, and when you save the project (see the previous task), these choices are saved along with it.

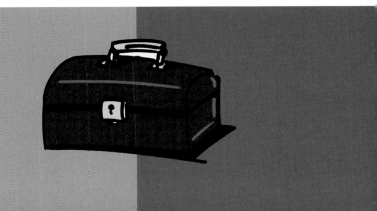

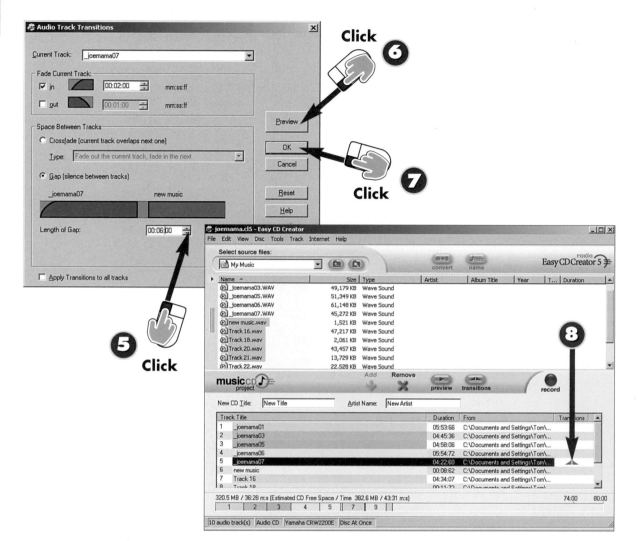

5 You can also change the length of the gap between tracks from the default of 2 seconds; click the arrows to change the value.

6 Click **Preview** to launch a player to hear the transitions you created.

7 Click **OK** to apply your choices to the tracks you selected.

8 A transition icon appears next to the track(s) to indicate that a transition has been applied.

End

HINT
If you change the gap length, your only record options will be to Close the Disc (Finalize).

TIP
To quickly apply a transition setting to all tracks at once, click the **Apply Transition to All Tracks** check box.

HINT
Double-click the **Transition** icon to open the transition and change it before burning.

Creating an MP3 Audio CD

Start

①

Click

Click

②

Click

Click

③

Easy CD Creator 5 platinum — **Select a Project**

SoundStream — The easiest way to create compilations of your favorite music from MP3, CDs, LPs and more.

musiccd project

make a music

make a data CD

make a photo or video CD

DIGITAL MEDIA SERVICES

roxio

Convert 4 Audio Track(s) to File(s)

File Edit View Disc Tools Track Internet Help

Select source files: New Title (I:)   convert   name   Easy CD Creator 5

CD Title: New Title   Artist Name: New Artist

Track Title	Number	Duration
Track01	<01>	05:53
Track02	<02>	05:47
Track03	<03>	04:45
Track04	<04>	04:42
Track05	<05>	04:58
Track06	<06>	05:54
Track07	<07>	04:22
Track08	<08>	05:28

musiccd project   Add   Remove   preview   transitions   record

New CD Title: Artist Name:

Track Title	Duration	From	Transitions

Add tracks and audio files here.

0 bytes / 0:00 m:s (Estimated CD Free Space / Time 703.12 MB / 80:00 m:s)   74:00   80:00

0 objects   Audio CD   Yamaha CRW2200E   Track At Once

① From the Project Selector, open **MusicCD Project** in CD Creator.

② Select tracks to "rip" or convert to MP3.

③ Click **Convert**.

See next page

INTRODUCTION

So far, we've burned CDs with true digital audio and saved digital audio as WAV files. We also found that the SoundStream music library files were highly compressed WMA (Windows Media) files. You've probably heard of MP3, which is a compressed audio format popular on the Internet and in portable devices that support its playback. Before we make an MP3 disc, we need to *rip* (another word for extract) the music. Then we burn a special type of audio CD.

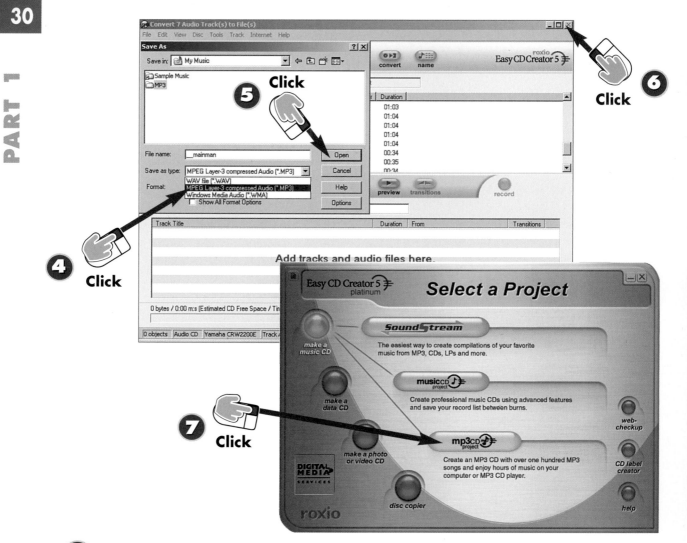

4 Choose a folder and a filename, and select the MP3 format.

5 Click **Open**. The files are "ripped" and named sequentially with the name entered.

6 Close CD Creator. (Save the project first to reuse it later, but give it another name to keep the original project.)

7 In the Project Selector (which has reappeared), click to open an **MP3CD Project**.

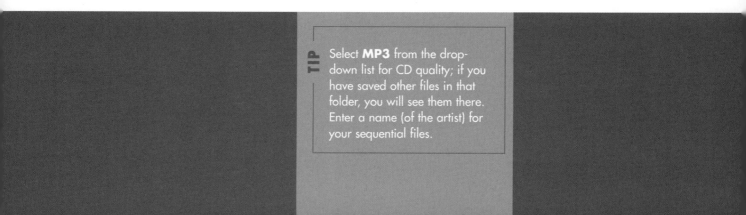

TIP

Select **MP3** from the drop-down list for CD quality; if you have saved other files in that folder, you will see them there. Enter a name (of the artist) for your sequential files.

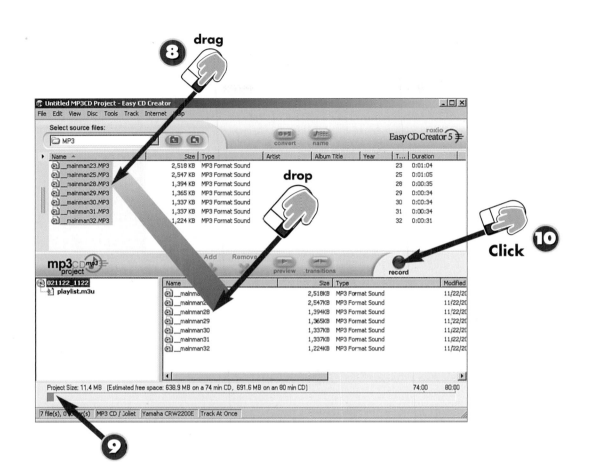

8 From the folder you selected to place your MP3s, drag and drop your stored MP3 files to the **MP3CD** project.

9 Watch your status bar; notice you can fit many more MP3s on a CD than CD-audio or WAV files.

10 Click the **Record** button to start the burn process.

End

Beginning DirectCD

Start

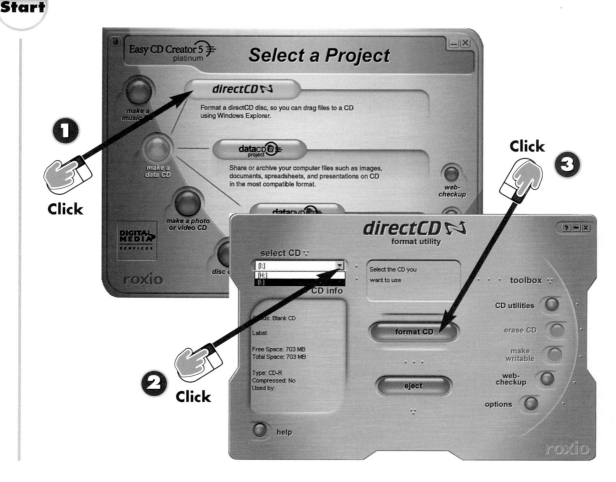

Click

Click

Click

1 Open a DirectCD project in Project Selector.

2 If you have more than one recordable drive, click the **drop-down arrow** to select the one that has the disc that you will be using. Review the disc information.

3 Click **Format CD**.

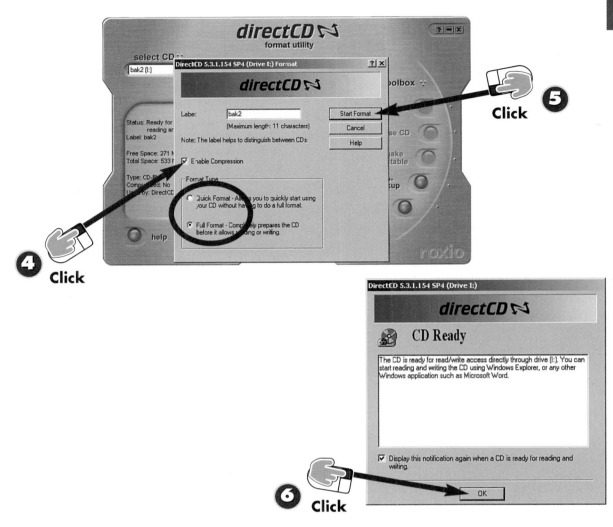

Click

Click

Click

4 Click **Enable Compression**, and then click and attempt **Quick Format** or do a **Full Format** (this can take a while).

5 Click **Start Format**.

6 Click **OK** when the CD Ready dialog box displays. You can now use the CD like a disc drive.

See next page

TIP The CD can be accessed for reading and writing by clicking **File**, **Save As** from any program or directly from Windows Explorer.

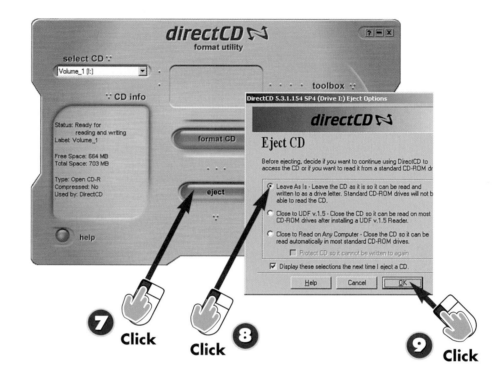

 Click **Eject**.

 Click to **Leave As Is**.

9 Click **OK** to continue.

End

HINT

With DirectCD, you automatically have a program that reads a UDF 1.5 formatted disc. But you can't always assume that others will have that capability, so if you want your discs to be accessible to others, don't use DirectCD. Instead, use the Data Disc feature of Easy CD Creator.

Working with DirectCD

Start

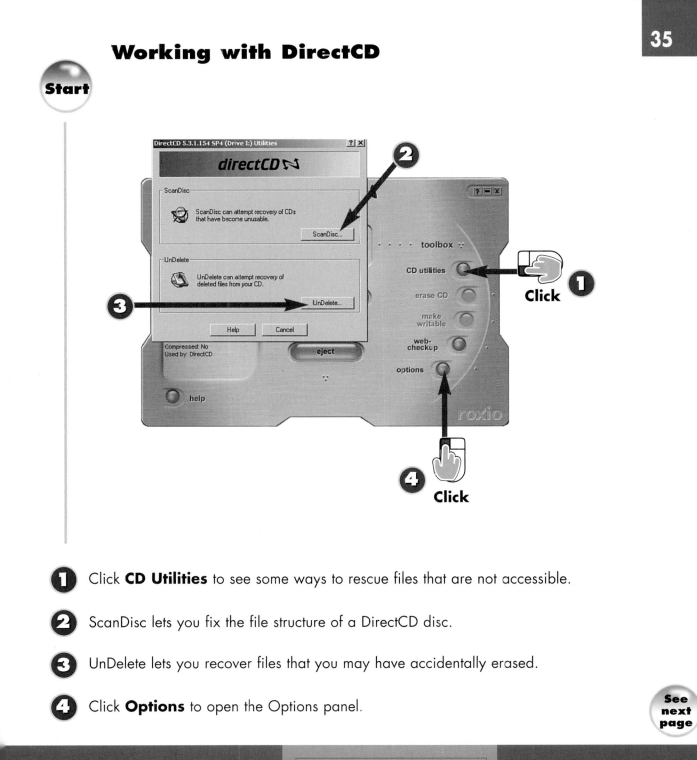

1 Click **CD Utilities** to see some ways to rescue files that are not accessible.

2 ScanDisc lets you fix the file structure of a DirectCD disc.

3 UnDelete lets you recover files that you may have accidentally erased.

4 Click **Options** to open the Options panel.

See next page

INTRODUCTION

DirectCD offers some features not found on a regular data CD. One of these features is the capability to compress files and fit more on a disc (available during formatting). Let's look at some other capabilities of DirectCD.

TIP

When you use DirectCD, you must follow the rules. Format your disc and use the software eject procedures. In Roxio DirectCD or Windows Explorer, right-click the disc and select **Eject**.

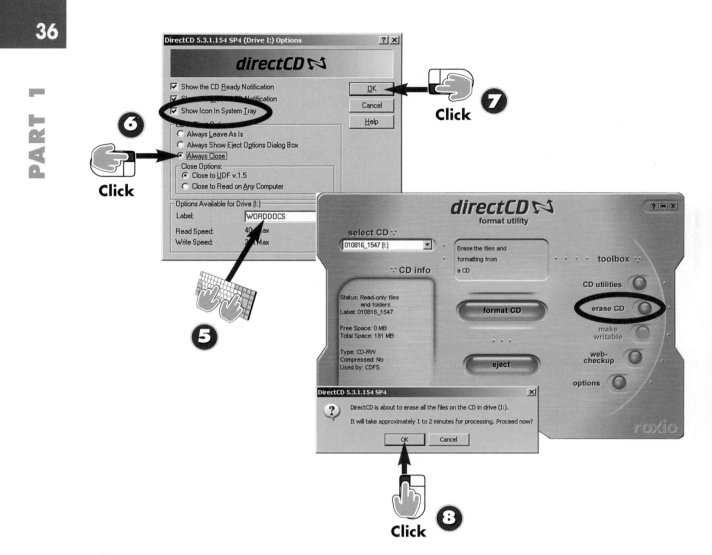

 5 Enter a new "Volume" to reference the contents.

6 Click **Always Close** to reset your CDR eject options.

7 If you really like DirectCD, you can check the option to add its icon to the System Tray for quicker access. Click **OK** when you're finished.

8 With a CD-RW or rewritable DVD, you can quickly erase its contents for reuse with DirectCD. Click **Erase CD** to start the process and **OK** to confirm.

HINT

When you delete files from a DirectCD disc, you actually revise only the CD directory. The file itself is still present and may be recovered; no disc space is actually restored. The only way to truly restore disc space with DirectCD is to erase or reformat a CD-RW or DVD rewritable disc.

Using the Disc Copier

Start

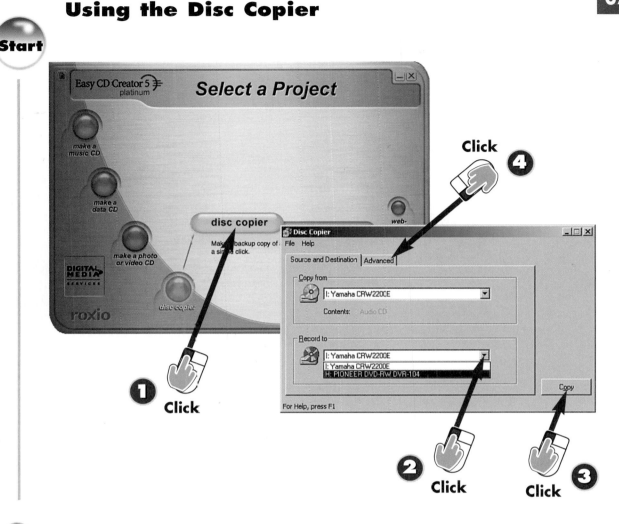

Click ④

Click ①

Click ②

Click ③

① Open **Disc Copier** in Project Selector.

② If you have more than one recordable drive, set one as Copy From and the other as Record To.

③ Make sure a blank CD is in the Record To drive and click **Copy**.

④ If you have just one recordable drive (CD-RW or DVD), no problem. Click the drop-down arrow to set the same drive for both Copy From and Record To. Then click the **Advanced** tab.

See next page

INTRODUCTION

Easy CD Creator has a special program that facilitates copying discs, but it will work only with CDs and DVDs that are not copy-protected. A nice feature of the Disc Copier is that you can easily copy your files to a temporary directory on the hard drive first if you have only one CD or DVD recorder, if it is slow, or if you want to make multiple copies.

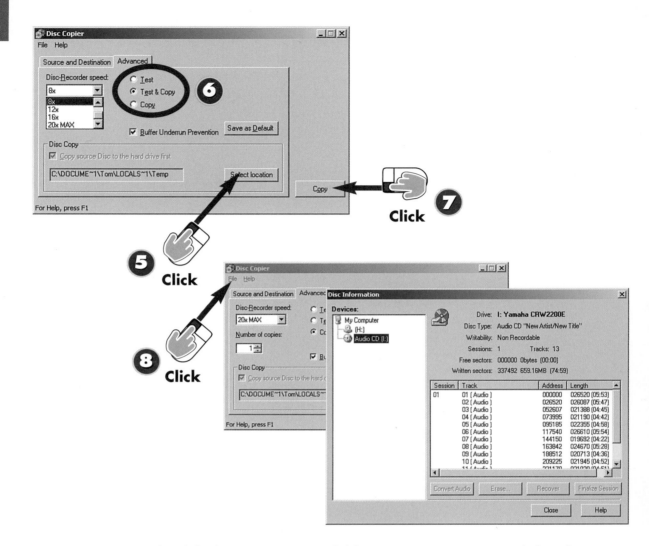

5   You can use the default temporary copy folder in My Documents, or click **Select Location** to choose another folder for reuse again later.

6   Select **Test**, **Test & Copy**, or **Copy**. Testing is always safer but will take longer to burn.

7   Click **Copy**.

8   To find out more about the source disc, click **File**, and then click **Disc Information** (not shown), and see the type of disc in the Copy From drive.

End

TIP
If you've already extracted music or used DirectCD, you should have no problem copying a music CD or a data CD disc. Choose **Test** or **Test & Copy**, click the drop-down arrow to set a record speed, and click **Copy**.

TIP
It's helpful to know the type of source disc you are copying for Photo CDs or video CDs because they require a CD-ROM XA drive (which is now quite common). Or if it's a DVD, it might be copy-protected.

HINT
Keep an eye on your hard disc space when using the CD Copier and other features of CD Creator. The disc space required for temporary files and disc images can quickly become full and cause disc errors and system freezes.

Creating an Enhanced CD

Start

Click ❶

Click ❷

Click ❸

❶ Click **DataCD Project** in Project Selector and open a data CD project.

❷ Click **File, New CD Project**, and select **Enhanced CD**.

❸ Click the **Empty Audio CD Project** in the compilation. It's ready for CD audio tracks just like regular music CDs.

See next page

INTRODUCTION

An enhanced CD is the best of both worlds—it works as an audio CD to play digital music, and it can also include data for a CD-ROM. With CD Creator, making an enhanced CD is easy.

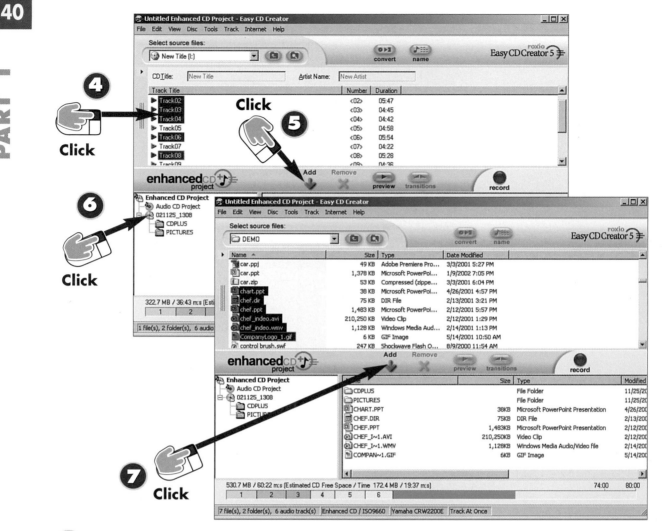

4 Select one or more source tracks.

5 Click **Add** to add these tracks into the audio CD folder.

6 Click to highlight the core data folder of the Enhanced CD. Notice the two blank folders ready to accept CD Plus data or Pictures (we'll cover those shortly).

7 Select your files and click **Add** to add your data from the disc drive selected in the top panel into the root folder of the new volume (or compilation).

TIP You can add your files by dragging and dropping, or use the Add button.

HINT In step 6, the core data folder of the Enhanced CD is the volume number, which is a number generated by the program based on the date—here, it's 021125_1308.

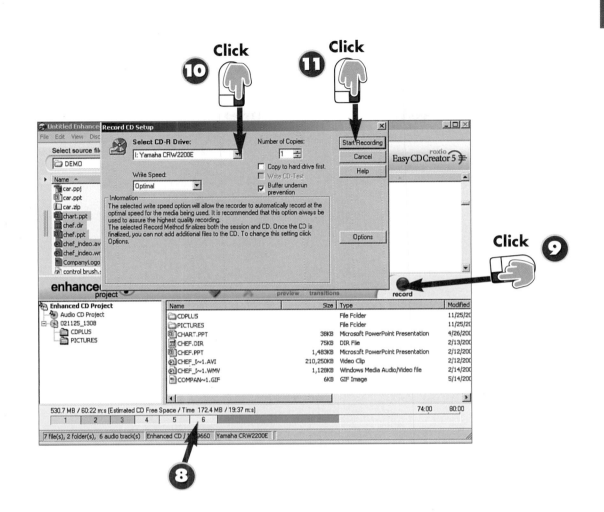

Click ⑩

Click ⑪

Click ⑨

⑧

---

⑧ Notice that the status bar at the bottom shows both CD audio tracks and megabytes of data.

⑨ Click **Record** to open the recording options.

⑩ Make sure your CD-R drive is selected by clicking **Select CD-R Drive**.

⑪ Click **Start Recording** to burn data to the disc.

End

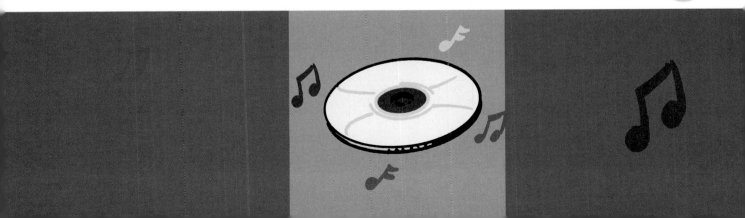

Creating a Mixed-Mode CD

Start

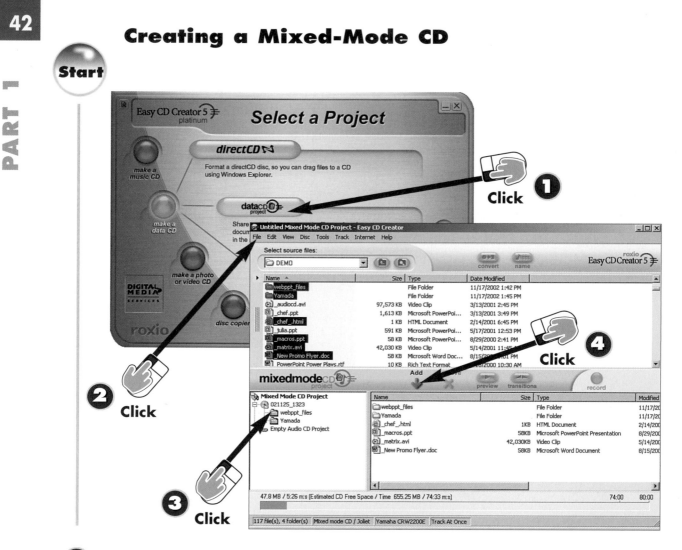

1. Click **DataCD Project** in Project Selector and open a data CD project.

2. Click **File**, **New CD Project**, and select **Mixed-Mode CD**.

3. Click the destination folder in the bottom panel.

4. From a disc drive or folder in the upper panel, select your files and folders and click **Add** to add them to the data folder of the mixed-mode compilation.

INTRODUCTION

A mixed-mode CD is a special kind of data CD that is often used in encyclopedias or other entertainment or educational programs that combine music and data.

HINT

The upper panel of a mixed-mode project again reveals the familiar Windows file structure, starting with the main C: drive. The lower panel has folders for data over the audio CD portion on the bottom.

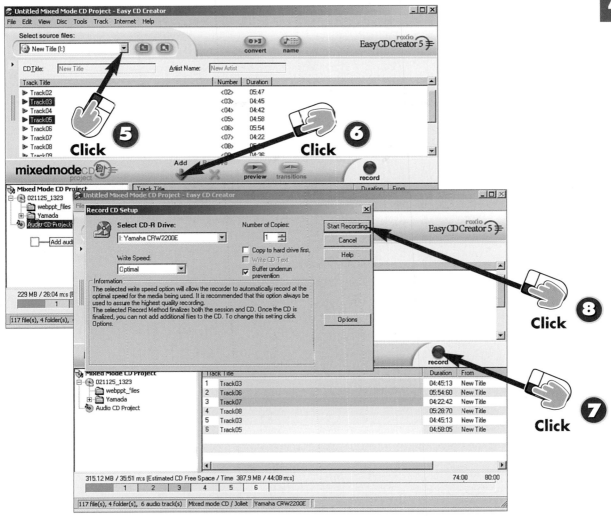

5 Click the **drop-down arrow** under **Select Source Files** to select your audio CD.

6 Select the tracks you want, and click **Add** to add them to the audio CD folder of your mixed-mode compilation.

7 Click the **Record** button.

8 Set your options and click the **Start Recording** button.

End

TIP
Because the data track is first, a mixed-mode disc lets you use the Autoplay feature of the disc so that a specified program opens when the disc is inserted. This isn't possible if a computer reads it first as an audio CD.

HINT
Don't put this disc into an audio CD player—you will hear loud static and no music. Notice that the data tracks precede the audio tracks on the disc.

Creating a PhotoRelay CD

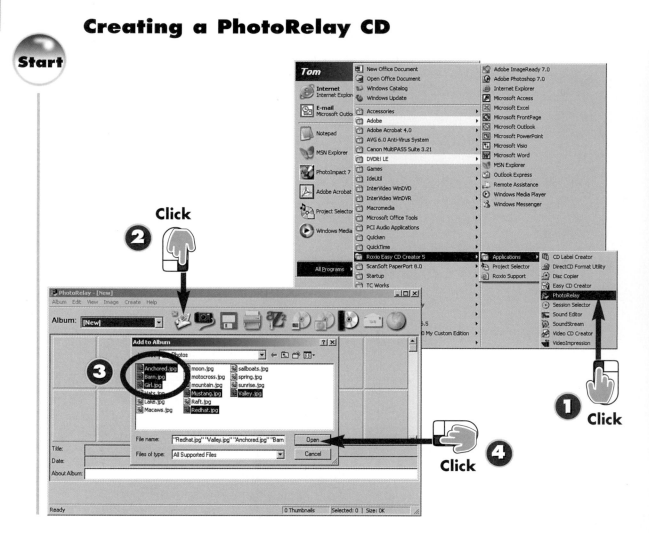

  Click **Start**, **All Programs**, **Roxio Easy CD Creator 5**, **Applications**, **PhotoRelay**. (See the Hint below.)

② Click the **Add Images** button to add your images.

③ Navigate to a folder with the images you want to burn to your PhotoRelay CD and select your images.

④ Click **Open** to add the images.

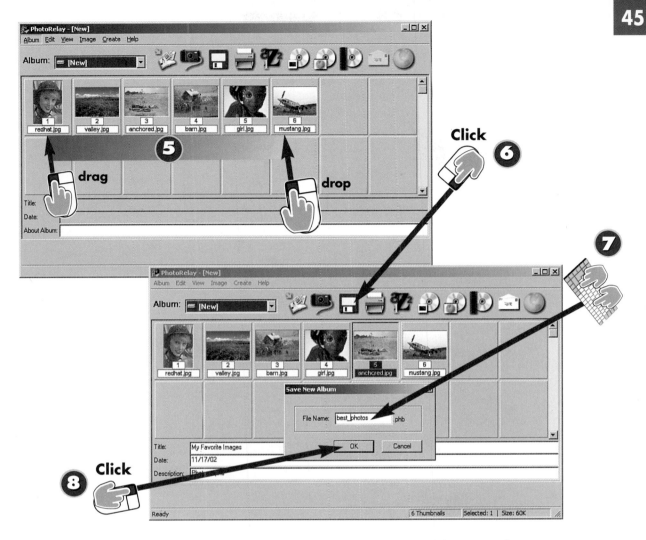

5   You can change the order of the images by dragging and dropping them to new locations.

6   Click **Save** to save your album.

7   Type in a name you'll remember.

8   Click **OK** to continue.

See next page

TIP   Click the **Acquire** button to use a scanner or digital camera to add more images, or repeat step 2 with another folder of images.

Click the **Sort** button to reorder your slides by name, size, date, or other parameters.

TIP   Use a descriptive name to refer to this collection (album) of images when you save your file as an album.

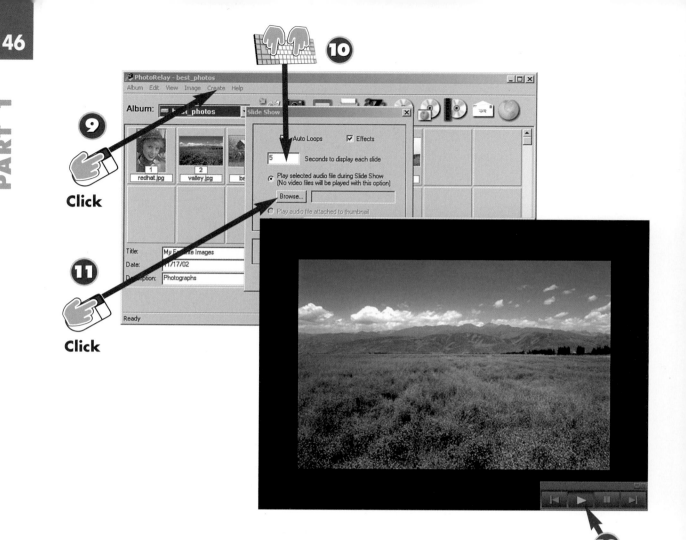

9 Click **Create**, **Perform Slide Show** (or **Ctrl+H**).

10 Set the timing for each slide.

11 Add an audio track (WAV or MP3 file) to accompany the slideshow.

12 A VCR-type of control lets you control the show at your own pace or just watch slides change automatically at the interval you set.

End

TIP
You can right-click individual slides to check their properties (size) and even attach audio clips to them individually.

Burning Your PhotoRelay CD

Start

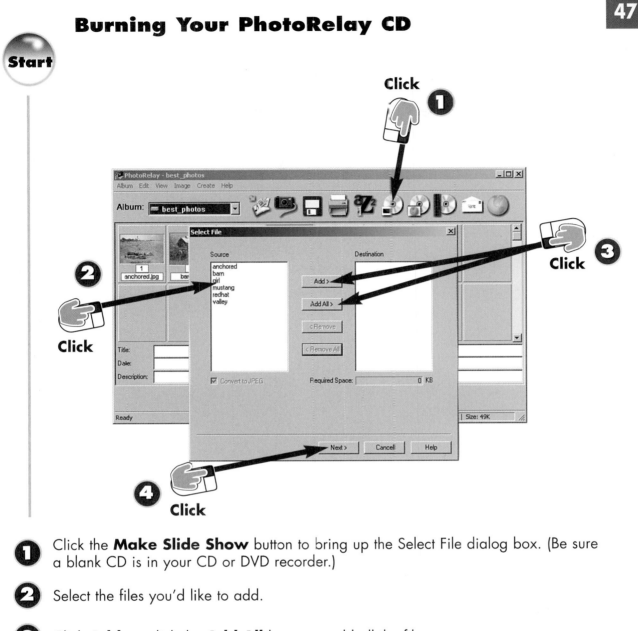

Click ❶

Click ❷

Click ❸

Click ❹

❶ Click the **Make Slide Show** button to bring up the Select File dialog box. (Be sure a blank CD is in your CD or DVD recorder.)

❷ Select the files you'd like to add.

❸ Click **Add**, or click the **Add All** button to add all the files.

❹ Click **Next**.

See next page

INTRODUCTION
Although watching your slideshow in PhotoRelay is nice, burning it to a disc that you can send to friends and family is really neat.

TIP
Notice the amount of space needed for the disc—don't let it exceed your CD capacity.

HINT
You will have to wait while the images are processed into PhotoRelay CD format.

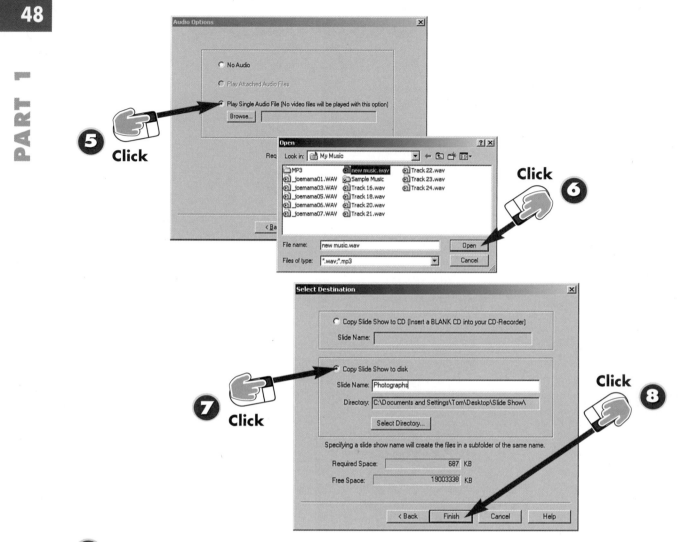

 Click **Play Single Audio File**.

Browse to the WAV or MP3 file you want and click **Open**.

Click **Copy Slide Show to Disk** and give your slideshow a name.

Finally, click **Finish**.

TIP If you want a soundtrack for your slideshow, you can attach an audio file to play in accompaniment.

TIP To burn directly to disc, choose the **Copy Slide Show to CD** option.

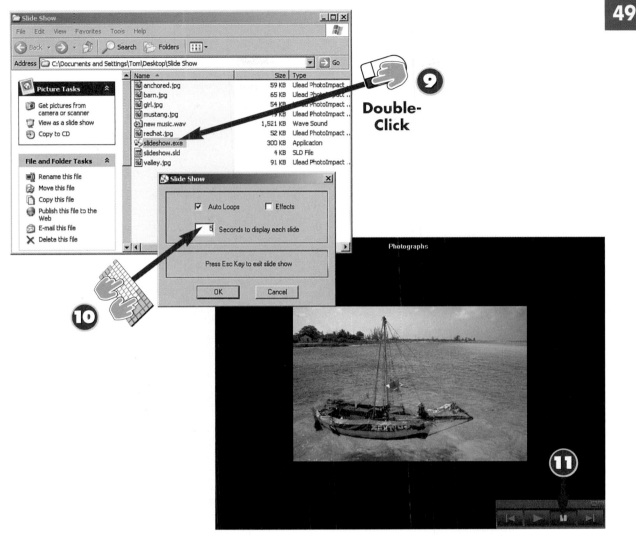

Double-Click

9 Now that you created it on a hard drive, you can double-click the **slideshow.exe** file in the folder where you saved it.

10 Then set the delay for each slide.

11 The name you gave the show appears on the first slide, the audio plays, and you can control playback or just sit back and watch.

End

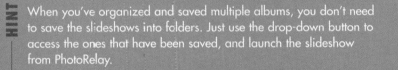

HINT
When you've organized and saved multiple albums, you don't need to save the slideshows into folders. Just use the drop-down button to access the ones that have been saved, and launch the slideshow from PhotoRelay.

Creating a Video CD

Start

Click 2

Click 3

Click 1

① Click **Start**, **All Programs**, **Roxio CD Creator 5**, **Applications**, and click **Video CD Creator**.

② A wizard splash screen opens up. Select **Simple Video Sequence**.

③ Click **Next**.

INTRODUCTION

A video CD is a special kind of CD that uses MPEG1 video files and an interactive menu to play movies. We will cover video capture and editing in more detail in later chapters (and further explain the VCD and SVCD formats). Let's quickly look at how CD Creator lets you make such a disc after you have MPEG1-compliant movie files.

HINT
We'll use interactive branching with MovieFactory to make sophisticated Video CDs, so let's just make a simple Video CD now as an introduction.

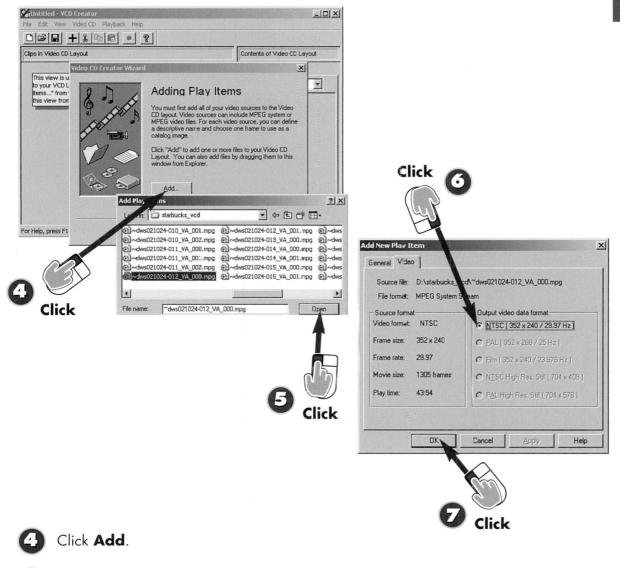

4 Click **Add**.

5 Select your video files from a folder, and click **Open** to add your MPEG files.

6 Unless the disc will go to Europe or Asia, click the **Video** tab and select **NTSC**.

7 Click **OK**.

See next page

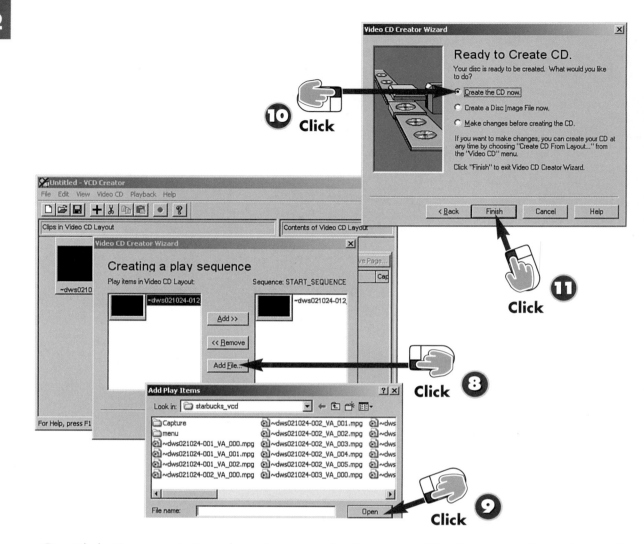

8 Click **Next** again (not shown) to open the Creating a Play Sequence dialog box and click **Add File** to add play items.

9 Click **Open** when you've selected your files then click **Next** to continue with the wizard.

10 Click **Next** again to play back the sequence as a test (not shown) then click **Next** a final time to be able to burn the disc. Select **Create the CD Now**.

11 Click **Finish** to begin burning your disc.

End

Creating a Disc Label or Cover

Start

2 Click

3 Click

1 Click

1 Click **Start**, **All Programs**, **Roxio CD Creator 5**, **Applications**, and then click **CD Label Creator**.

2 Select **CD Label** for your project.

3 Select an item or element on the disc to modify it. When an item is selected, selection squares surround it.

See next page

INTRODUCTION

After you've burned your masterpiece, you might want to cap it off with a nice label for the disc, or perhaps with inserts for the case. Many templates or styles of labels and inserts are available, and CD Creator lets you work with almost all of them.

TIP

If you are using a number of elements (CD label, inserts, and so on), on the main menu click **File**, **Print Preview** to see how it will look. When you like what you've done, use **Save As** to use it again.

Click **5**

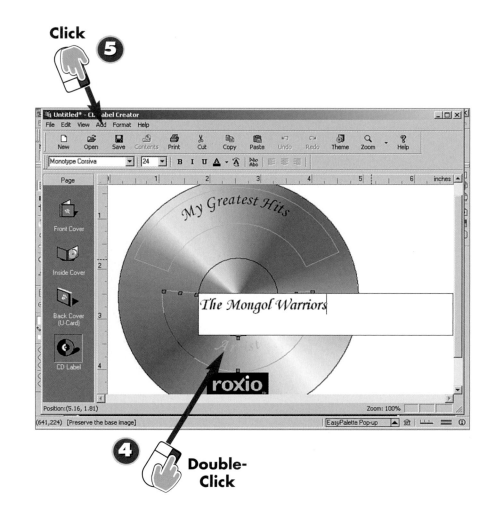

4 **Double-Click**

4 To revise text placeholders, double-click a selected text placeholder to change the text to what you want.

5 To add a picture, from the Main Menu click **Add**, then click **Picture** (not shown).

TIP The best way to label a compilation of data is to use **Format**, **Change Background (span across both panels)** (not shown) to make the insert white.

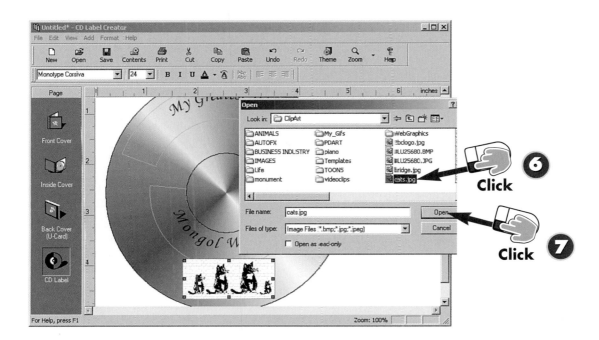

6 Select an image file you want to put into the label.

7 Click **Open**.

See next page

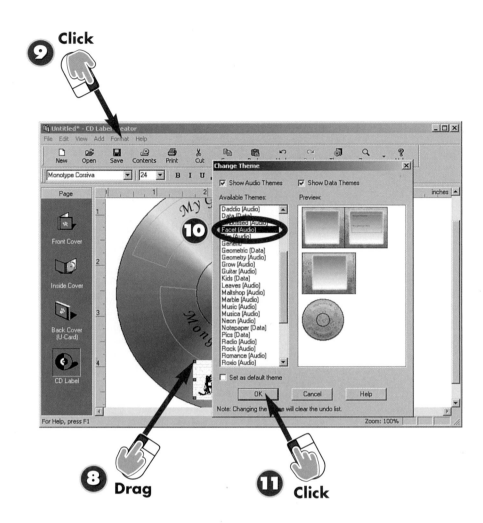

8 Drag the rectangular corners to resize it or the center of the image to reposition it.

9 To change the theme, from the Main Menu click **Format**, **Change Theme** (not shown).

10 Choose another look. Note that some are for audio CDs and some for data CDs.

11 Click **OK** to apply the theme.

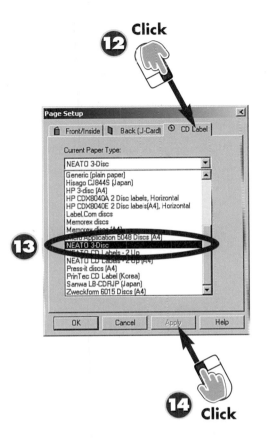

Click 12

14 Click

12 To use the layout you want, in the Main Menu click **File** and **Page Setup** (not shown) then click the **CD Label** tab.

13 Select the exact industry layout you will print to on the drop-down menu.

14 Click **Apply** and you're ready to print.

End

How to Use Nero 5

Nero Burning ROM is one of the most popular digital disc production programs on the planet. Besides supporting a true *.CDA file format to recognize digital audio, it also can burn a true DVD (or VCD or SVCD) disc when the interface has been created elsewhere and the movie files are formatted properly as MPEG2 video. But we'll cover these formats with DVD MovieFactory and DVD-It later on.

For now, we're going to concentrate on burning audio CDs with our favorite music, and creating data CDs to safeguard our most precious files. We'll also learn to create combination discs and even print custom labels and sleeves.

There are a few ways to approach Nero. We're going to start with the main program, Nero Burning ROM, and two components, the wizard and the main interface.

Here's a bonus hint: For those of you who either get bogged down in the main program or just want to get in and out quickly, skip to the section, "Using Nero Express."

The Main Nero Program Interface (Audio CD)

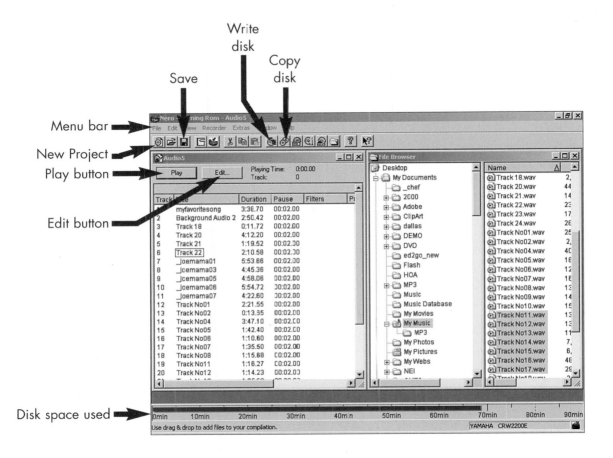

Creating a Data CD in Nero

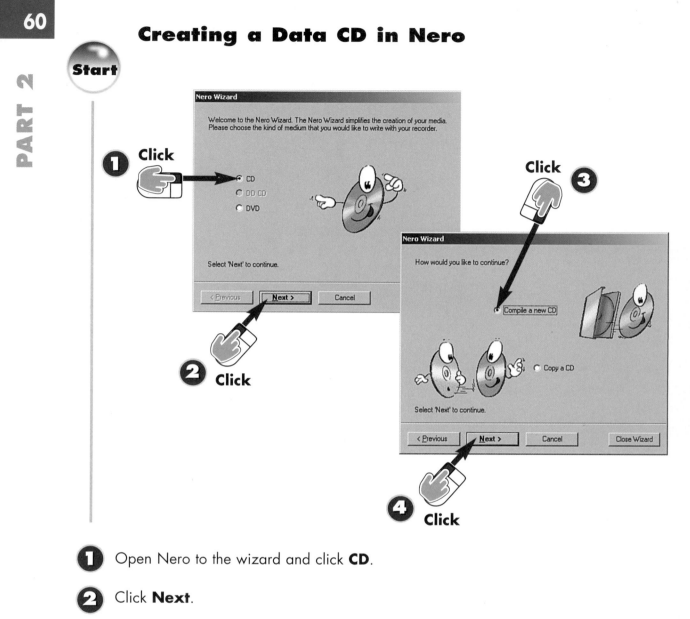

1 Open Nero to the wizard and click **CD**.

2 Click **Next**.

3 Click **Compile a New CD**.

4 Click **Next** to continue.

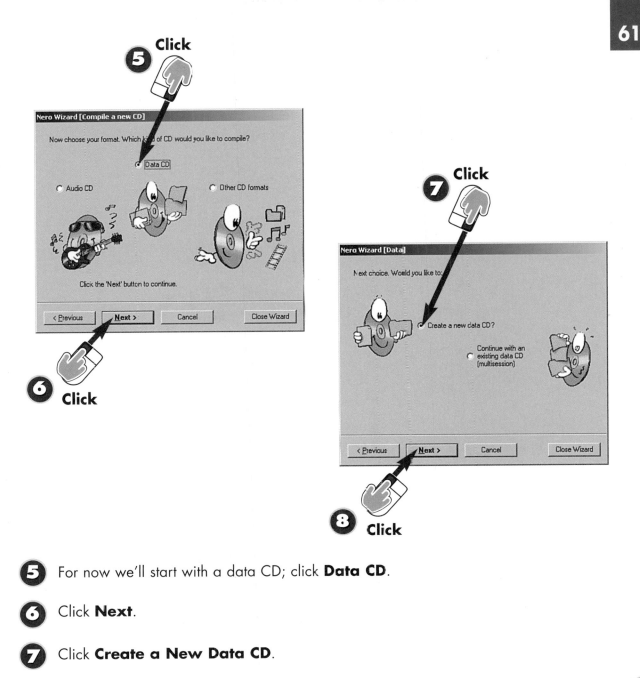

Click 5

Click 7

Click 6

Click 8

5 For now we'll start with a data CD; click **Data CD**.

6 Click **Next**.

7 Click **Create a New Data CD**.

8 Click **Next**. Another wizard window will appear (which isn't shown). Click **Finish**.

See next page

HINT
In the main program (next page), a status bar at the bottom shows you the available disc space for a blank disc for this type of project.

HINT
How you add the folders and files in the main program (next page) reproduces their structure in the root folder of the CD.

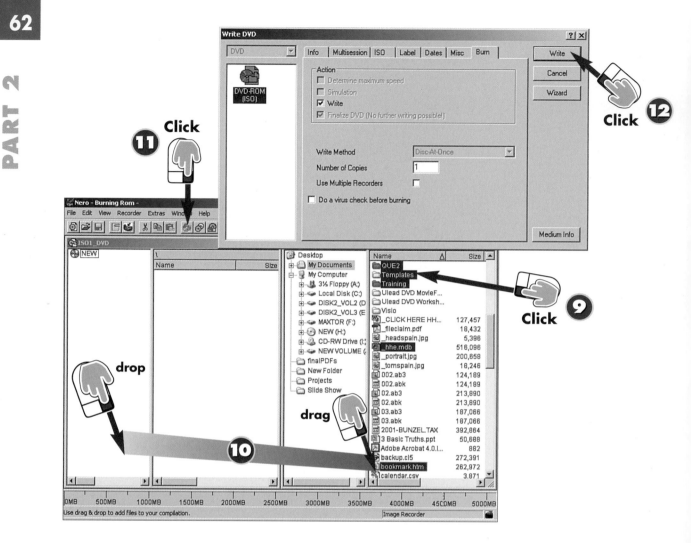

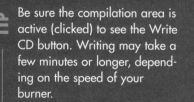

Click **11**

Click **12**

Click **9**

drop

drag

10

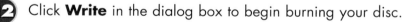

9 Review the familiar interface. Select your files and folders from the **My Documents** folder—most of your important files are probably there.

10 With the files and folders selected, drag and drop them into the compilation.

11 Be sure you have a blank CD in your drive and click the **Write CD** button to begin.

12 Click **Write** in the dialog box to begin burning your disc.

End

TIP Be sure the compilation area is active (clicked) to see the Write CD button. Writing may take a few minutes or longer, depending on the speed of your burner.

HINT If you drag the slider along the bottom of the File Browser, you can see more column headings at the top. Click to sort by date, size, or type, which can help locate the items you want to burn and back up.

TIP To select files, hold down the **Ctrl** key as you click to choose individual items. Hold down the **Shift** key as you select consecutive folders or files.

Creating an Audio CD with Nero

Start

Click ①

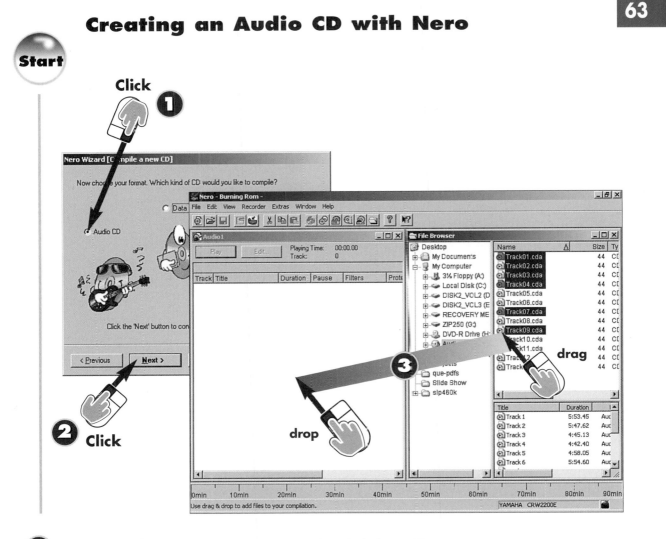

② **Click**

drag

3

drop

① Open Nero Burning ROM to the wizard and click **Audio CD**.

② Click **Next** until you are at the program screen.

③ Locate and click the icon for your audio CD and select the tracks you want to include in your greatest hits album. Drag and drop them into the compilation area.

See next page

INTRODUCTION

I'm sure you're anxious to make your own "greatest hits" audio CD. You'll need the music you want to compile (source audio CD discs) and a blank CD-R or CD-RW disc. Put your blank audio CD into your CD-RW drive.

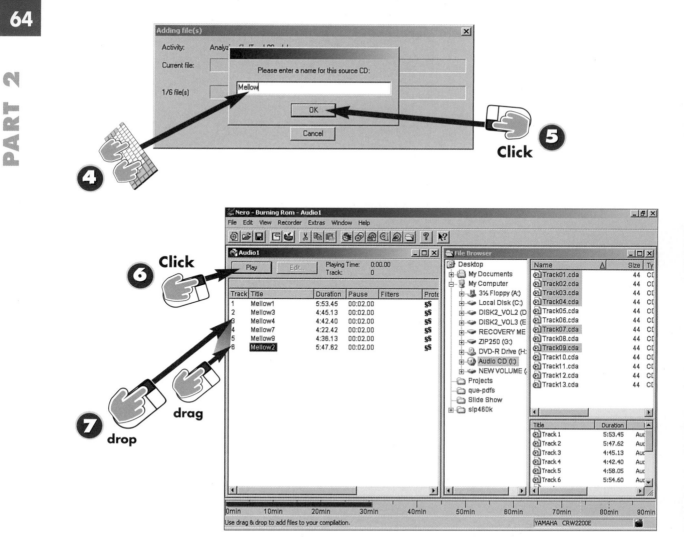

④ Click **Cancel** (not shown) to close the database. A window will pop up, prompting you to name your audio CD. Type in a name.

⑤ Click **OK** to continue.

⑥ Select a track and click the **Play** button to make sure it's the right one.

⑦ Drag and drop a track to a new location to change the play order.

TIP You can always stop the wizard from appearing by clicking **Help** and unchecking **Use the Wizard**.

HINT Windows XP will sometimes pop up and prompt you for action when you insert a new CD of any kind. It's a good idea to select **Take No Action** in the middle of a project; later, you'll learn how to "train" Windows XP to make that the default.

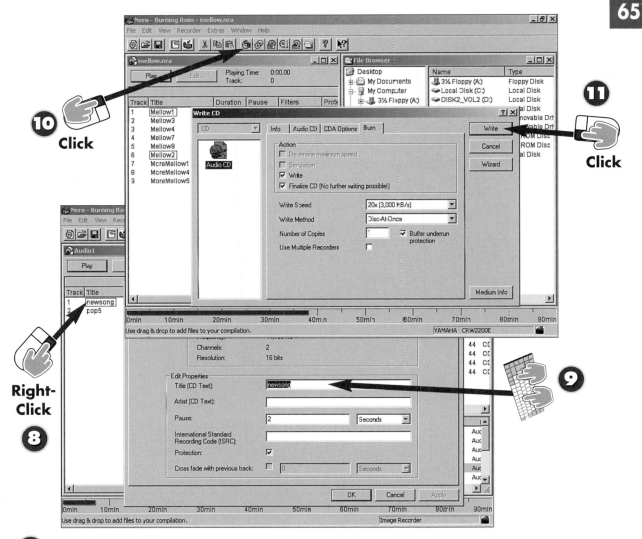

8 Right-click a track and click **Properties**.

9 Enter a descriptive name for the track.

10 Insert a blank CD and click the **Write CD** button.

11 Click **Write** to create your disk.

See
next
page

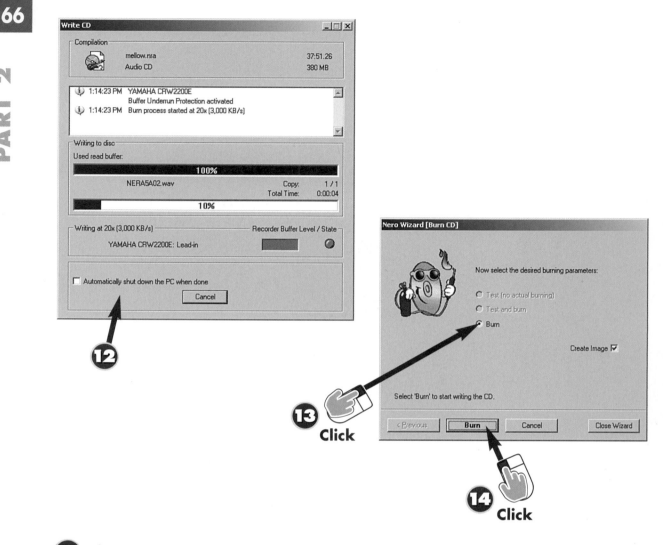

12 If you've disabled the wizard, your disc begins the burn process right away.

13 If the wizard is active, click **Burn**.

14 Click **Burn** to create your disk.

End

HINT In the Write CD dialog box, choose the best speed for your burner and your blank media. If you have disc space and might want to add tracks later, uncheck **Close Disc** and save your compilation.

TIP The audio tracks in your compilation are temporary files. To continue with the project file and reuse these tracks, you will still need the original audio CD(s) when the program prompts you for them.

HINT Another way to reuse the files is to use the wizard and select **Create Image**. As you'll see, a disc image is a file that can then be "reburned" over and over.

Creating a Music Collection in Nero

Start

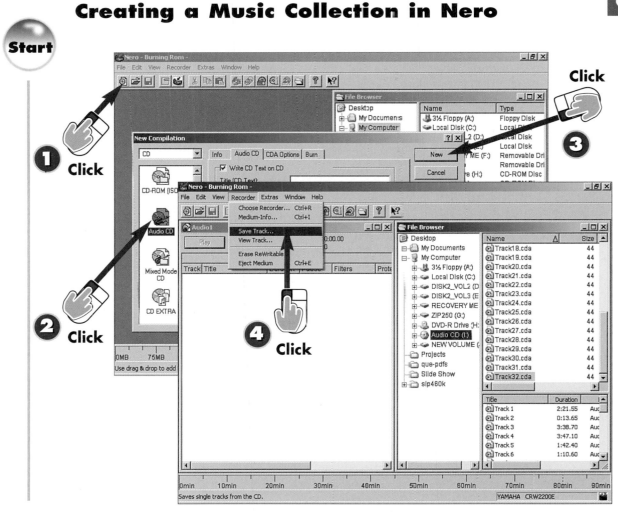

1 Within the main Nero interface (not the wizard), click **New**.

2 Click **Audio CD**.

3 Click **New**.

4 Click **Recorder**, **Save Track**.

See next page

INTRODUCTION

What if you want to keep your tracks available to play or to burn again in different combinations? You need to save the audio tracks as computer files on your hard drive. Let's take a look at creating a personal collection.

HINT

There is a dialog box that explains that the Nero MP3 converter can be used only 30 times without a program upgrade (available at www.nero.com).

Nero's title and CD database

List of corresponding CD entries in the Nero CD database:

Artist	Title

📖 : Internet database entry   📁 : Program database entry

🖿 : User defined entry   📁 : User database entry

🖳 : Windows CD player entry

Tracklist of the currently selected CD:

Artist	Title

Create a new CD entry...	Edit CD entry...	Access Internet Database
Print CD Cover	Cancel	Selected CD

☐ Never show this message again   Remaining time until autoclose (sec): 56

5 Click

Choose Drive

Device	SCSI ID	Adapter	Adapter No.
🖴 PIONEER DVD-RW DVR-104	0	siside	2
🖴 YAMAHA CRW2200E	1	siside	2

Max. read speed: 40x   OK   Cancel

Click **6**

Click **7**

5 Select the drive that holds your audio CDs.

6 Click **OK**.

7 A database menu will open; click **Cancel** to close it for now.

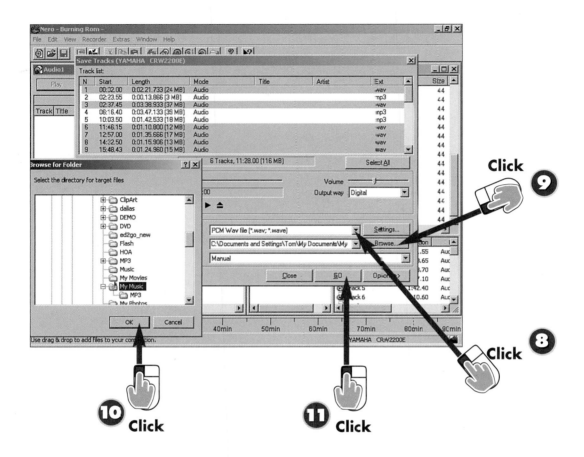

8 By default, all the audio tracks on your CD are selected. To deselect them, click a single track to select it. Click the drop-down arrow to make the files WAV or MP3 format.

9 The converted tracks will go to your My Documents folder. Click **Browse** to select a new folder (such as My Music).

10 Click **OK** to accept the new folder.

11 Click **Go**.

End

Creating and Using a Music Database in Nero

Start

Click 2

Click 4

Click 3

Click 1

1. In My Documents, select **New**, **Folder** to create a new folder. Name it **Music Database**.

2. In Nero, click **Extras**, **Create a New User Database**.

3. Select your new **Music Database** folder under My Documents.

4. Click **OK**. Nero will begin creating the file. When it asks you to accept it, click **Yes**.

So far we have seen and cancelled out of the Database window in Nero as we performed various tasks. Some of you advanced users will love the database, so we'll summarize it here. The database is like a file cabinet that keeps track of your CDs, album titles, artists and tracks—but it takes effort to create and maintain.

HINT

The database will be a file that needs a folder for a home. That's what we're creating in step 1.

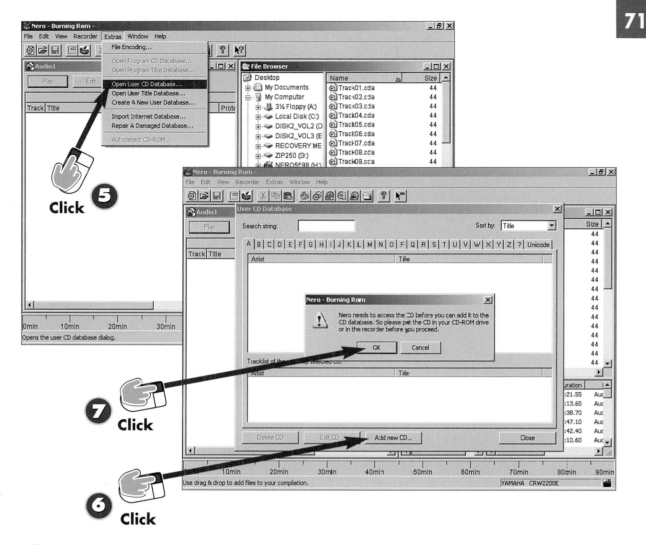

5 Click **Extras, Open User CD Database**.

6 Click **Add New CD** and make sure your audic CD is in your drive.

7 Click **OK** if Nero asks to access the CD (sometimes it can read the information directly for the disc's CD text).

See next page

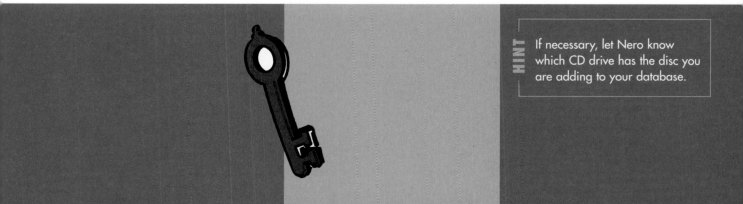

HINT

If necessary, let Nero know which CD drive has the disc you are adding to your database.

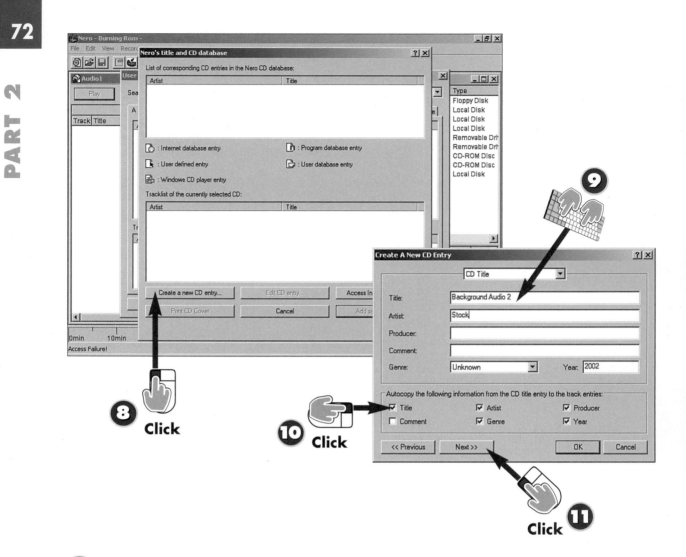

8 Click **Create a New CD Entry**.

9 Fill in the **Title** information.

10 Click to set the check box for **Title**.

11 Click **Next**.

If the database is more trouble than it's worth, you can turn off the database pop-up window permanently. Click **File**, **Preferences** on the main menu. Then click the **Database** tab and click to disable the three open database options.

Click 15

Click 14

Click 13

Click 12

 Click the drop-down arrow next to **Track**, and then scroll down and highlight the last track before you close the list.

13 Click **OK**.

14 In the main database window, click **Add Selected CD**.

15 Click **OK** to confirm that the entry has been successfully added.

See
next
page

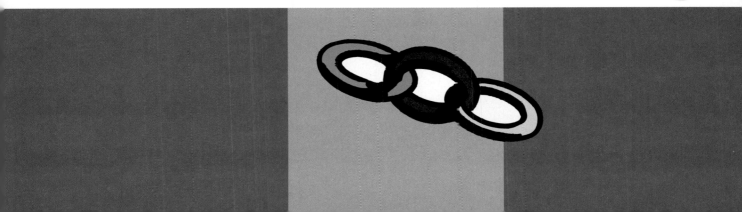

Click 17

Click 16

Click 18

16 Click the drop-down arrow to sort by Title or Artist. Click the appropriate alphabetical tab and look at the entries.

17 Now begin to extract audio and click **Recorder**, **Save Track**.

18 When the database opens, you see that it has found your CD! Click **Selected CD**.

HINT Now that you've seen the database, you can understand how CD text works. When you click to open a new audio CD as a project, use the CD Text window to enter information.

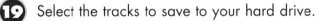

19 Click

Click 20

Click 21

19 Select the tracks to save to your hard drive.

20 Pick a file format (**WAV**) from the drop-down arrow.

21 Now, with the title and artist filled in from the database, click **Go**.

End

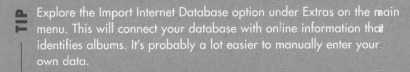

TIP
Explore the Import Internet Database option under Extras on the main menu. This will connect your database with online information that identifies albums. It's probably a lot easier to manually enter your own data.

HINT
Be sure you also click **Write CD Text on CD** and when you insert the disc (after it has been burned), you can instantly add your new album to your user database as a new entry.

Burning Your Audio Data Files

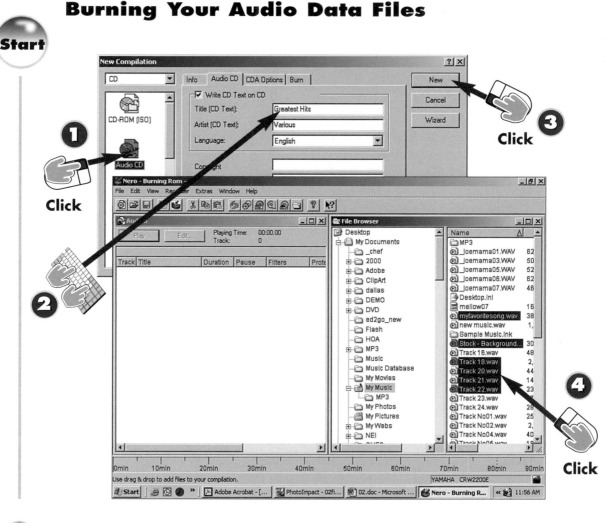

1 Begin a new compilation and select **Audio CD**.

2 Fill in the CD text information.

3 Finally, click **New**.

4 Click the folder that holds your music files and select your tracks.

So far you've compiled an audio CD from other CDs and seen the advantage of first *extracting* the files and moving them to the hard drive. You've also explored the database feature and found that it helped name your audio data files by using the field entries, or perhaps you've just renamed the files in your own music folders. Now you're ready to use and reuse them.

HINT
Hold down the **Ctrl** key as you select individual tracks or the **Shift** key as you select consecutive tracks.

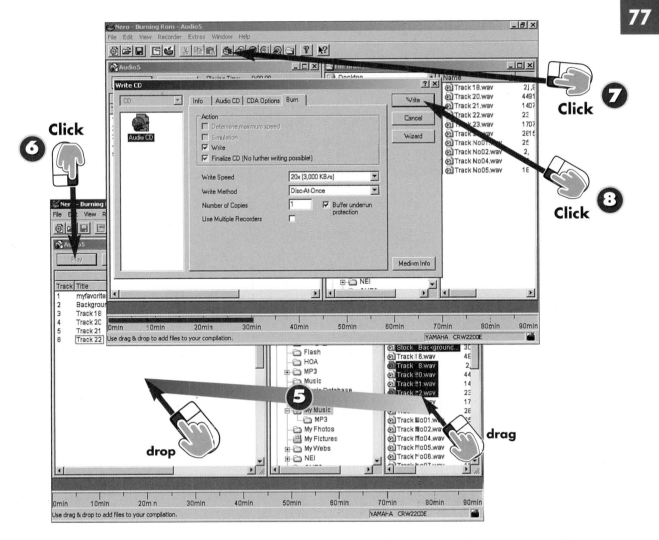

Click 6

Click 7

Click 8

drop

drag

5 Drag and drop the selected files into the new audio CD compilation. (Notice how much faster it is now that they're on your hard drive!)

6 Click **Play** to preview the tracks. Check the status bar to see that you have not exceeded CD capacity.

7 Click the **Write CD** button.

8 Set your speed and other options, and click **Write**. (If you have not disabled the wizard, it will pop up. To burn with the wizard, click **Wizard**.)

See next page

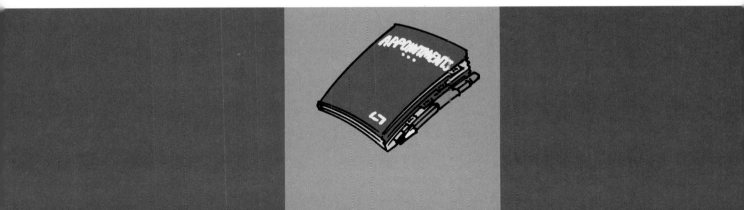

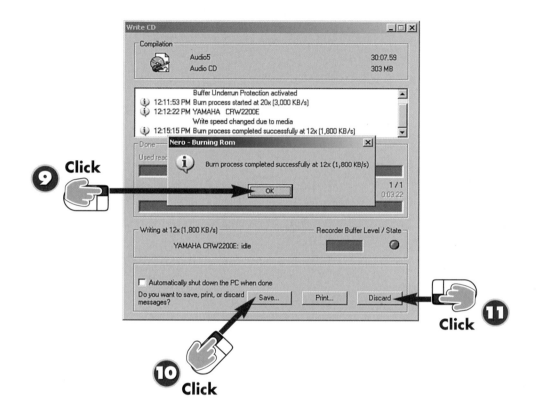

9 Click **OK** for a successful burn.

10 Click **Save** if you'd like to save the burn process messages.

11 Click **Discard** to close the window and eject your new disc.

End

TIP Now if you open **CD Database** under Extras and click **Add New CD**, the information from the CD text is imported into the database automatically.

Converting Your Audio Files

Start

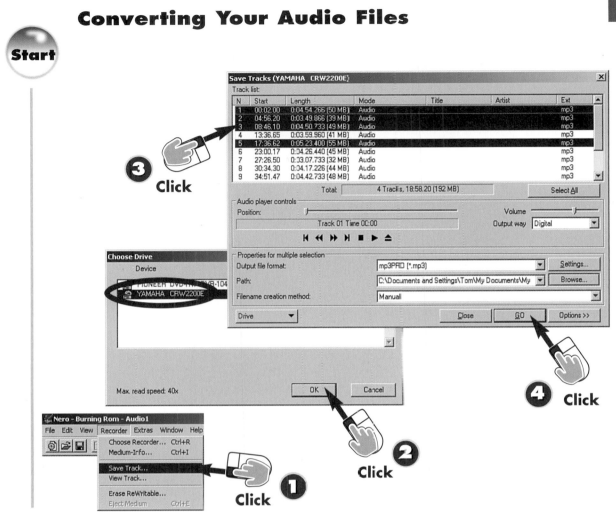

③ Click

④ Click

② Click

① Click

Click

① Open an audio CD project, insert an audio CD, and then click **Recorder**, **Save Track**.

② Select the CD with the audio tracks and click **OK**.

③ Select the tracks you want to save as MP3 files.

④ Set the destination folder and click **Go** to start the extraction process.

See next page

INTRODUCTION
So far when you've saved (extracted) audio files, you've saved them as WAV audio files, which preserves their full digital quality but results in large files. Other formats, notably MP3, are very popular for compressing audio files while preserving quality.

TIP
Nero includes only a 30-times use demo of its MP3 converter. To use it more extensively, you must download a full plug-in (and pay for it) from the Ahead Web site (www.nero.com).

HINT
When you use Save Track, other file options appear besides *.WAV and *.MP3. *.AIF is the Apple audio standard.

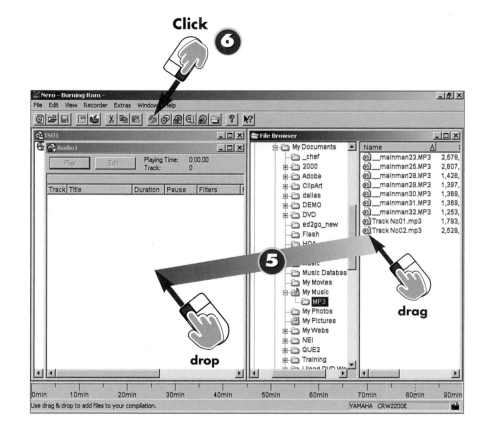

Click

drag

drop

With the files converted and saved, you can drag and drop them to a new compilation.

Click the **Write CD** button.

End

TIP *.VQF is another compressed format like *.MP3 but not nearly as popular. *.WMA is a highly compressed format promoted by Microsoft for Web streaming and is used with Windows Media Player (see Chapter 9, "Tips and Techniques").

Converting Your Audio Data Files

Start

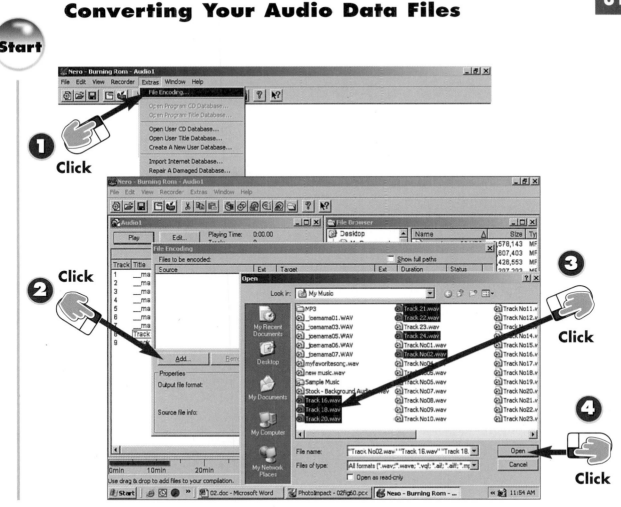

1 Click

2 Click

3 Click

4 Click

1 Open Nero and click **Extras**, **File Encoding**. You're going to convert some WAV files to MP3.

2 To add your source files, click **Add**.

3 Browse to your file folder with your extracted WAV audio files and select the files you'd like to convert.

4 Click **Open**.

 See next page

INTRODUCTION

Now that you've seen the benefits of having full-sized digital audio on your hard drive as WAV files and compressed MP3 files, let's see how you can convert (*encode*) from one format to another. (So far you've only converted files you've extracted from a CD.)

HINT

We've covered different ways to rename your audio files from "Track 1" and such. If you persist in using Track as your filename, during conversion you will be asked if you want to overwrite files with the same name—you might delete audio files you've previously extracted from another CD.

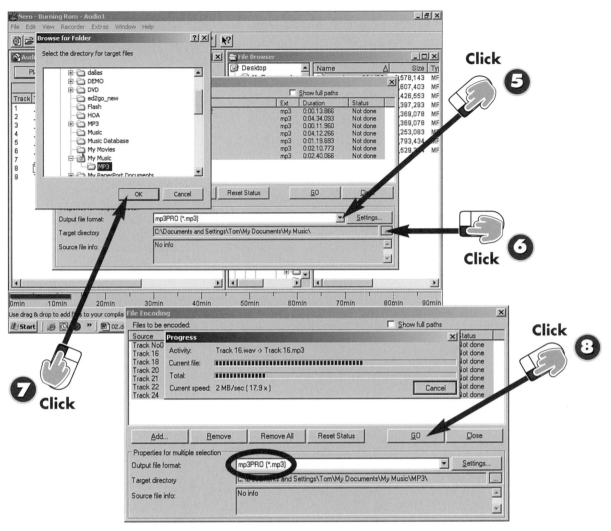

5 Click the drop-down arrow to change the format to MP3.

6 Click the ellipses (…) to browse a folder for MP3 files, and click to select the folder.

7 Click **OK** to continue.

8 Be sure the output file format is MP3 and click **Go**. The files are converted.

End

TIP
Audio quality is very subjective. If you are happy with the sound of an audio CD created from compressed MP3 audio files, you can use this format and delete or avoid using WAV audio files entirely. (Remember, you will need to buy the Nero MP3 plug-in.)

HINT
Either format will play on your PC, letting you use your hard drive as an "audio jukebox" in Windows Media Player (See Chapter 9).

Setting Your Recording Options

See next page

Start

Click 1

Click 2

Click 3

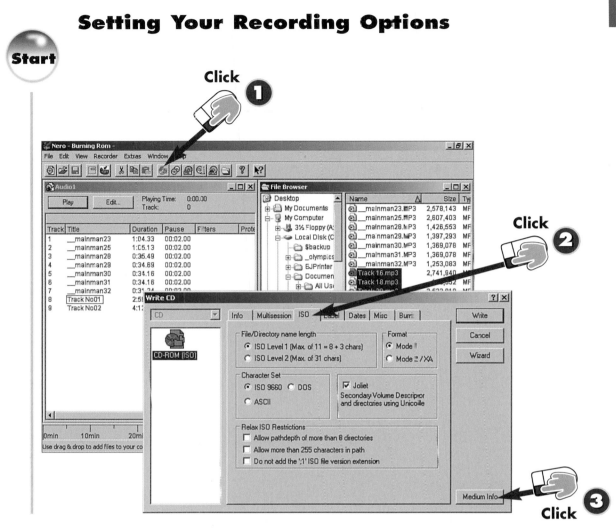

1 Create a compilation in Nero and click the **Write CD** button.

2 Click the **ISO** tab. Like many of the defaults, this is more than you want to know. ISO is the CD standard. Leaving these settings will maximize the readability of your files.

3 Click **Medium Info** to see the status of your blank disc.

See next page

INTRODUCTION

I wanted to wait with this topic until you've created data and audio CD compilations. Using the Write CD defaults will work for most of you, and these options are fairly universal to the different projects you will create.

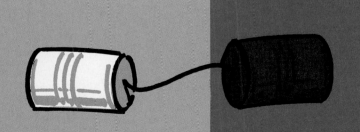

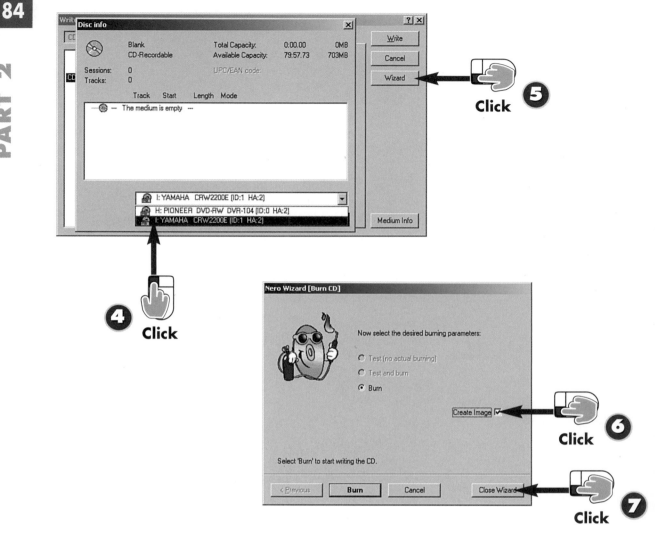

Click ➎

Click ➍

Click ➏

Click ➐

➍ Click the drop-down arrow to select another CD or DVD recorder.

➎ If it makes you feel better, click the **Wizard** button. (It gives you an important option: creating an image.)

➏ Click **Create Image** to create a file to reburn this exact compilation many more times.

➐ Click **Close Wizard** to go back to the options screen.

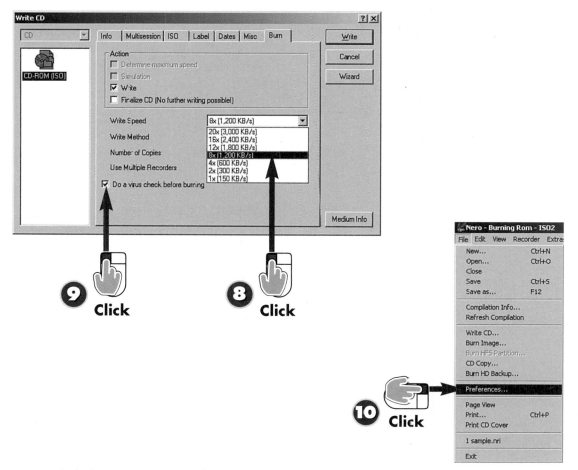

8 Click the **Write Speed** drop-down menu to select a burning speed that matches your media. (Nero may opt to lower this speed later.)

9 Click **Do a Virus Check Before Burning** to ensure you won't copy a virus.

10 If you get errors or want to fine-tune your system, investigate your preferences by clicking **File**, **Preferences**.

End

TIP
If you run a virus check, be sure you don't have conflicting virus checking programs. Turn off virus check if it interferes with your burning.

If you have Buffer Underrun Protection as an option, be sure it is checked.

HINT
The General tab under Preferences lets you disable the virus plug-in if it's causing problems. The Cache tab lets you set a location for temporary files. If you have too little hard-drive space (for DVD recording in particular), adjust this location to a drive that has enough room.

TIP
If you are able to burn only an image file, be sure your virtual Image Recorder is selected under **Recorder**, **Choose Recorder**.

Working with InCD

Start

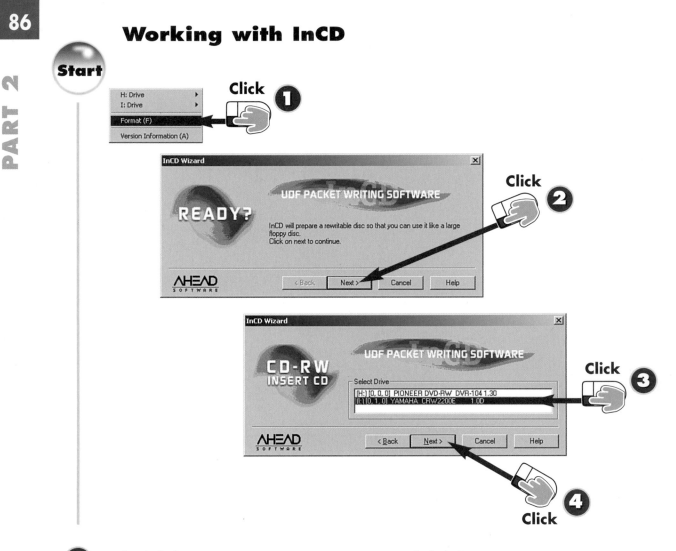

① Right-click the InCD icon on your system tray and click **Format**.

② The UDF Packet Writer opens. Click **Next**.

③ If you have more than one recordable CD or DVD drive, click to select one in which you've inserted a CD-RW disc.

④ Click **Next** to continue.

INTRODUCTION

Nero has another option, InCD, which turns your CD or DVD recorder into another disc drive, allowing any program to save files directly to your media. This takes advantage of a technology called UDF (Universal Disc Format), or *packet writing*.

TIP

With InCD installed as a separate installation option, you automatically have a program that reads and writes to a UDF 1.5 formatted disc, but you can't always assume that others will have that capability.

HINT

If you want your discs to be accessible to others, don't burn them with InCD; instead, use Nero's Data Disc feature.

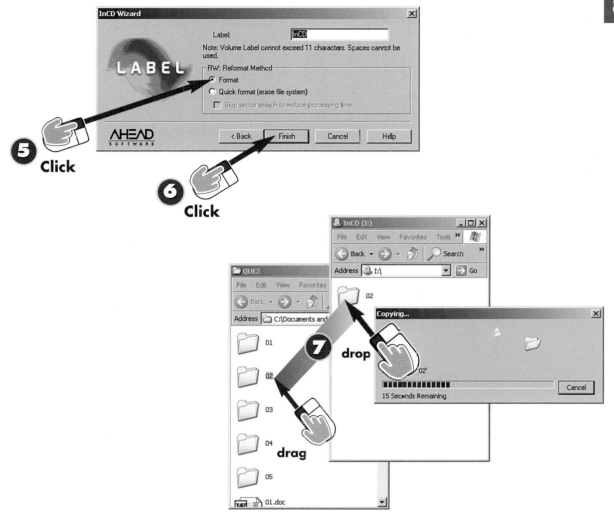

5 Click the **Format** option button.

6 Click **Finish**. Formatting a CD-RW disc can take some time. (Reformatting a used CD-RW took almost 20 minutes!)

7 In Windows Explorer, drag and drop files to the formatted disc, or save to it from programs such as Microsoft Word.

End

TIP When you use InCD, label your discs (or use color-coded labels or discs) to differentiate your UDF (InCD) discs from conventional CDs. Also, right-click and eject the discs using Windows Explorer for best results.

TIP To go back to using Nero Burning ROM, be sure there are no InCD discs in use.

Using Copy CD

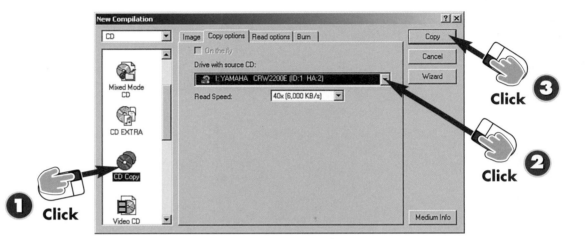

1 Open a new project and select **CD Copy**.

2 Under the **Copy Options** tab, select your source CD.

3 Click **Copy** to continue. Nero creates a temporary image file of the contents of the disc.

TIP

If you have a single CD recorder, using the wizard will lead you through the process of saving an image file and burning it afterward.

HINT

With an audio CD, if the database opens, click **Cancel** (or make any entries you like).

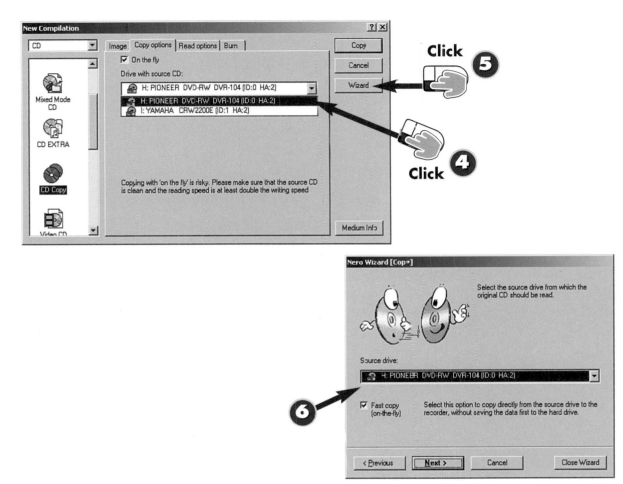

Click **5**

Click **4**

4 Put in the destination disc that will accept the copied data, and let copying proceed. If you have two CD (or DVD) recordable drives in your system, click to make one the source drive and the other the destination drive.

5 You can also click **Wizard** to use the wizard.

6 If you have kept the wizard enabled, you get a CD copy option, and then a Fast Copy setting if you have two recorders.

End

HINT With two drives, you can click the **On-the-Fly** option after clicking the **Copy** tab of **CD Copy**, but note it's risky and requires the speed of the recording drive to be *double* the speed of the source drive. (Without On-the-Fly, copying is slower and steadier.)

TIP Remember that reproducing copyrighted material, whether it is music, video, or computer programs, can get you into a lot of trouble.

Creating Image Files

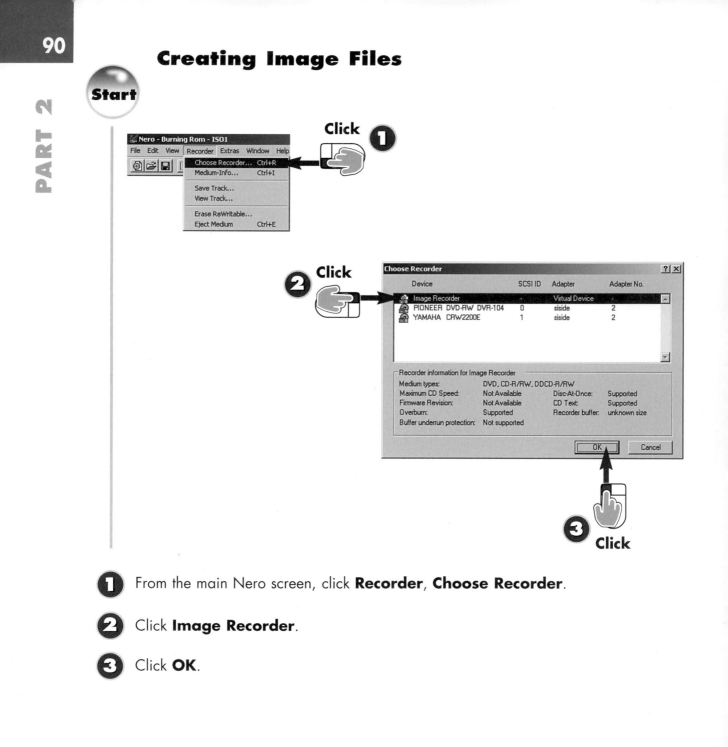

Start

Click ①

② Click

③ Click

① From the main Nero screen, click **Recorder**, **Choose Recorder**.

② Click **Image Recorder**.

③ Click **OK**.

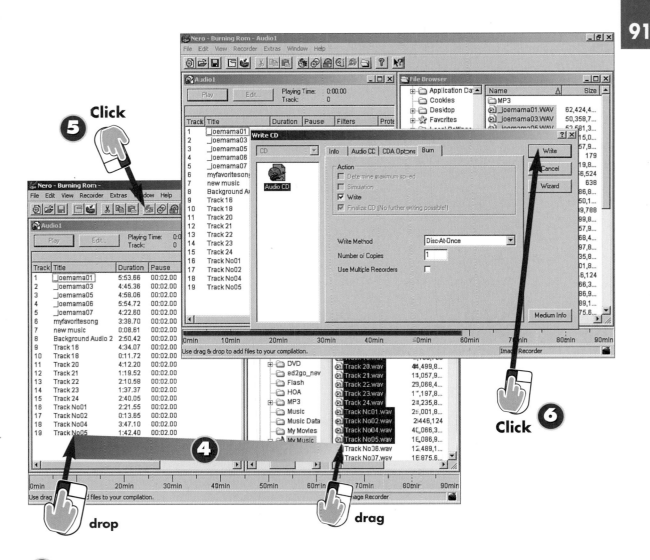

4 Select and then drag and drop your audio or data tracks to create a compilation.

5 Click the **Write CD** button. (If it's grayed out, be sure you are in the compilation panel by clicking it.)

6 Unless you have specific recording needs, click **Write**.

See next page

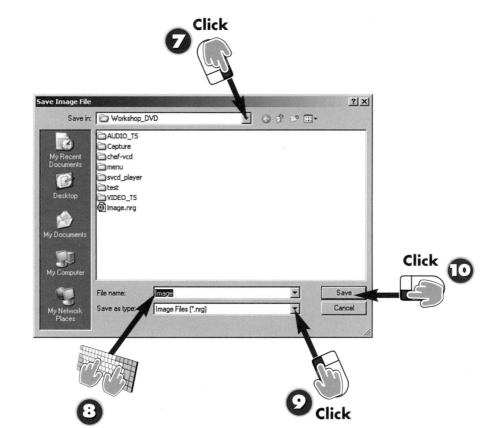

7 Choose a folder in which you want the image to be saved.

8 Give the image a name.

9 Select a file type. (The default image format for Nero is *.NRG.)

10 Click **Save** to create an image file of your compilation on your hard drive.

End

TIP   If you burn a lot of disc images, create a special folder for them to keep them organized, and delete them when they're done.

HINT   When you're ready to burn discs again, change your Recorder option back from Virtual to one of your actual CD burners—or you will only be able to burn disc images!

Reburning Your Image Files

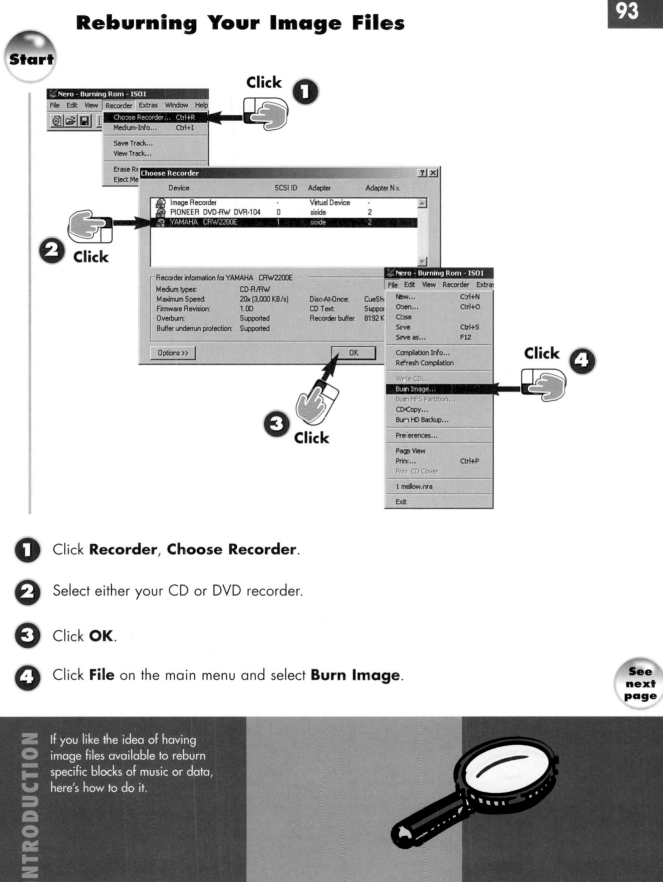

1 Click **Recorder**, **Choose Recorder**.

2 Select either your CD or DVD recorder.

3 Click **OK**.

4 Click **File** on the main menu and select **Burn Image**.

See next page

INTRODUCTION

If you like the idea of having image files available to reburn specific blocks of music or data, here's how to do it.

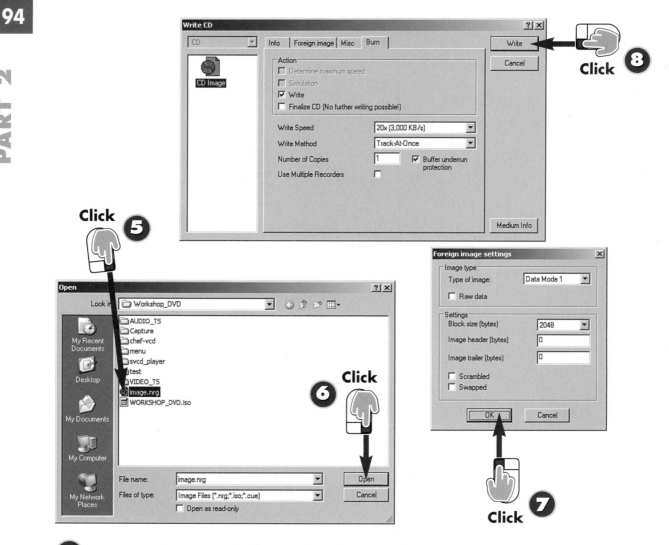

5 Browse to the correct folder to select the image file.

6 Click **Open**.

7 Unless you have specific recording needs, click **OK** for the Foreign Image Settings.

8 Make any final changes to burn speed or other options, and then click **Write**.

Enc

TIP The default format for Nero is NRG, but it supports ISO and CUE-Sheet formats. This means that you can burn images created by other programs.

HINT The full retail version of Nero 5 includes a program that lets you look inside disc images to remind you of their contents. To install Nero ImageDrive, go to the **Start** button, **All Programs**, **Ahead**, and **Install Nero ImageDrive**.

Creating a CD Extra

Start

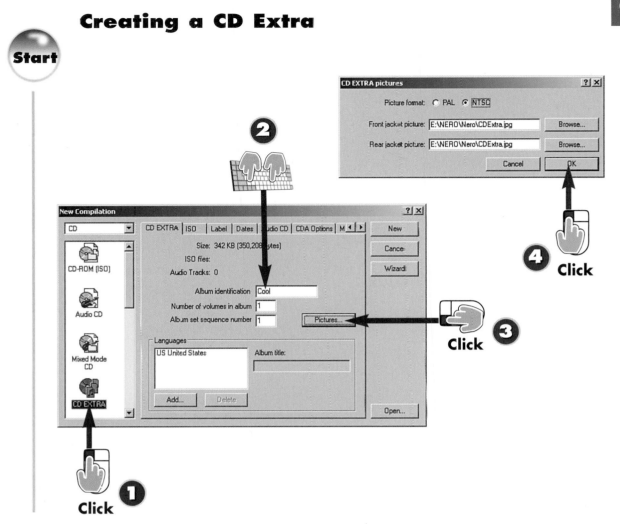

Click

Click

Click

Click

1 Create a new compilation and select **CD Extra**.

2 In the CD Extra tab, add information in **Album Identification**.

3 Click the **Pictures** button to add front and back images.

4 CD Extra is popular abroad, so PAL is the default. Change to **NTSC** for U.S. audiences, then click **OK**.

See next page

INTRODUCTION

A CD Extra is sometimes called an enhanced CD. It works in a conventional audio CD to play its digital music, and it can include data for a CD-ROM. With Nero, making a CD Extra disc is easy.

HINT

CD Extra is popular in other countries, and different devices have the capability to read these discs differently. To find out more about this format, consult the Nero manual included on your disc.

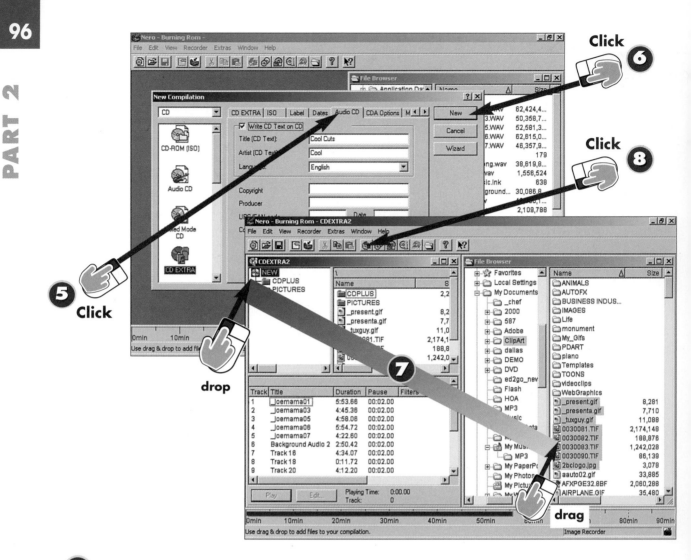

5 Click the **Audio CD** tab to add CD text to the audio portion.

6 Click **New**.

7 Drag and drop your data files onto the New icon in the data portion, not into the subfolders. Your audio tracks can be added as usual to the audio panel.

8 Click the **Write CD** button, and click **Write** to burn the disc.

End

HINT

Notice that the status bar at the bottom shows both CD audio tracks and megabytes of data. When you have filled the disc (but not exceeded its capacity), the wizard will also take you to the CD Extra option; go through it and pick **Other Data Formats** and **Audio + Data Mixed**.

Creating a Mixed-Mode CD

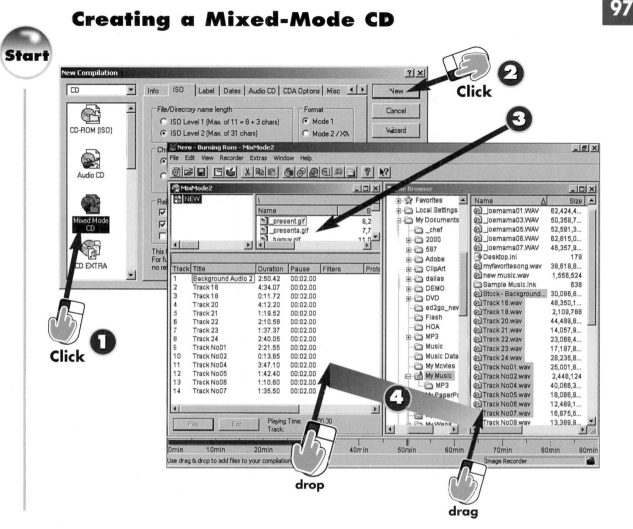

Start

Click ②

③

Click ①

drop

drag

④

---

① Click the **New Compilation** button and select **Mixed Mode** from the drop-down list.

② The default options on the ISO tab will generally be okay. The Audio CD tab enables you to enter CD text. When you've made your entries, click **New**.

③ Add your data files to the upper panel as you would any data-CD compilation.

④ Locate a file folder (or audio CD) with your audio files or track. Then drag and drop them into the lower panel.

See next page

INTRODUCTION

A mixed mode CD is a special kind of data CD that is often used in encyclopedias or other entertainment or educational programs that combine music and data. Older CD-ROM drives can't differentiate these tracks, so the CD Extra (enhanced CD) mode was developed (see the preceding section). Both of these are somewhat advanced, but it's cool to combine digital audio and data.

TIP

Don't put this disc into an audio CD player—you will hear loud static and no music. Notice that the data tracks precede the audio tracks on the disc.

HINT

A mixed-mode disc lets you use the Autoplay feature. We will cover how to create an Autoplay disc in Chapter 9.

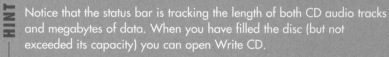

5 Click the **Write CD** icon.

6 Select **Disk-At-Once**.

7 Click **Write** to burn the mixed-mode disc.

HINT Notice that the status bar is tracking the length of both CD audio tracks and megabytes of data. When you have filled the disc (but not exceeded its capacity) you can open Write CD.

You can still make additional changes to the Options tab in the Write CD dialog box.

Using Nero Express for Data

Start

1 Click

2 Click

3 Click

1 Open Nero Express and click to select a CD or a DVD recorder.

2 Click the **Data** arrow and look at the choices.

3 Read the explanation of the data CD and click to select **Data Disc**.

See next page

INTRODUCTION

Nero Express is like the AOL of CD burning. It puts a friendly face on the process of CD creation and hides what's under the hood.

TIP

Notice that there are also image recorders for both DVD and CD projects (that let you burn image files for continued reburning).

To burn a disc image, use one of the image recorder options in the drop-down menu.

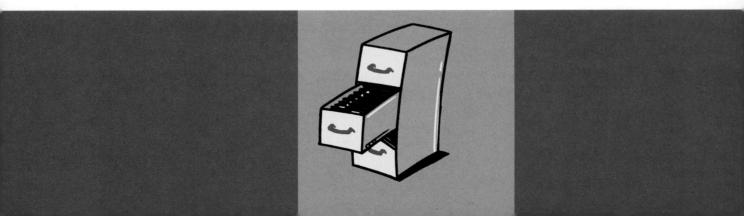

4 Click **Add**.

5 In the File Browser, select your folders or files.

6 Click **Add**.

7 Click **Finished**.

Nero Express

Final Burn Settings

Click 'Burn' to start the recording process

Current Recorder: I: YAMAHA CRW2200E [CD-R/RW] ▼ Browse...

Disc Name: My Disc

Title (CD Text):

Artist (CD Text):

Writing Speed: 12x (1,800 KB/s) ▼

Number of copies: 1

☑ Allow files to be added later (multisession disc)

☑ Verify data on disc after burning

❓ 🔥 Nero 📀 More >> ⬅ Back 🔥 Burn

Click **10**

8 How much easier can it get? Give your disk a name.

9 Set your Writing Speed and options—select **Allow Files to Be Added Later (multisession disc)** and **Verify Data on Disc After Burning**.

10 Then click **Burn**.

End

HINT You can always click the **Back** button to return to your compilation to make changes. Click the **New Folder** icon to create and name a new folder in your compilation (into which to drag files or subfolders).

You can use the **Save** button to save your compilation (not your disc image) to a file.

Using Nero Express for Audio

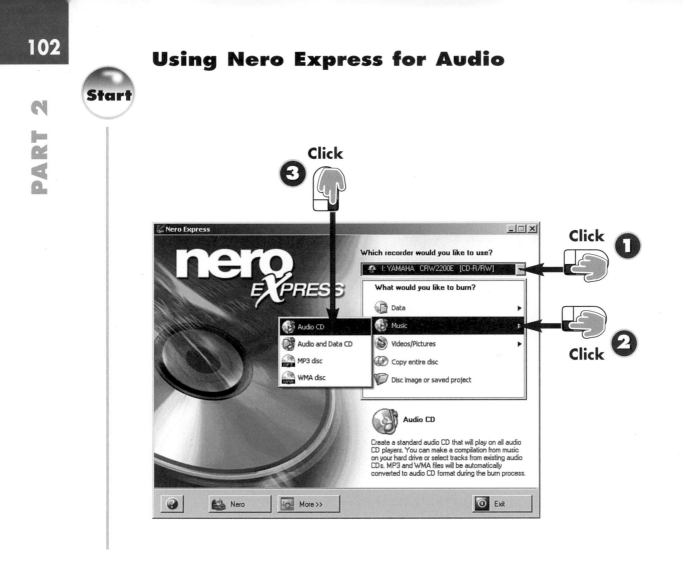

Start

Click 3

Click 1

Click 2

1. Open Nero Express and click to select your recorder.

2. Click the **Music** arrow, and examine the choices. (We work with some of the other types in the main section on Nero.)

3. Read the explanation of the audio CD and click to select **Audio CD**.

INTRODUCTION

Now that you've seen how easy Nero Express is, let's try it with an audio CD. This time we'll explore a few more bells and whistles.

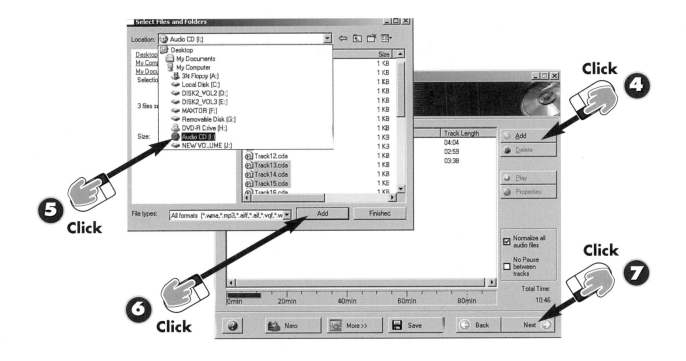

Click 4

Click 5

Click 6

Click 7

4 Click **Add** to begin adding your sound files.

5 In the File Browser, select your audio CD source drives (or music files).

6 Click **Add** (click **Cancel** to close the database if it opens).

7 When the tracks you want have been added, click **Finished**, and then click **Next**.

See next page

TIP Click the **More** button for options. Saving your files to your hard drive will make them more easily accessible. You can also erase a rewritable disc, quickly set Nero preferences (Configure), get disc information, or open the Cover Designer.

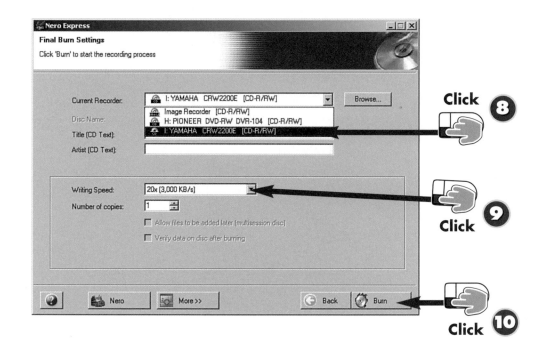

Click **8**

Click **9**

Click **10**

 8 Select your recorder from **Current Recorder**.

9 Set your **Writing Speed**.

10 Click **Burn** to create your audio CD.

End

TIP If you are getting audio from a CD, the time for the extraction process depends on your source drive.

HINT Click the drop-down arrow to select a different destination recorder or image file.

Note the check box options under music: Normalize all audio files and No Pause between tracks.

Creating a Video CD in Nero Express

Start

① Open Nero Express and click the **Videos/Pictures** arrow to begin a video CD project.

② Read the explanation of the Video CD.

③ Click to select **Video CD**.

See next page

INTRODUCTION

A Video CD is a special kind of CD that uses MPEG1 video files and an interactive menu to play movies. We will cover video capture and editing in more detail in later chapters (and explain the VCD and SVCD formats), but let's quickly look at how Nero lets you make such a disc after you have MPEG1-compliant movie files.

PART 2

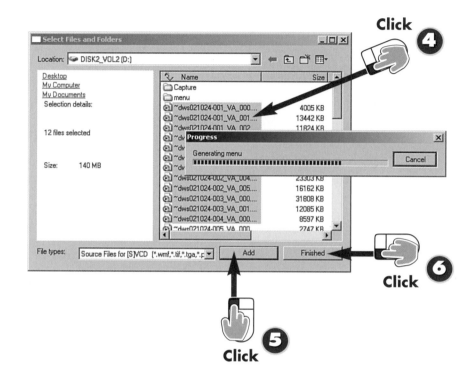

4 Click **Add**, and then select your MPEG1-compliant video files.

5 Click **Add**. As the files are being added, if you look quickly, you can see a menu being automatically generated.

6 When the files you want have been added, click **Finished**.

HINT

If you have selected non-MPEG1–compliant files (such as Windows AVI video files), Nero will encode (convert) them. This can take some additional time, and the results will depend on your source video quality.

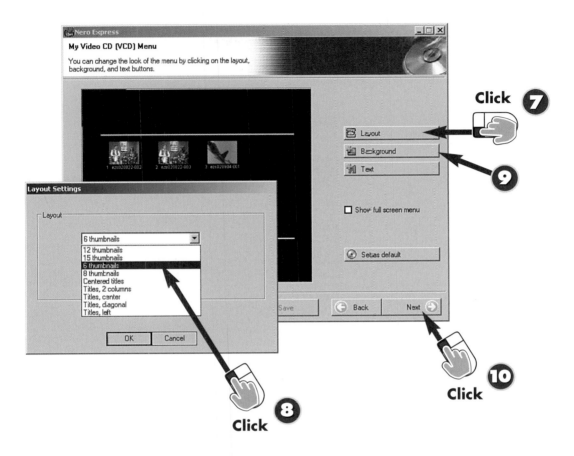

Click **7**

Click **8**

Click **10**

7 Click the **Layout** button to adjust the look by the number of thumbnails (first frame of the videos) and titles (filenames).

8 The largest thumbnail size is six per menu. Select a layout from the drop-down list.

9 To change the menu text and background, click the **Text** and **Background** buttons and examine the choices.

10 When you're done, close the windows and click **Next**.

See next page

TIP
If you change the sample text and click **Font**, you can change the color of the text. In the Background panel, you can change the color and/or add an image.

HINT
By experimenting with the Background and Text option panels, changing the video file-names, and adding a photo, you can get some nice results.

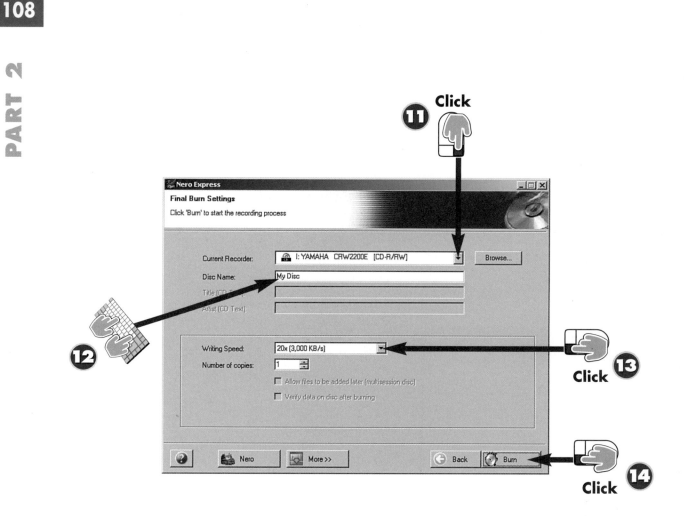

Click

11

12

13

Click

14

Click

11 Select your recorder from **Current Recorder**.

12 Type in a label for your video disk.

13 Set your **Writing Speed**.

14 Click **Burn** to create your disk.

End

TIP

With VCDs, the user menu selections are always made by their numbers. We'll work with both VCD and SVCD in more detail in the DVD MovieFactory 2.0 sections of the book.

Creating a Photo CD in Nero

Start

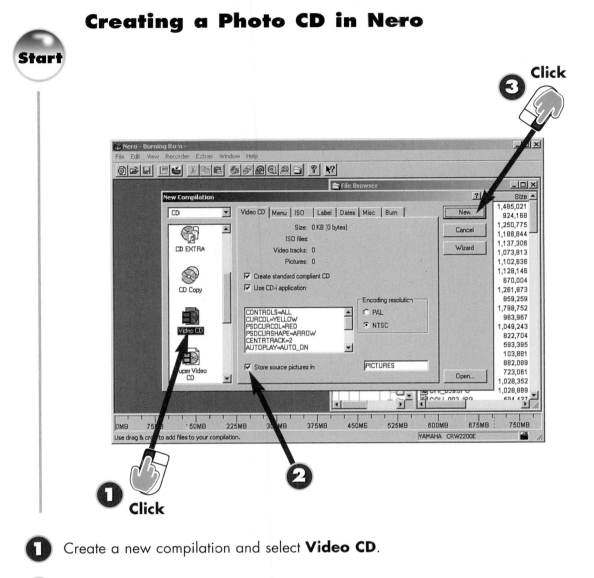

Click

Click

① Create a new compilation and select **Video CD**.

② Be sure that **Use CD-I Application** and **Store Source Pictures In** are selected.

③ Click **New** to begin.

See next page

A Photo CD is like an album of images. You can combine it with MPEG1 video on a Video CD or just add your pictures. This time, let's use the main Nero program.

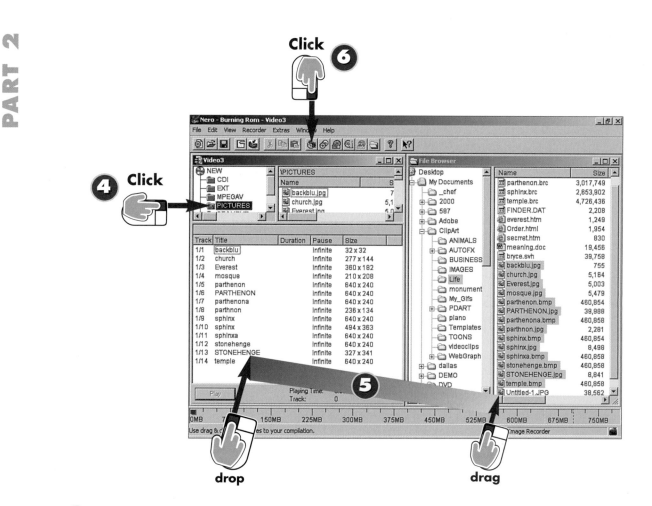

4 Click the **Pictures** folder in the upper panel.

5 Find your pictures in the File Browser and drag and drop them into the bottom of the Pictures folder in the left panel.

6 Click the **Write CD** icon.

Click ⑦

8 **Click**

9

⑦ On the Menu tab, click **Enable Menu**.

8 Click **Preview First Page**.

9 Type a title in the **Header Text** field.

See next page

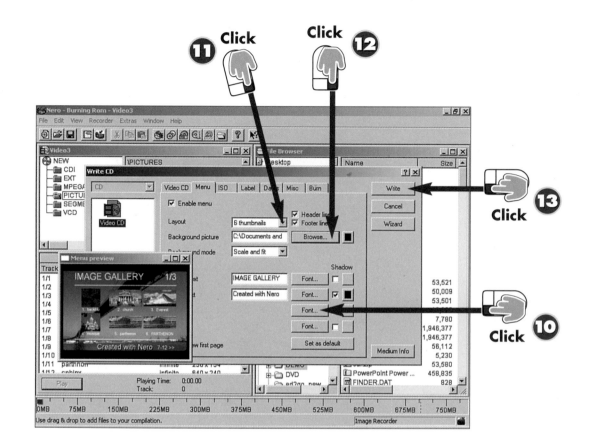

10 Click the **Font** button to change the font and/or its color.

11 Set the number of thumbnails to show the images as well as captions.

12 To add a photo background, click the **Browse** button to add an image for the menu background.

13 Click the **Write** button to begin recording.

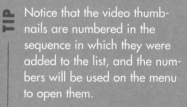

TIP Notice that the video thumbnails are numbered in the sequence in which they were added to the list, and the numbers will be used on the menu to open them.

How to Create a Disc Label or Cover

Start

1 Click

2 Click

3 Click

4 Click

1 Open Nero Cover Designer and click on the **Standard** CD label.

2 Click **Audio**, **Data**, or **Audio+Data** to see the template choices.

3 Click **OK**.

4 Click the **Disc** tab to start with the actual disc label. Then right-click a text place-holder and select **Data** to begin to change the text.

See next page

INTRODUCTION

After you've burned your master-piece, you might want to cap it off with a nice label for the disc, or perhaps an insert for the case. Many templates or styles of labels and inserts are available, and Nero Cover Designer lets you work with almost all of them.

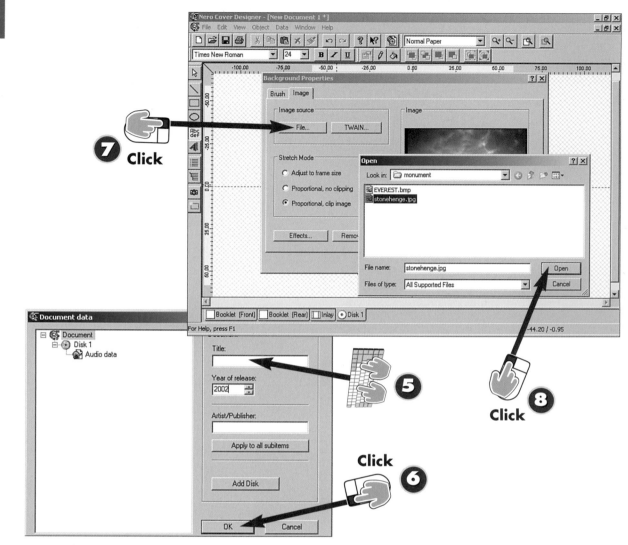

⑤ The text window will come up for the label text. Enter the text for the field that you want to change.

⑥ Click **OK**.

⑦ Double-click the label itself to bring up the Background Properties window. Then, click **File** to load an image file and browse to one you like.

⑧ Click **Open** after you've selected your file.

HINT

If you are using several elements (CD label, inserts, and so on), click **Print Preview** under **File** on the main menu to see how they will look.

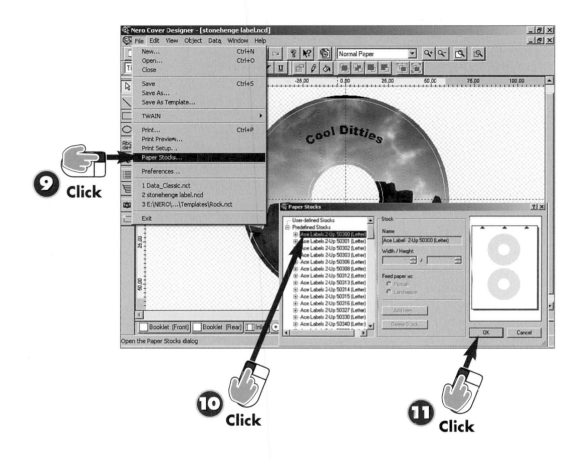

9 Under the **File** menu, click **Paper Stocks** to bring out a list of popular layouts for labels you intend to print.

10 Choose the right one for your project.

11 Click **OK**, and then print your label.

End

TIP
When you like what you've done, use Save As a File or Template to use it again later.

HINT
The best way to label a compilation of data is to click **Data**, **Document Data** on the main menu. You can add folders and files from the compilation to a field on the back or front cover to remind you which files and folders are on your data CD.

Completing Three Simple CD Projects

In this chapter, we're going to de-emphasize the tools and concentrate on common projects. We'll address some universal problems and work on concepts that you should find helpful in your professional or personal computer life.

First, now that you know how to back up data, we'll do a project that also shows which files and folders are important to safeguard. (In Chapter 9, "Tips and Techniques," we'll cover DVD, multimedia work, and backup strategies in even more detail.)

We've covered different ways to archive and burn a music collection. Now we'll think through our own personal collection and burn it to disc.

Finally, we want to combine some of the main data formats on the PC to create an interactive project, so we'll make a CD-ROM that we can burn on the smaller "business card"-sized discs that you can buy at electronic stores. We'll do this by concentrating on the projects themselves.

By now, even if we happen to select one of the programs for a specific task, you'll understand the concepts well enough to achieve the same results with the program you use. These projects are meant to teach you tasks so you can apply them to your own situation at home or at work.

Using the Roxio Project Selector

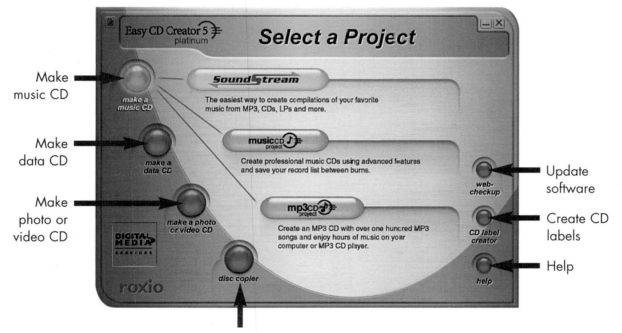

Make music CD

Make data CD

Make photo or video CD

Update software

Create CD labels

Help

Copy disk

Easy CD Creator 5 platinum

Select a Project

SoundStream

The easiest way to create compilations of your favorite music from MP3, CDs, LPs and more.

musiccd project

Create professional music CDs using advanced features and save your record list between burns.

mp3cd project

Create an MP3 CD with over one hundred MP3 songs and enjoy hours of music on your computer or MP3 CD player.

make a music CD

make a data CD

make a photo or video CD

web-checkup

CD label creator

help

disc copier

DIGITAL MEDIA SERVICES

roxio

Preparing a File and Folder Backup

Start

Click ❶

Click ❷   **Click** ❸

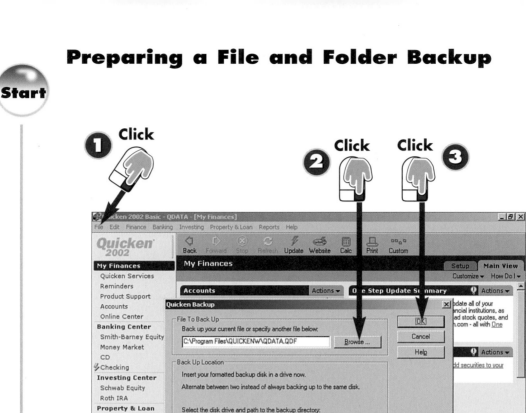

❶ To back up finances in Quicken, click **File**, **Backup**.

❷ Browse to the folder in which you want to store the file on your C: drive.

❸ Click **OK** to create the backup file.

Because I have reinstalled Windows (95, 98, 2000, and XP) many times, I have lost all faith in backup programs. I assume that when I crash, I will need to reinstall everything. I need to protect my stuff the best way I can, so I concentrate on two things: data and settings. You should also think about these issues.

Click

4

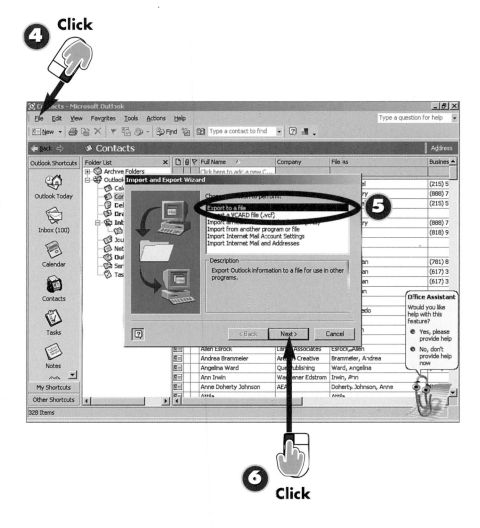

5

6

Click

4 To back up the Contacts (and Calendar), in Outlook, select either one and click **File**, **Import and Export**.

5 In the wizard, choose **Export to a File**.

6 Click **Next**.

See next page

TIP

You can save a complete Outlook.PST file to reopen later. But this is what I do for my addresses (and Calendar); the important thing is that you back up whatever database you use.

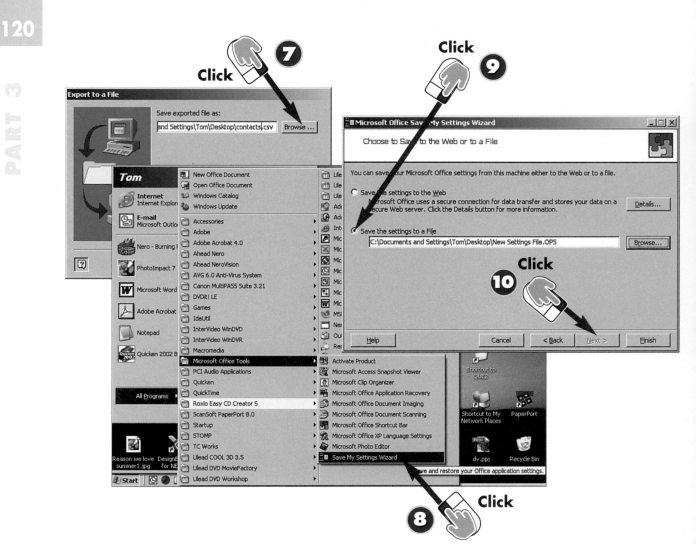

 Choose and name a file; the format that I select is **Windows Comma Delimited (CSV)** because it's easy to import to other programs.

 To back up all your Office settings, click the **Start** button, click **All Programs**, select **Microsoft Office Tools**, and select **Save My Settings Wizard**.

9 Again, this results in a single file that the wizard can restore after you have reinstalled Windows and Office. Click **Save the Settings to a File**.

10 Click **Next** to save your settings.

Click 11

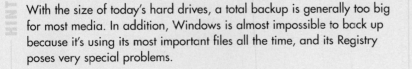

11 In MS Word, click **Tools**, **Options**, **File Locations**.

12 Select **User Templates** from the File Locations list.

13 Click **Modify** to locate the Templates folder.

End

With the size of today's hard drives, a total backup is generally too big for most media. In addition, Windows is almost impossible to back up because it's using its most important files all the time, and its Registry poses very special problems.

Normal.DOT is the most important file MS Word users have, especially if they have autotext settings and macros. You must know where the current version is stored—and back it up conscientiously.

Compiling the Backup

Start

Click **1**

Click **3**

2 Click

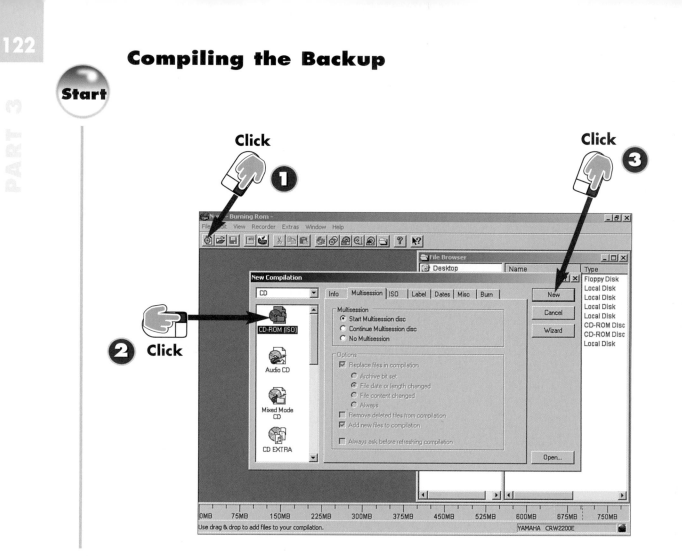

1 Click the **New Compilation** button to begin.

2 Select **CD-ROM** and choose either **Multisession** or **No Multisession.**

3 Click **New** to continue.

INTRODUCTION

By now you should be comfortable compiling a data CD in either of the CD-burning applications we've covered. In both programs, the interface features a compilation panel and a file browser. Let's compile our files in Nero for the purpose of illustration.

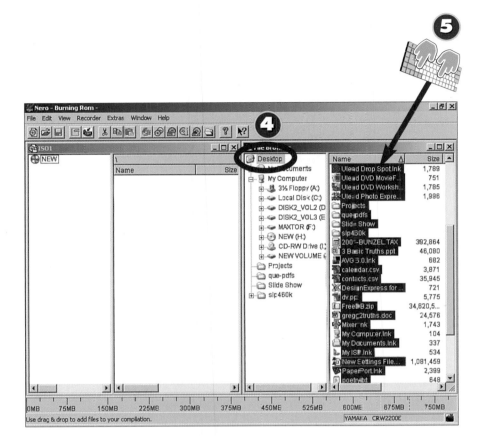

 In the File Browser, click **Desktop**.

 Press **Ctrl+A** to select everything on your desktop (even shortcuts—they're tiny).

See
next
page

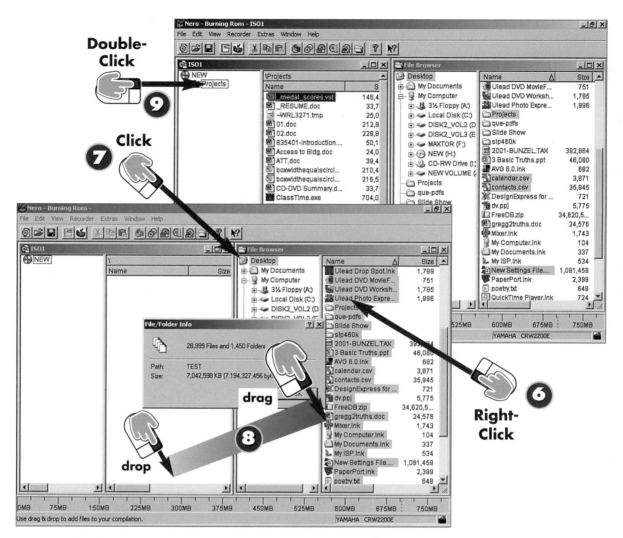

Double-Click

9

Click

7

Right-Click

6

drag

drop

8

6 Right-click the selected files and folders and click **Properties**. The folders and files on my desktop are more than 7GB in size—way too much data.

7 Click **Desktop** again and select fewer files and folders.

8 Drag and drop to add them to the compilation. Don't forget to save your files in the **My Documents** folder or other folders where you have important files!

9 Double-click the folder icon in the compilation to display its contents.

End

Notice that I have selected and compiled the three files I saved in my preparation task (Office Settings, Calendar, and Contacts) and a projects folder. See how the folder is separate from the files.

Individual files will join the ones from my desktop in the root folder. (If they have the same names, they may be overwritten.)

You could do the same thing with the UDF format (DirectCD or InCD), but if you wanted to use it in two years with a different PC, you might have a different CD-recording program that couldn't read your disc.

Completing the Data Backup

Start

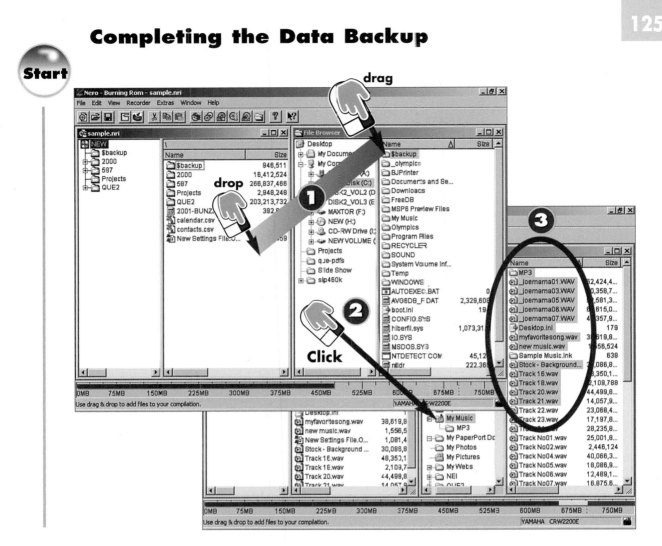

drag

drop

Click

1. We backed up our Quicken data into a folder called $backup on the C: drive. Click **C:**, click the folder, and then drag and drop it into the compilation.

2. Now for the audio tracks saved as WAV and MP3 files: Click **My Documents**, find the **My Music** folder, and drag and drop in the audio tracks from those folders.

3. Whoa! That exceeded the capacity—those files are huge If you go over your limit, click **Ctrl+Z** (Undo), select fewer files, and start over.

See next page

INTRODUCTION

At this point you can continue adding files until you get close to the most common 650 (or 700) megabyte limit of your disc. If you're using a DVD recorder and media, you can cram up to 4.7 gigabytes onto your disc.

TIP

Notice that if I double-click the folder in the compilation, the MP3 files are included within it.

HINT

CD Creator doesn't have Undo; you must delete the folders manually.

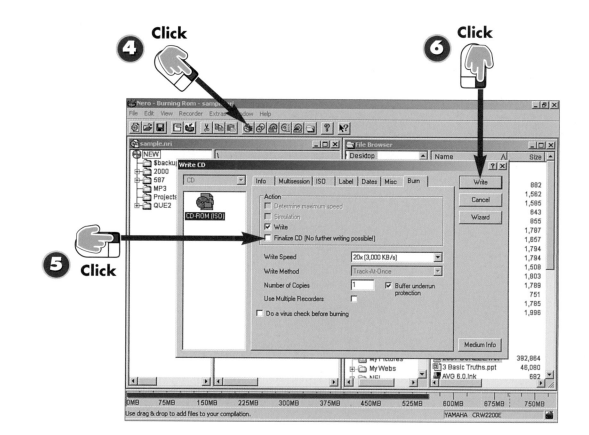

Click 4

Click 6

Click 5

4 Now, insert a blank CD into your burner and click **Write CD**.

5 Check **Finalize CD** if you are finished adding files to this disk.

6 Finally, click **Write**.

End

In the Write CD dialog box, choose the best speed for your burner and your blank media. If you have disc space and you might want to add more tracks later, uncheck Close Disc.

You can have Nero Cover Designer add the info from your data.

There are disc image programs (such as Norton Ghost) that can make an image file of your whole hard drive and restore it from DOS. If you use a program like that, you can explore the bootable CD option.

Backing up part or all of a Program File Folder can be useful—some programs store your settings or personal files by default in a subfolder (although most now use My Documents).

Creating a Diversified Music Collection

Start

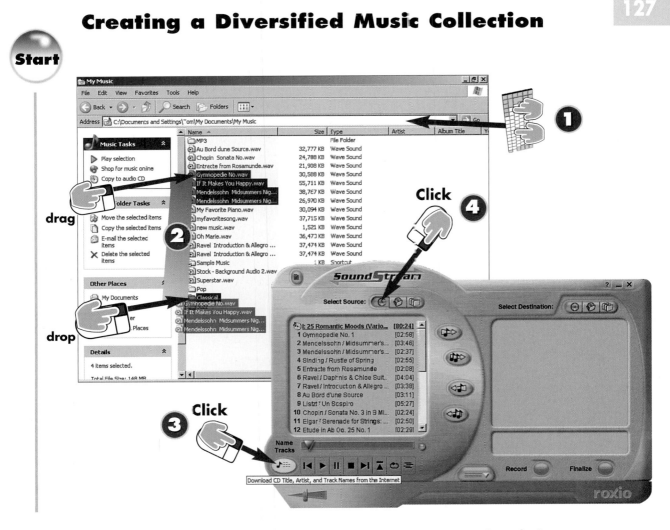

drag

drop

Click

Click

---

1 In your My Music folder, create new folders, naming them **Pop**, **Classical**, and **Jazz**.

2 Drag and drop your extracted files into the correct folder. To distinguish MP3 files, you can use another subfolder.

3 Open SoundStream and click **Name Tracks**. (To use the online Roxio database you must be connected to the Internet.)

4 With your audio CD in your drive, your tracks should appear. If not, click the **CD** tab in the Source panel.

See next page

INTRODUCTION

Now let's organize a music collection from different types of CDs to burn different combinations or to play directly from our hard drive. Because I like the ease of using SoundStream and the Roxio online database to name the files, I'm going to use CD Creator. But because we've also covered how to name files in Nero, these concepts will also work with that program.

TIP

If you have files named Track 1, Track 2, and so on, right-click to rename them.

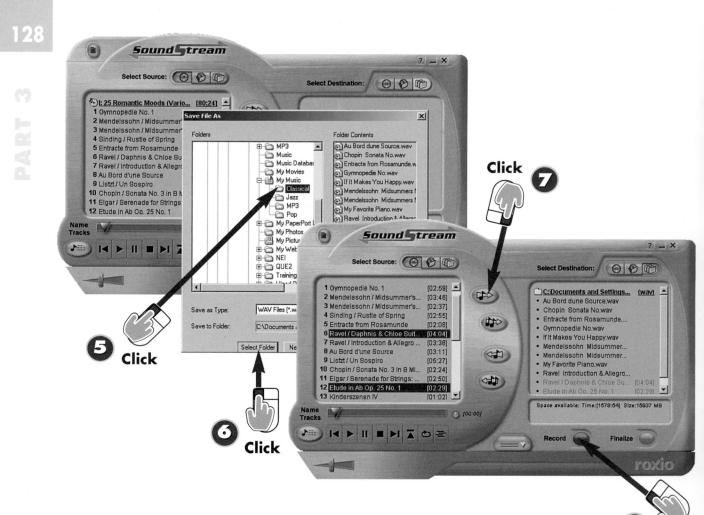

(5) Click the **Folder** icon in the Destination panel, and then select the subfolder in My Music with the music you want to add (**Classical**, in this case).

(6) Click **Select Folder**.

(7) Click in the Source panel to select the tracks you want to add. Then click **Add**.

(8) Finally, click **Record**. Your new additions will be added to the folder you have selected.

End

One way to use your collection is to open SoundStream anytime you want a particular type of music; open the Destination folder, select the tracks you want to play, and click the **Play** button.

You can use your audio CDs in the car and play your music at home on the PC.

Notice that files you have already added appear; they need not be duplicated. The default file format is WAV. You can also select MP3 from the **File Types** drop-down list.

Starting a Business Card CD

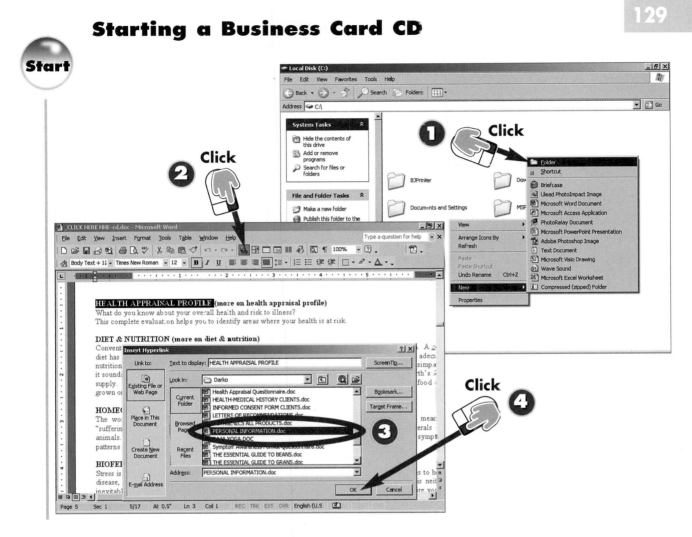

Start

Click **2**

Click **1**

Click **4**

3

1. Create a new folder (preferably in the root folder of a drive [C:]) to hold your business-card files.

2. Start with a main Word document, which includes some images and hyperlinks. Select a phrase you'd like to add a link to, and click the **Hyperlink** button.

3. Select a Word document to make it link to.

4. Click **OK** to continue—don't forget to save your work!

See next page

You might have seen the business-card shaped CDs available in stores; they hold about 180MB of data. You can burn your folders to one of those, and if you simulate a Web site, with a home page and subpages, you can create a simple interactive business-card presentation.

HINT
These will include the main document, linked documents, images, and maybe even video.

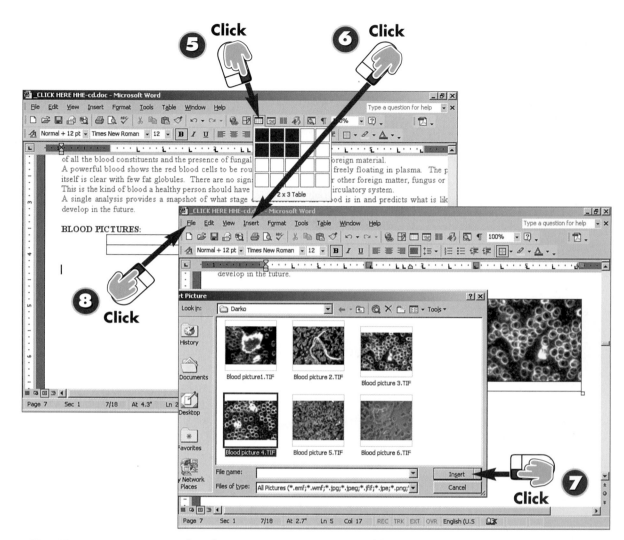

5 To put images into the document, you can use tables to create a layout and hold the pictures. Click **Insert Table** to create a table.

6 Click **Insert** on the main menu, then click **Pictures**, **From File**.

7 Browse to the image(s) you want to insert. Select an image and click **Insert**.

8 Now save your new Web page by clicking **File**, **Save As**.

TIP
You could keep everything in Word; hyperlinks generally will work. But saving as a Web page will let anyone with a Web browser look at your presentation.

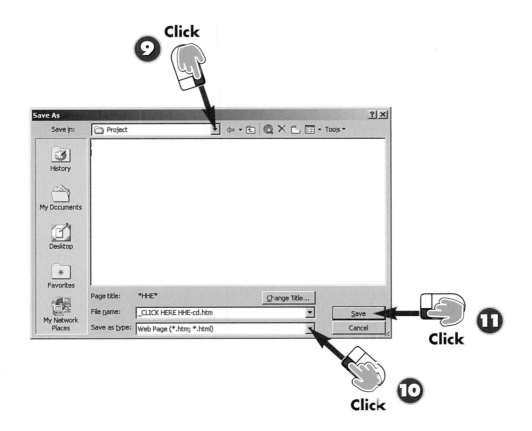

Click 9

Click 10

Click 11

9 Choose the folder you selected for your Web project.

10 Under Save as Type, select **Web Page**.

11 Click **Save** to continue.

End

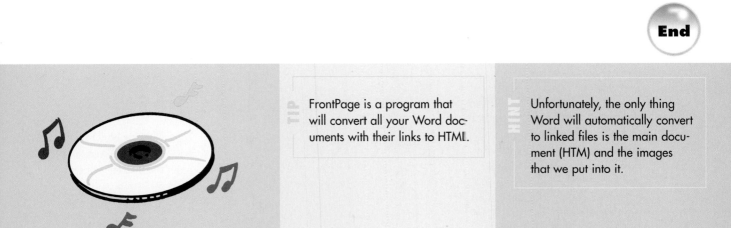

FrontPage is a program that will convert all your Word documents with their links to HTML.

Unfortunately, the only thing Word will automatically convert to linked files is the main document (HTM) and the images that we put into it.

Completing a Business Card CD

Start

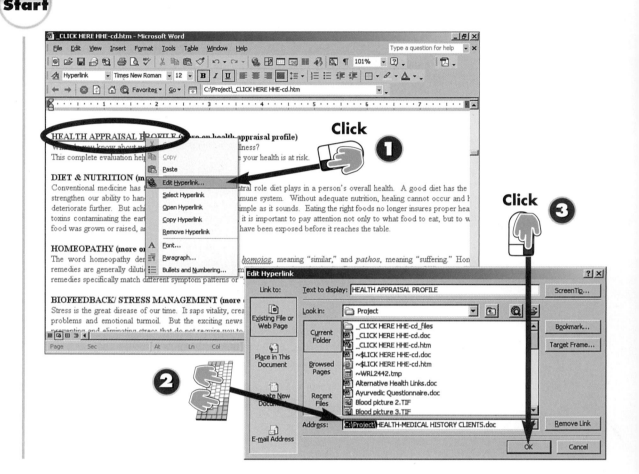

1 Locate the hyperlink you created and right-click it. Then click **Edit Hyperlink**.

2 In the hyperlink Address box, drag your mouse to select everything but the filename and press **Delete** on your keyboard. (You are deleting the drive and folder reference.)

3 Click **OK** to continue. Remember to save your work in the same folder.

INTRODUCTION

Now that you're in Word and have the HTM document (not the Word document) open, you need to edit the hyperlinks so that they have no references to your local drives and folders (because the person using the disc will have a different directory structure on his or her machine).

HINT

This "site" is meant to be accessed from a CD. In Chapter 9, you'll learn how to make the first page display automatically when the disc is inserted into the drive.

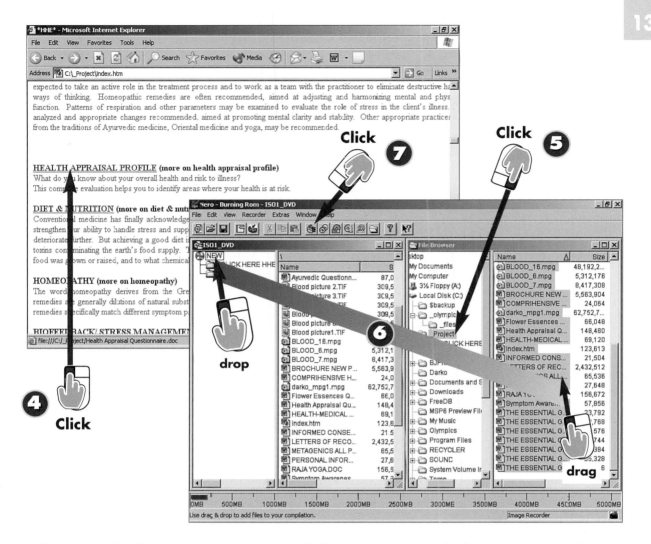

4 Open the document in a browser and click on the hyperlinked text. Internet Explorer opens the document to which it was linked.

5 In Nero (or Easy CD Creator), select your project folder in the File Browser.

6 Drag and drop the contents of the project folder directly to the root folder of the compilation, including all files and subfolders.

7 Click **Write CD**.

End

To make sure that the link is read from the disc and not from your hard drive, you can temporarily rename or move your project folder to test the links.

Doing a Web site is outside the scope of this book. This structure will work from a disc in a PC if the user surfs with Internet Explorer (not Netscape). That's because the linked documents are still Word (DOC) files.

Dragging the contents to the root folder will preserve the directory structure and will let anyone surf the contents, starting with the first (main) HTM page. Do not drag the folder (Project) to the compilation; instead, select its contents.

Starting to Capture with DVD MovieFactory 2.0

Now that we've worked a bit recording to CDs and DVDs with music and data, we're going to work with movies using a very simple but extremely powerful tool, Ulead MovieFactory 2.0. Remember that on an audio CD, the music is not really a PC file type, but rather a special digital format that can be *extracted*, or burned. The files we edited or stored were generally WAV audio files.

DVD is similar in that the computer files we store and edit are usually MPG or AVI video files. However, the digital content we burn will be either DVD or its cousins, VCD or SVCD. These are very precise forms of digital video *encoded* (or converted and stored) on a disc in specific folders and according to very strict rules. They will play on computer DVD-ROM drives and, in most cases, on commercial DVD players.

In MovieFactory we will learn four basic steps that are universal in creating a digital video disc: acquiring video, editing video, creating an interface, and finishing the disc.

MovieFactory 2.0's Add/Edit Media Window

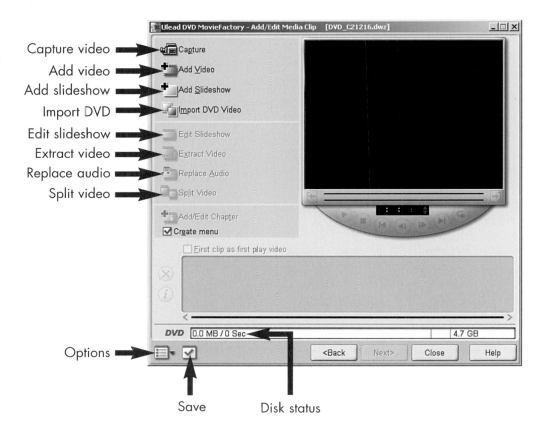

Capture video

Add video

Add slideshow

Import DVD

Edit slideshow

Extract video

Replace audio

Split video

Options

Save

Disk status

Starting DVD MovieFactory 2.0

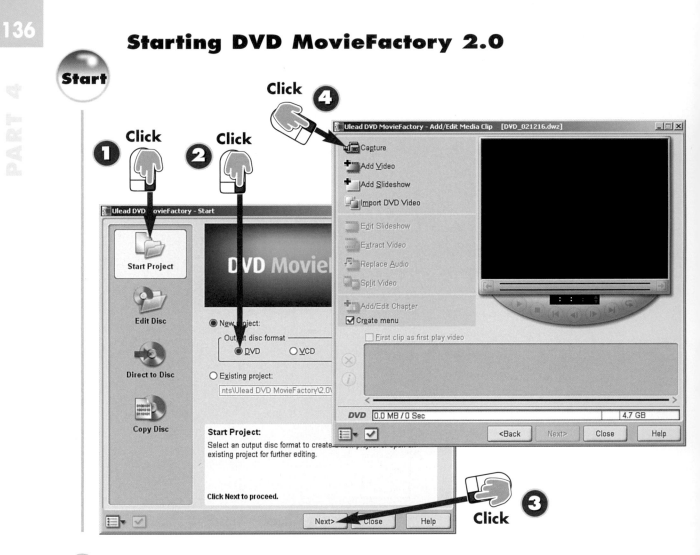

① Open MovieFactory and click **Start Project**.

② Under New Project, choose an Output Disc Format (for now, click **DVD**).

③ Click **Next** to continue.

④ The Add/Edit Video window opens. Click **Capture** to open the Capture Video window.

Opening MovieFactory 2.0 is the first key stop in our journey. You should have either a Firewire (DV) or an analog capture device and camcorder or VCR configured to begin acquiring video.

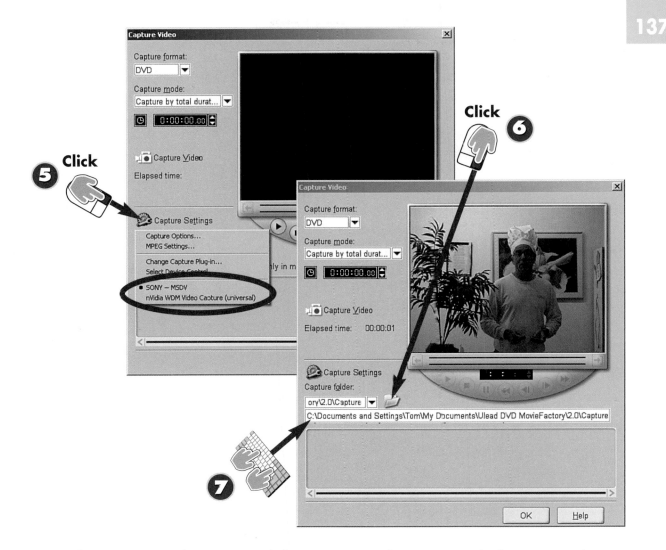

Click ⑤

Click ⑥

⑦

⑤ The Capture window opens. Click **Capture Settings** to see whether your analog capture device or your Firewire capture device is active.

⑥ Click the folder to select or note your capture folder (this is where your source video files will be stored).

⑦ You can type the path to your folder here.

End

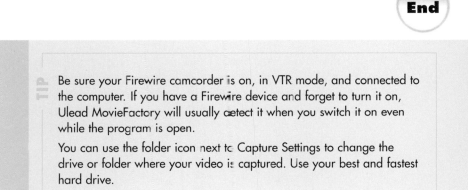

Be sure your Firewire camcorder is on, in VTR mode, and connected to the computer. If you have a Firewire device and forget to turn it on, Ulead MovieFactory will usually detect it when you switch it on even while the program is open.

You can use the folder icon next to Capture Settings to change the drive or folder where your video is captured. Use your best and fastest hard drive.

Previewing in MovieFactory

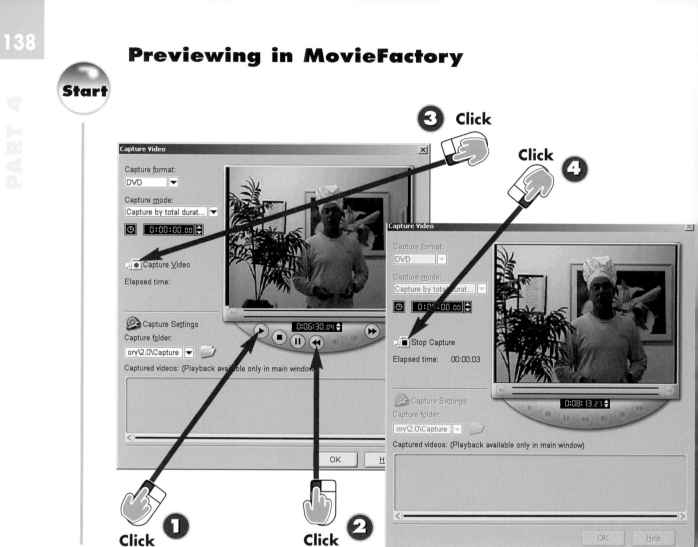

Start

③ **Click**

Click ④

Click **①**

Click **②**

① To play your video, click Play in the program (FireWire) or push the Play button on the camcorder or VCR (analog).

② To find a segment of your video, click **Pause**, **Fast Forward**, or **Rewind** on the navigation buttons (Firewire) or use the controls on your camcorder or VCR.

③ Start Capture by clicking the red **Capture Video** button.

④ Wait until you pass the desired end point, and then click **Stop Capture** or **Esc**.

You will have to use the manual controls of an analog capture device. Firewire (or DV) capture devices can be controlled directly by using the navigation buttons under the Preview window. In any case, using the capture capabilities of MovieFactory is just about as hard as pressing the Record button on your VCR. So let's get ready to capture our first video clip.

INTRODUCTION

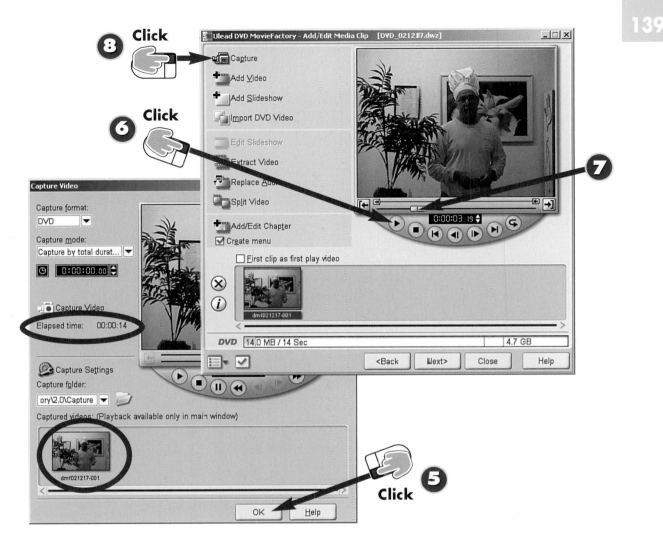

5 Your first clip is in the Video Strip, and the elapsed time of the clip appears in the Options panel. Click **OK** to return to the Add/Edit Media Clip window.

6 Click **Play** in the navigation controls under the Preview window to preview your captured clip (analog and/or Firewire/DV).

7 Watch the jog shuttle move.

8 Click **Capture** again if you want to go back and capture more clips.

If any frames are dropped, a message is displayed.

You can preview your video by using the navigation control buttons back in the Add/Edit Media window.

The thumbnails on the Video Strip are references to your captured video. Deleting the thumbnail does not delete the captured video, which is fortunate because you may later decide to use it. To see your captured videos, open the designated capture folder and open a video file.

Configuring Capture in MovieFactory

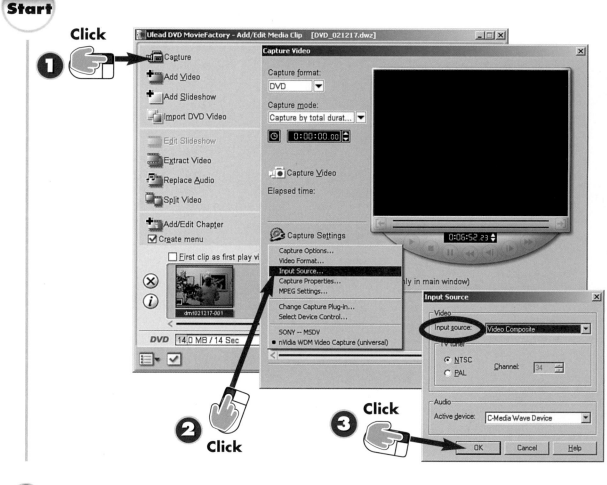

Start

Click ①

Click ②

Click ③

① Click **Capture** to return to the Capture window.

② For analog video, click **Capture Settings** and click **Input Source**.

③ Select the source. You can capture from a TV tuner (if installed), composite (yellow plug), or S-VHS (pin connector). Then click **OK**.

MovieFactory usually will detect the Firewire or analog video capture driver by default. However, if you don't get a preview in the Preview window when you push Play, or if you don't hear your audio in preview or playback, you can check some settings.

HINT

Your video source generally will correspond to the type of cable and plug that connects the Video Out plug on your camcorder or VCR to the input of your capture device—composite or S-VHS.

If you're using a camcorder for *live capture* (in camera mode rather than VCR mode) be sure the lens cap is off before you begin to troubleshoot the lack of a preview in the Capture step.

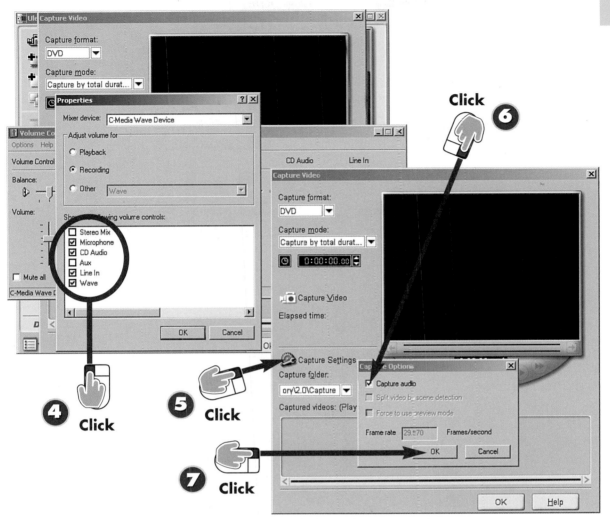

Click

6

4 Click

5 Click

7 Click

4 If you have no sound (analog), right-click the volume control on your System Tray to open the Recording (not just Playback) options. Be sure Line In is enabled and the devices are active in the Properties panel.

5 If you have no audio in captured files, click **Capture Settings.**

6 Click to enable **Capture Audio** within the Capture Options dialog box.

7 Click **OK** to continue.

End

TIP For analog video, most defaults based on format choices (DVD) will work fine. Use the Windows controls to make sure that your audio is not muted.

HINT Firewire audio might not be audible during preview before capture. After it has been captured, however, it should play through your system speakers.

TIP When capturing from tape (VCR or VTR mode on a camera), start your video far enough before clicking Capture so that you don't cut off the beginning; then leave a few seconds at the end.

Capturing with Firewire/DV

Start

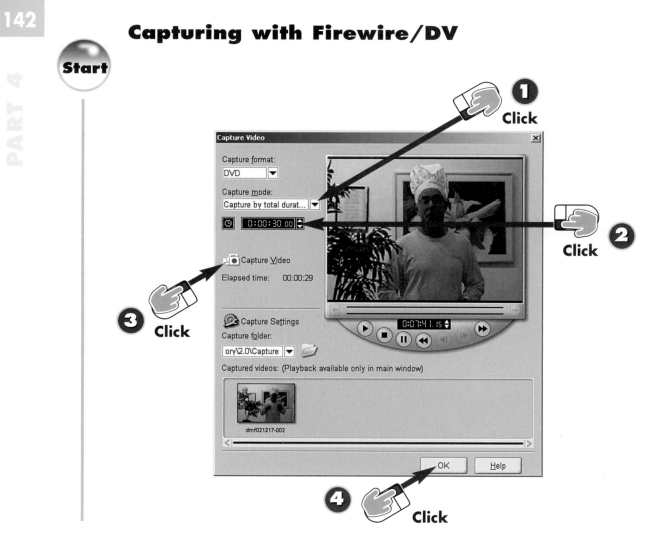

1 Click

2 Click

3 Click

4 Click

1 In the Capture Video window, click **Capture Mode** and select **Capture by Total Duration**.

2 To set a capture duration, click in the timer and enter the duration on your keyboard.

3 Click **Capture Video.**

4 Capture will stop at the length of time you indicated, and the thumbnail appears in the Video Strip. Click **OK** to return to the main window.

For those of you with Firewire/DV camcorders and capture devices, MovieFactory makes video capture even easier and more precise. MovieFactory can automatically calculate captured Firewire sequences and even split scenes for you.

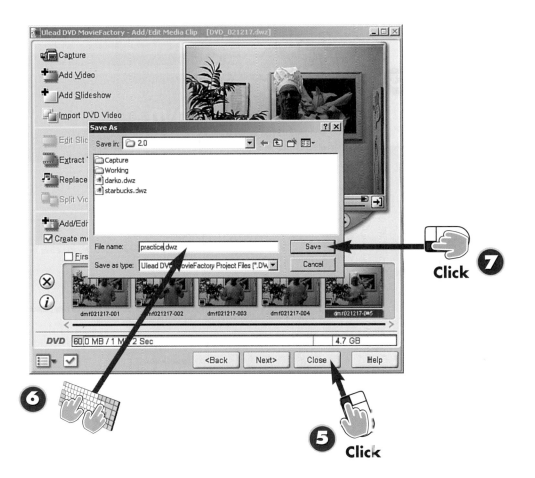

5 Now all your captured clips are available in the Video Strip. Click **Close** to close MovieFactory.

6 Save your project and give it a name you'll remember. Note its location.

7 Click **Save** to save your project.

End

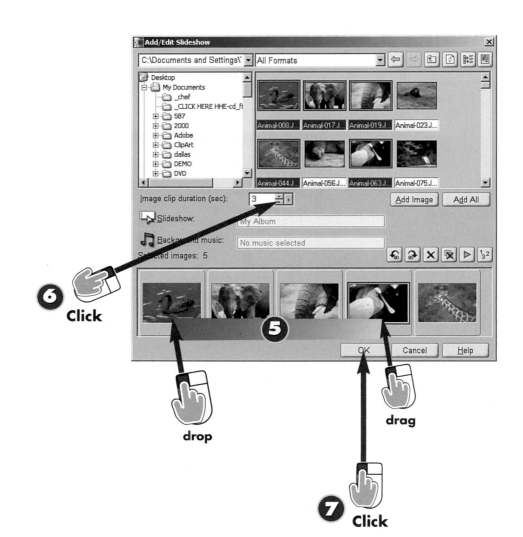

5 Drag and drop images to change their order.

6 Click to adjust the **Image Clip Duration**.

7 Click **OK** to add the Slideshow to the MovieFactory project (and return to Add/Edit Video).

End

You can change the duration of selected images (in seconds) under Image Clip Duration. You can change the show's name by clicking the **Slideshow** icon and replacing My Album with your own name.

Add background music by clicking the music symbol and attaching an audio clip.

To reopen a slideshow (and add images or make changes), select it in the Add/Edit Video window and click **Edit Slideshow**.

Importing DVD Video

Start

1 Click

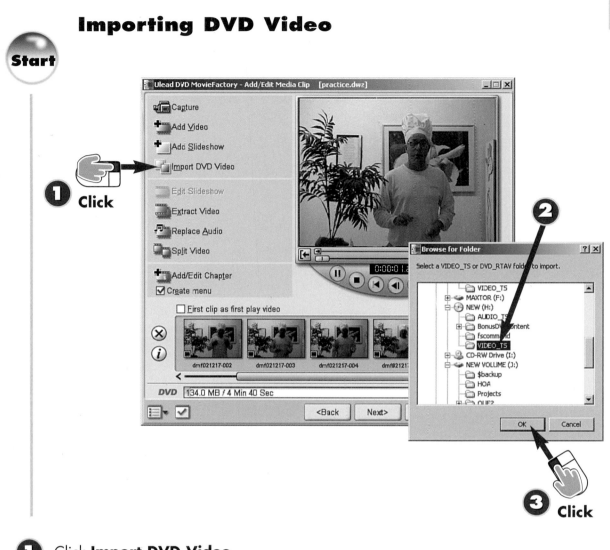

2

3 Click

---

1 Click **Import DVD Video**.

2 Select the **VIDEO_TS** folder of the DVD (usually automatic).

3 Click **OK** to continue.

See next page

INTRODUCTION

Incredibly, with MovieFactory 2.0 you can get MPEG2 video files directly from a DVD! (Except for copyrighted movies.) Insert a DVD into your DVD-recordable drive (you should still be in the Add/Edit Window).

TIP

The first time you import DVD video from a disc, finding the VIDEO_TS folder is automatic. As you will see, however, you can create your own additional DVD folders on your hard drive, making it necessary for you to choose the one you want.

HINT

When you click Finish to import DVD video, it will take a few minutes (depending on the amount of video) for the files to be added to your Add/Edit Video window.

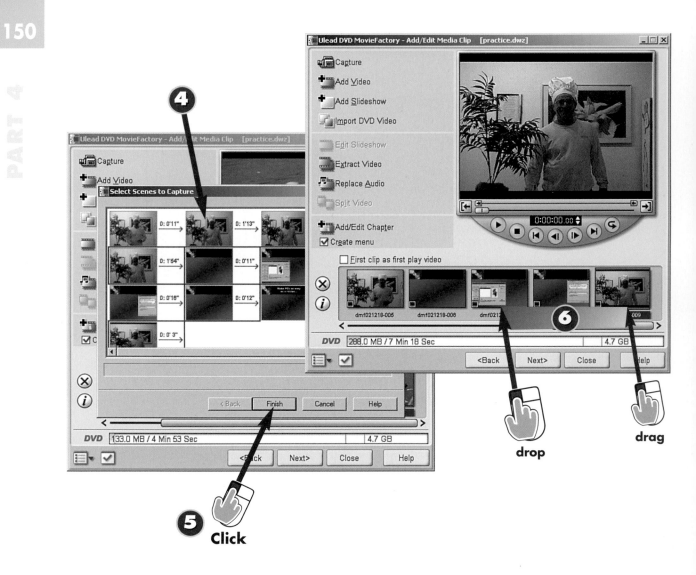

 ④ Select one or more video clips to add. (Remember the tips on keyboard click selection options listed previously.)

⑤ Click **Finish**.

⑥ DVD video clips are added to the Video Strip. You can drag and drop them to change the order.

 End

Preparing to Edit in MovieFactory

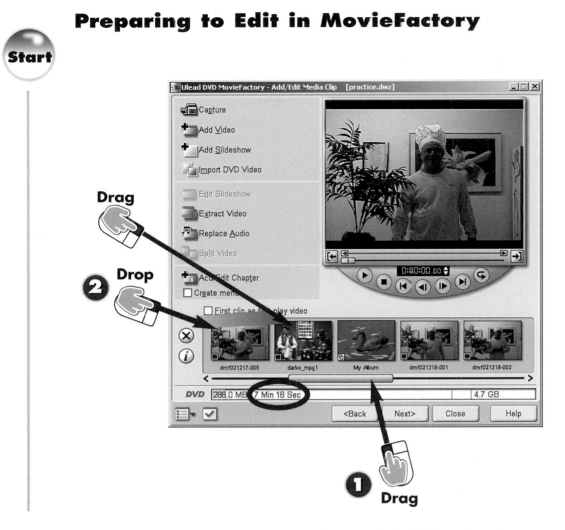

Start

Drag

2 **Drop**

1 **Drag**

1 Drag through the Video Strip to see your clips, and check the video duration on the status bar.

2 Drag and drop clips to change their order.

See next page

INTRODUCTION

You can see now how the Video Strip in MovieFactory will become populated with your captured and imported clips.

Before we begin editing these clips—and creating menus—let's get comfortable in the Add/Edit Menu.

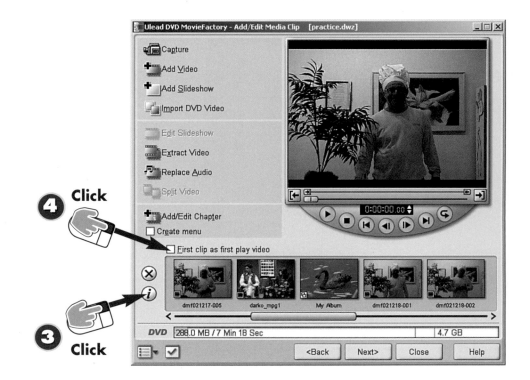

Click ④

Click ③

③ Click **Info** to check the properties of a selected clip.

④ Click to make the first clip a First Play video.

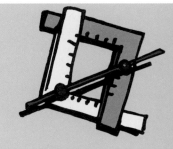

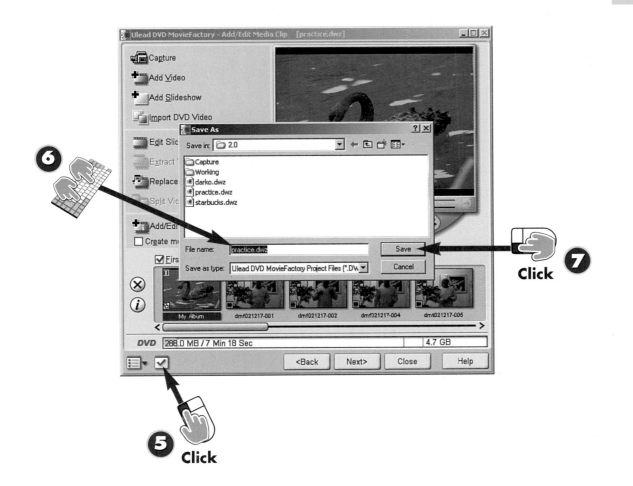

5 Save your work! Click the box to open the Save As window.

6 Type in a name you will remember.

7 Click **Save** to save your project.

End

HINT Now that you've learned to assemble all your video and slideshow assets and arrange them as a storyboard on the Video Strip, it's time to fine-tune the material by editing these video clips.

Editing with DVD MovieFactory 2.0

After we've acquired our video and still image (slideshow) assets we're ready for the fun part. Remember, to get the entire segment, we left a bit of *preroll*, or began our capture before the precise segment we wanted, and ended capture slightly after.

Now just as we might crop a picture after we scan, we will trim our videos to give them a precise in and out point. This will make sure that Aunt Sue's big moment doesn't begin with her eyes closed, or with Uncle Fred hogging the shot.

Edit Videos with Individual Scenes

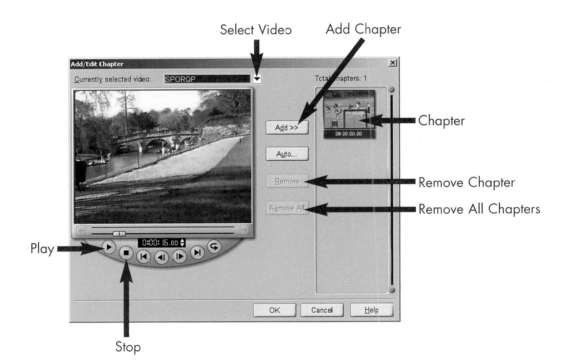

Begin Trimming Video in DVD MovieFactory

Start

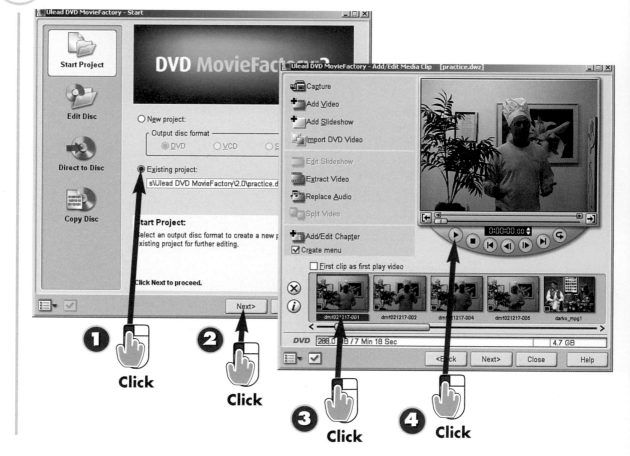

Click

Click

Click

Click

① Click **Existing project** to reopen your project to the Add/Edit window.

② Click **Next** to continue.

③ Click a video to put it in the Preview window.

④ Click the **Play** button to play the clip (or press the **spacebar**).

INTRODUCTION

You can return to your DVD project in MovieFactory by opening the program and selecting it from the Existing Project list.

TIP

You can use the **left** and **right arrow** keys on your keyboard to move between key frames.

Pressing the spacebar on the keyboard will begin and pause playback. You can also learn other keyboard shortcuts for editing steps.

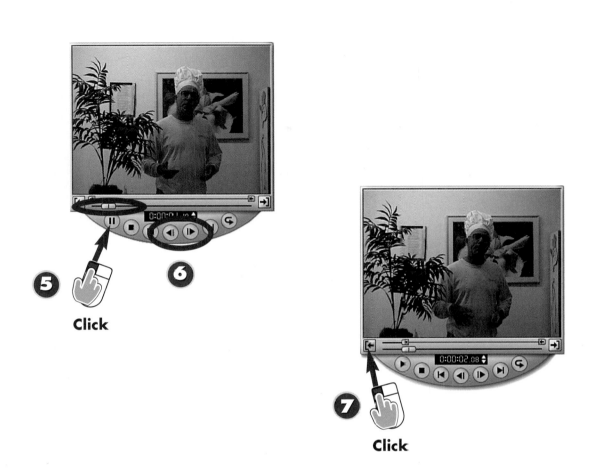

5 Click

6

7 Click

5 Click the **Pause** button to pause the clip (or press the **spacebar**).

6 Adjust the position of the jog bar with the **Go To Next** and **Previous Frame** buttons.

7 Click the **Set Mark-In** button to make the current position the new beginning frame of the clip.

End

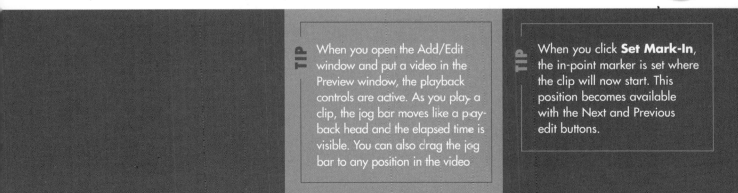

TIP When you open the Add/Edit window and put a video in the Preview window, the playback controls are active. As you play a clip, the jog bar moves like a playback head and the elapsed time is visible. You can also drag the jog bar to any position in the video

TIP When you click **Set Mark-In**, the in-point marker is set where the clip will now start. This position becomes available with the Next and Previous edit buttons.

Finish Trimming in MovieFactory

Start

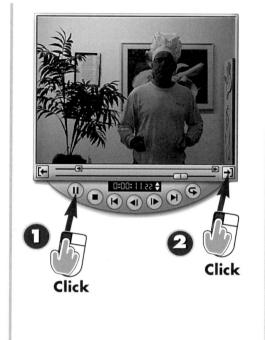

1 Click

2 Click

3 Click

4 Click

1 Play your video to where you want it to end, and then **Pause** the video or press the **spacebar**.

2 If you like the ending, click **Set Mark-Out** (or adjust the position with the **Next** and **Previous Frame** buttons).

3 To return to the first edit point or the beginning of the unedited clip, click **Home**.

4 Now that you've made significant editing decisions, click the icon, and then select **Save as** to save your work.

End

Extracting Segments from Long Clips

Start

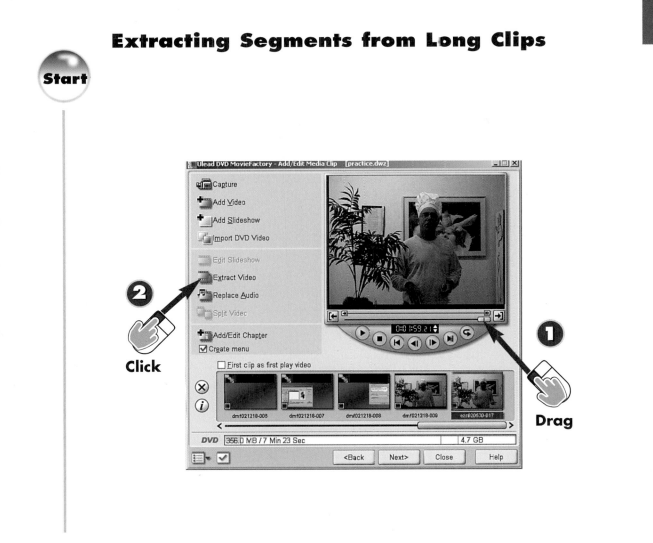

2 Click

1 Drag

1 Check the length of a clip by dragging its jog bar to the end.

2 Click **Extract Video**.

See next page

INTRODUCTION

Trimming shorter clips is fine—they become a series of titles that will either play consecutively in your project or return to a previous menu from which they began. But your longer clips can have points within them accessed as chapters from a menu or extracted into shorter titles.

HINT

You can do a visual quick trim by dragging the **In** and **Out Point** buttons under the Preview window to where you want them, but be careful of how the audio may play. When you trim a clip dramatically, the total length of your DVD project changes on the status bar.

You can preview just the trimmed segment by clicking **Repeat** and then holding down the **Shift** key as you press **Play**.

Click

3

4

Click

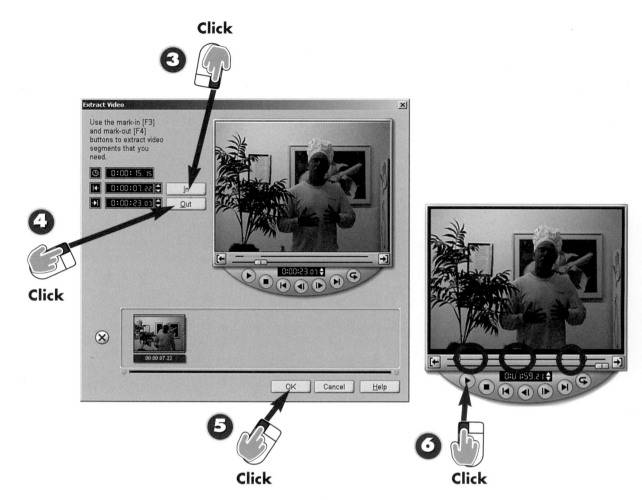

5

Click

6

Click

3 In the Extract Video window, play the video to the first in point, and click **In**.

4 Now play further and set an out point for the first segment.

5 Continue to play the clip and add segments with new in and out points. Click **OK** when you're done.

6 Click **Play** to preview the clip in the Add/Edit window. The entire clip will play with extracted portions marked.

End

TIP You can alter the segments in an extracted video anytime by clicking it in the Video Strip and clicking **Extract**.

HINT When you move an extracted clip along the Video Strip, the extracted segments all move together (unless you split them—see the next task).

Splitting Extracted Videos

Start

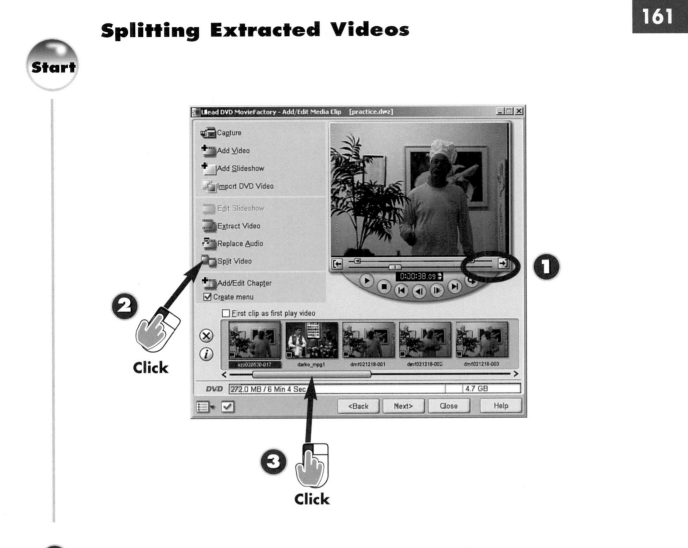

2 Click

3 Click

1 Check the length of a clip by dragging its jog bar to the end.

2 Drag back to a spot between two extracted portions. Click **Split Video**.

3 You might have to drag back through the Video Strip to locate the two new segments split from the original.

See next page

INTRODUCTION

The beauty of extracted videos is that you can now split them up to move portions to different parts of the Video Strip.

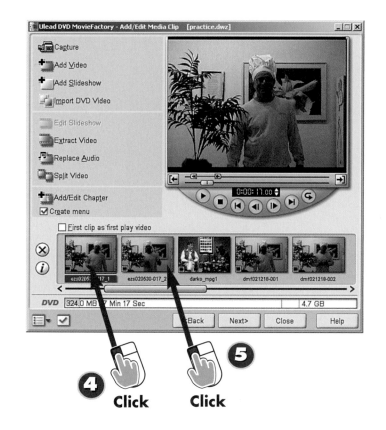

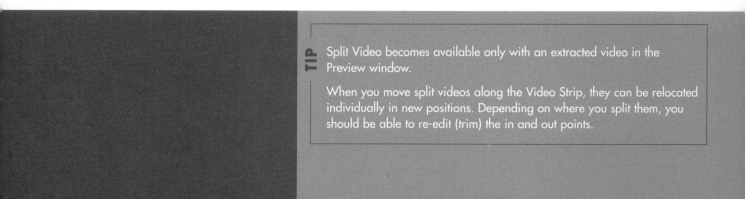

4 Click the shorter of the split videos to put it into the Preview window. Notice that your edits are intact.

5 Click the split video with multiple extractions to put it into the Preview window. Notice that your edits are intact.

TIP Split Video becomes available only with an extracted video in the Preview window.

When you move split videos along the Video Strip, they can be relocated individually in new positions. Depending on where you split them, you should be able to re-edit (trim) the in and out points.

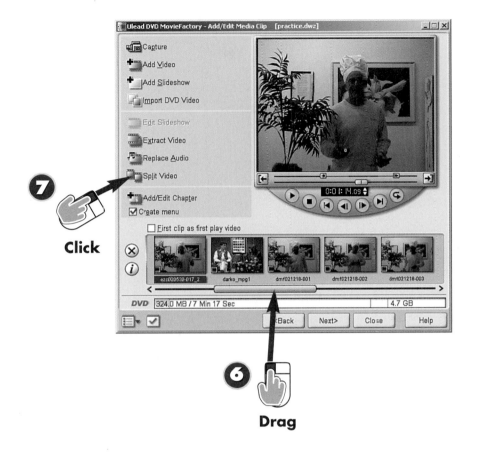

Click

7

6

Drag

6 Drag between the extracted portions and notice that Split Video is active.

7 Click **Split Video** to split them again.

End

Setting Chapters in Longer Clips

Start

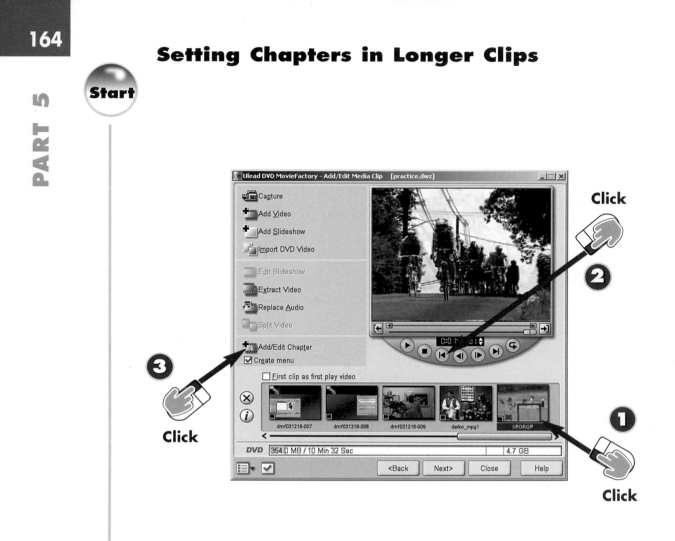

Click

Click

Click

Click

1 Find a longer clip or one with several portions within it. Click to put it into the Preview window.

2 Click **Home** to return to the beginning.

3 Click **Add/Edit Chapter**.

INTRODUCTION

In anticipation of creating menus for your project, think about using chapters to let viewers access specific portions of some of your longer clips. (This will be clearer when we go to the menu creation area in the next chapter, but let's prepare for it now.)

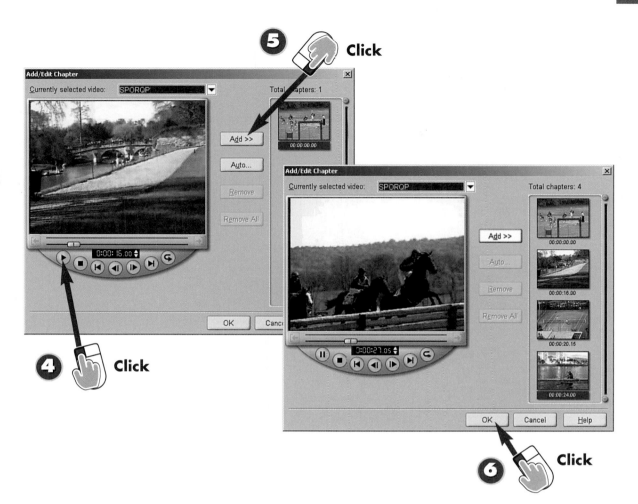

5 Click

4 Click

6 Click

End

④ In the Add/Edit Chapter window, play a frame (or drag the jog bar to a frame) that begins a new "chapter."

⑤ Click **Add** to make that frame a chapter point. A new chapter is added to the chapter list.

⑥ Continue adding chapters to the video. When you're done, click **OK** to return to the Add/Edit Video window.

HINT
Chapters are additional portions of those titles that you will also be able to make accessible from your menus.

The first frame of any title is automatically also a chapter point (unless you choose another one—you'll soon learn how).

TIP
The titles on the Video Strip will play one after the other when your DVD is inserted into a drive; they also can be accessed from menus if you choose to create them.

HINT
You don't need to pause or stop the video to click Add; you can do it on-the-fly as the video plays.

In the Preview area, you will have a chance to see the results of your project settings before you burn your disc and to return to make any changes.

Replacing Audio

Start

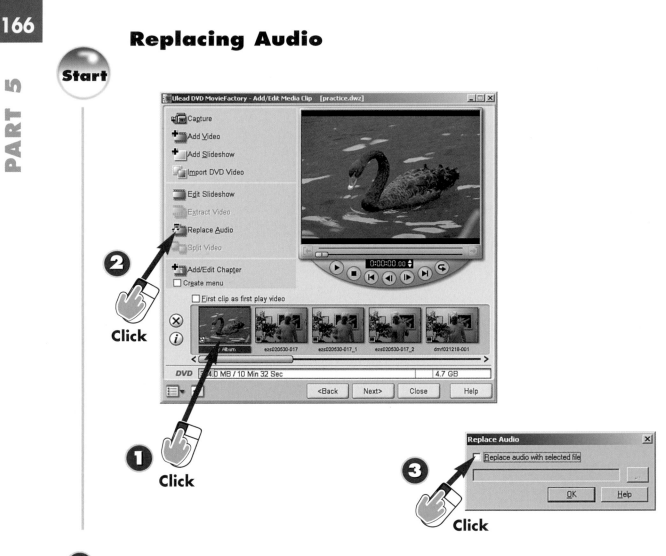

② Click

① Click

③ Click

① Click to put the clip whose audio you want to replace into the Preview window.

② Click **Replace Audio**.

③ Click the box that says **Replace Audio with Selected File**.

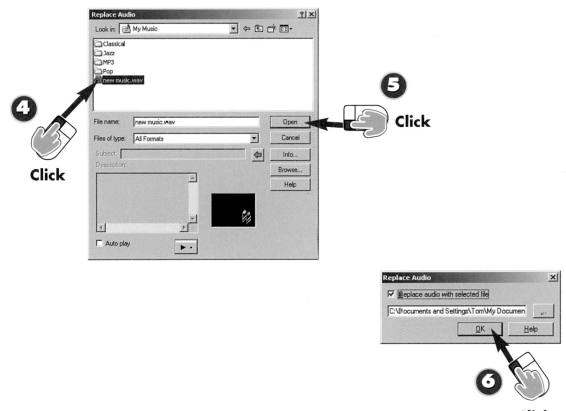

Browse to and locate the narrative or musical audio file you want to use. Click to select it.

Click **Open**.

With the file set, click **OK**. You'll notice a music icon on the clip in the Add/Edit Video window.

End

TIP

See the section on music CDs for your DVD or CD recording software for more information on using music.

Check Ulead's video editing programs for more sophisticated effects and audio synchronization capabilities.

Reviewing Our Project Settings

Start

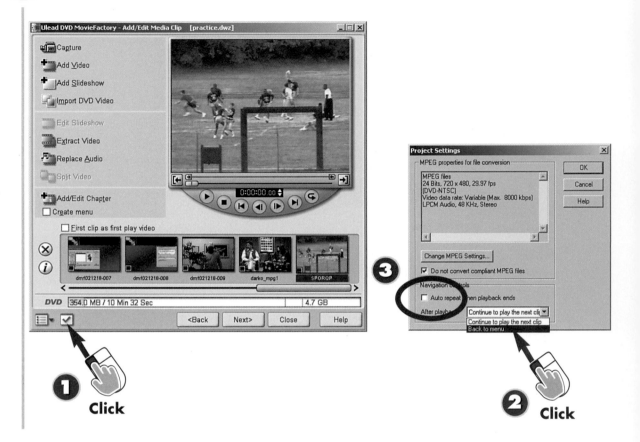

1 Click

2 Click

1 In the Add/Edit Video window click the check mark box to open the **Project Settings**.

2 Click the **drop-down arrow** and choose **Back to Menu** to select a different project option for title playback.

3 Review the other settings. (Leave the defaults.)

INTRODUCTION

Now we're almost ready to make our menus, but we need to review some other items and decide what our titles will do when they finish. (We can either have them return to a menu, which we will create, or continue on to the next title on the Video Strip.)

TIP

You can still use just a main menu and let the titles run into one another by leaving the default project settings.

HINT

Letting the titles continue one after the other is a good idea if you have one long, cohesive storyboard on the Video Strip (like a "real" movie).

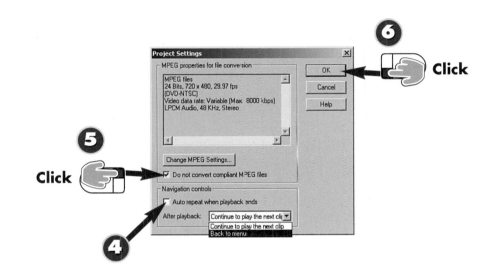

4. Do not check Auto Repeat unless you want all videos to keep playing over and over. (Users may proceed to the next video by clicking the **Next** button on the remote control.)

5. There is no reason to convert MPEG files that are already fine; check the **Do not Convert Compliant MPEG Files** box.

6. Click **OK** to return to the Add/Edit Video window.

End

HINT Next, we will examine the ways of using menus to let users navigate through the video segments.

Creating a DVD Interface

At this point, we've acquired our video and still images and assembled them on our Video Strip in the order in which they would play consecutively without any menus. However, you probably will want to present the viewer with some choice as to what to see first—and which content to view.

A Hollywood movie DVD is usually one main title (the entire movie), but there are menus that let you skip directly to selected chapters (parts of the film—or main title). In the beginning, a main menu usually lets you choose to watch the movie, go directly to specific scenes, see some outtakes, or watch an interview with the director. In DVD terms, these are other titles, with the movie itself—again—being the main title.

Let's see how this is done.

Using Templates to Modify a Menu

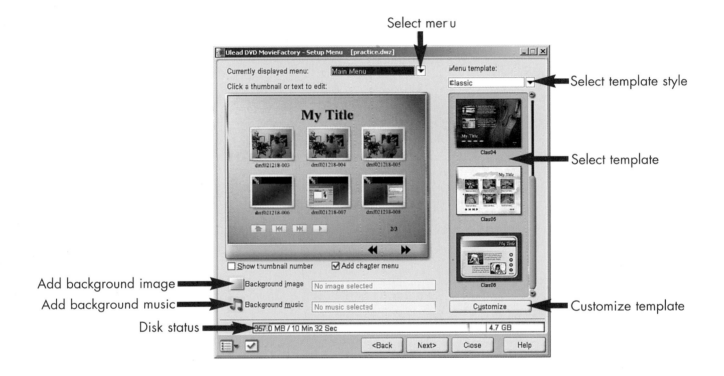

Select menu

Select template style

Select template

Add background image

Add background music

Disk status

Customize template

Starting Our Menus

Click

Click

Click

1 Click **Create Menu** to begin.

2 Click **Next** to open the Setup menu.

3 The Setup menu opens. If you have created any chapters, Add Chapter Menu is checked. Click to see the next title menu (if you have more than six titles).

You will access the Setup menu to create your video from the Add/Edit Video window.

TIP

If you uncheck **Create Menu** and click **Next**, you bypass menu creation and go directly to preview and burn a disc. Your clips will simply play consecutively, the titles following one another in the order they appear on the title list. *Any chapters you created will be inaccessible.*

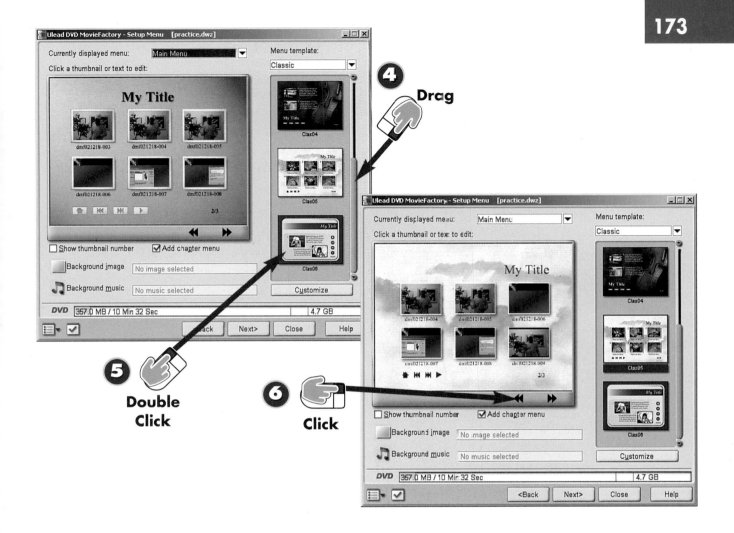

Drag

Double Click

Click

4 Drag through the **Classic** templates to find another with six title placeholders.

5 Double-click a template to apply it to the menu.

6 The new template is applied to the menu. Now click back to the first page of the Main Menu to see that the template is applied to all the menu pages.

End

Adding Text to the Main Menu

Start

Click

1

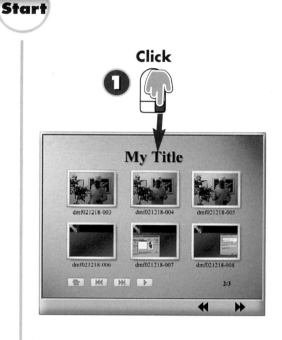

My Title

dmf021218-003   dmf021218-004   dmf021218-005

dmf021218-006   dmf021218-007   dmf021218-008

2/3

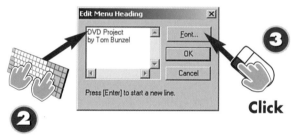

Edit Menu Heading

DVD Project
by Tom Bunzel

Font...

OK

Cancel

Press [Enter] to start a new line.

2

3

Click

1 Click **My Title** to open the Edit Menu Heading screen.

2 In the Edit Menu Heading screen, click and use the **Delete** key to erase and replace My Title with your own new title. (Press **Enter** for a new line.)

3 Click **Font** to access the Font dialog box.

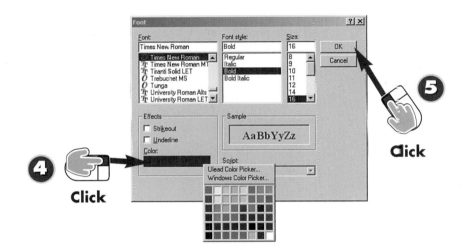

Click

Click

④ You can make the font larger and make it bold or italic. Click the **color chip** to change the color.

⑤ To return to the Main Menu editing area, click **OK** twice. Your new title is now on the first page of the Main Menu.

See next page

Click

6

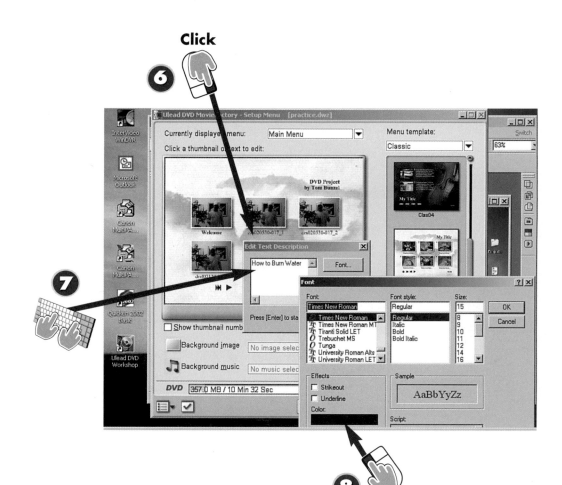

7

8

Click

6 Now click the captions to edit them the same way.

7 Type in a new caption.

8 Choose a new color for your text.

End

TIP You can find many more template choices by clicking the drop-down arrow under the **Menu Template** heading—investigate the other categories such as Cool, Romantic, and Nature.

HINT Changing the title on one page of the Main Menu does not affect the other pages in the same way as applying a template. Each page can have its own title.

Creating Chapter Menus

Start

Click

Click

2

1

3

Click

4

Double-Click

1 Click the drop-down arrow next to **Currently Displayed Menu**.

2 Select a title that has chapters.

3 Under **Menu Template**, click the drop-down arrow and select another category.

4 Double-click one of these templates.

See next page

As we mentioned, if you created chapters for any of your titles, the Add Chapter Menu check box is active. This means that beside your Main Menu, you can create and design menus for any titles that contain chapters.

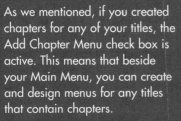

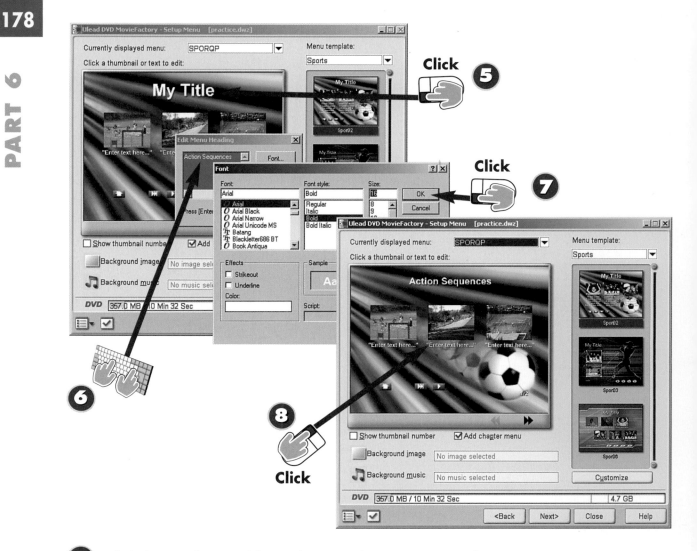

5 Click the words **My Title** to change it the same way as the Main Menu.

6 Type **Action Sequences** in the edit box.

7 Click **OK**.

8 Click to change the captions as well, or leave them all unchanged to be blank and let the thumbnails speak for themselves.

HINT

Checking Show Thumbnail Number will *not* enable the numbered keypad for DVD discs. (This option is automatic if you select VCD and SVCD format discs.)

You will see that unchanged captions do not appear on menus in the Finish step. You must leave all captions unchanged on a menu to keep them blank (and leave the menu without captions).

Customizing Menus

Start

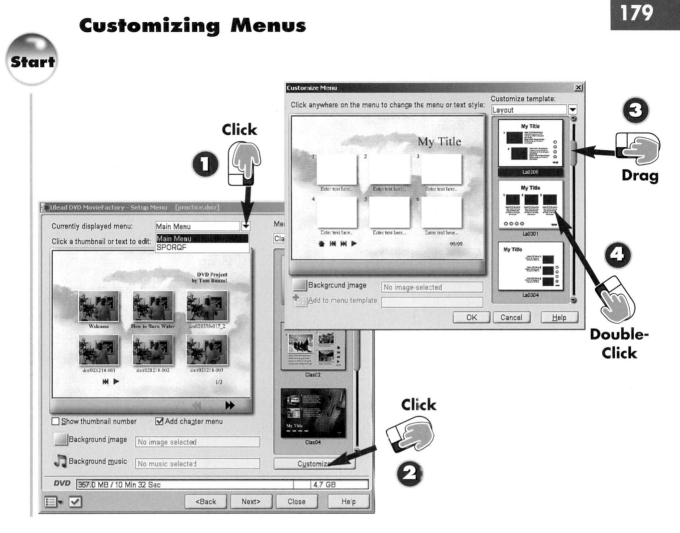

Click ①

③
Drag

④
Double-Click

Click ②

① Click the drop-down arrow for **Currently Displayed Menu** to return to the Main Menu.

② Click **Customize**.

③ Drag through the layouts to find one you like.

④ Double-click the layout with three thumbnails and more text to apply it to the menu.

See next page

INTRODUCTION

So far we've used the various templates to create our Main Menu and Chapter Menu. Let's add some bells and whistles.

PART 6

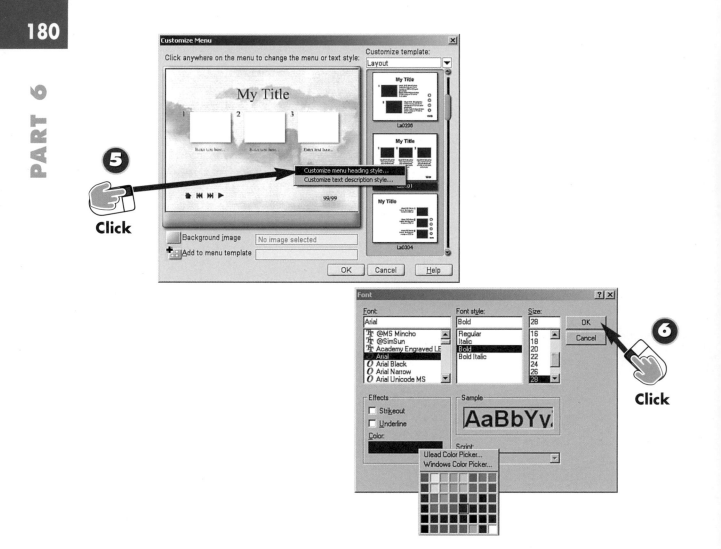

5 Click

6 Click

5 Click in the menu area and choose **Customize Menu Heading Style**.

6 Use the Font dialog box to choose a new look for the heading. Then click **OK**. The new customized look is applied to the first and second menu pages (dividing the six thumbnails). Note the page number and click back to see the results.

End

HINT

The reason the customized font is not applied to the first page is because we modified it from the original in an earlier step.

Continuing to Customize Menus

Start

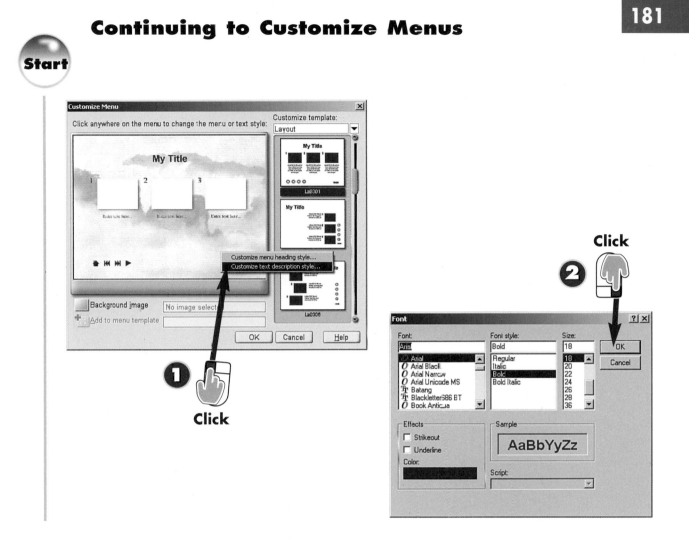

Click

Click

1 Click in the menu area and choose **Customize Text Description Style**.

2 Use the Font dialog box to choose a new look for the text description. Then click **OK**.

See
next
page

INTRODUCTION

So far, we worked only with the Layout part of the Customize feature. Let's finish up and change the appearance of the text descriptions. First, click to make sure you're back in Customize.

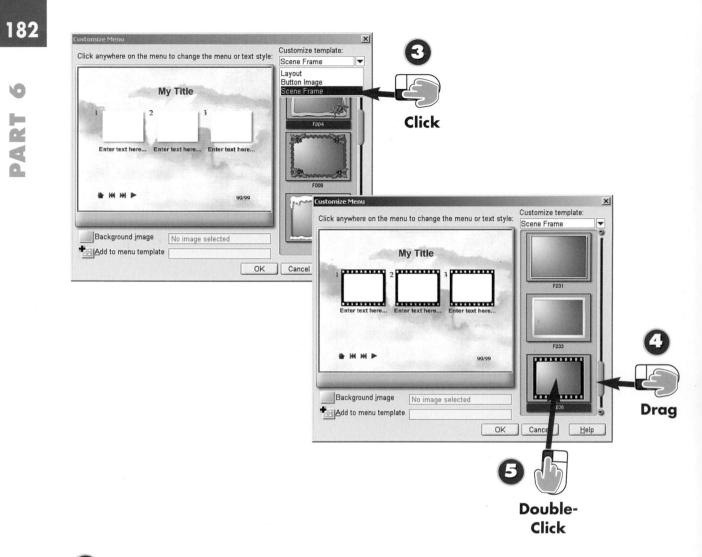

3 Click the **Customize Template** drop-down menu and select **Scene Frame**.

4 Drag down through the gallery and find a new frame.

5 Double-click to apply your new frame.

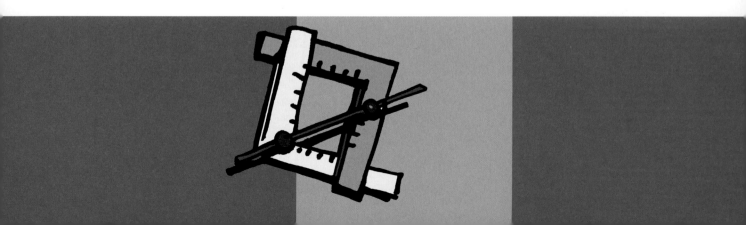

Click

6

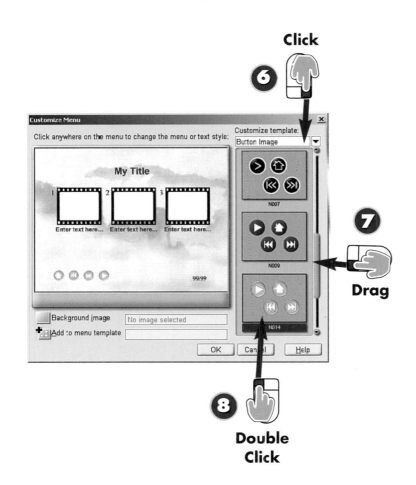

7

Drag

8

Double Click

6 Click the **Customize Template** drop-down menu and select **Button Image**.

7 Drag down through the gallery and find a new button style.

8 Double-click to apply your new button style.

End

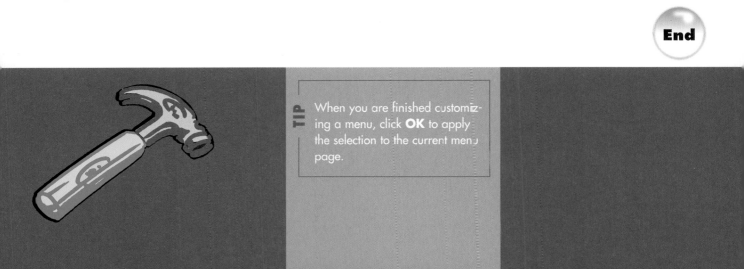

TIP
When you are finished customizing a menu, click **OK** to apply the selection to the current menu page.

Finishing Our Customized Menu

Start

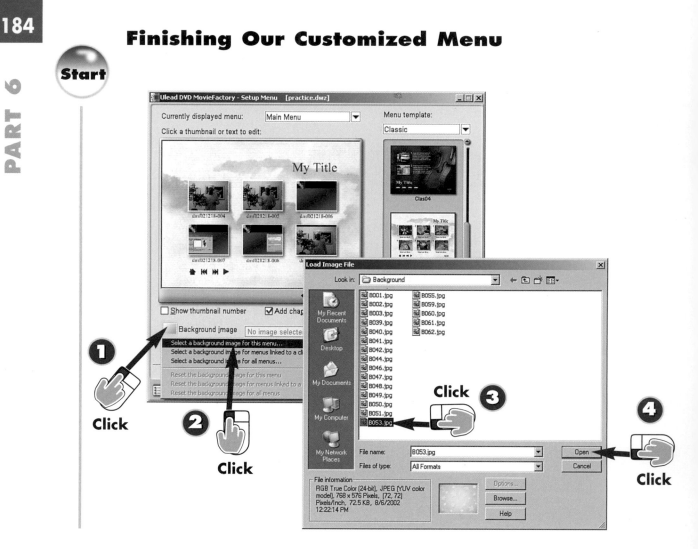

Click

Click

Click

Click

① Click **Background Image** to add a background image.

② Click **Select a Background Image for This Menu**.

③ Click to locate a nice new image in the MovieFactory Background folder. Notice the preview.

④ Click **Open**.

HINT

When you apply a template or a customized style to a menu, it affects all the pages of that set of menus.

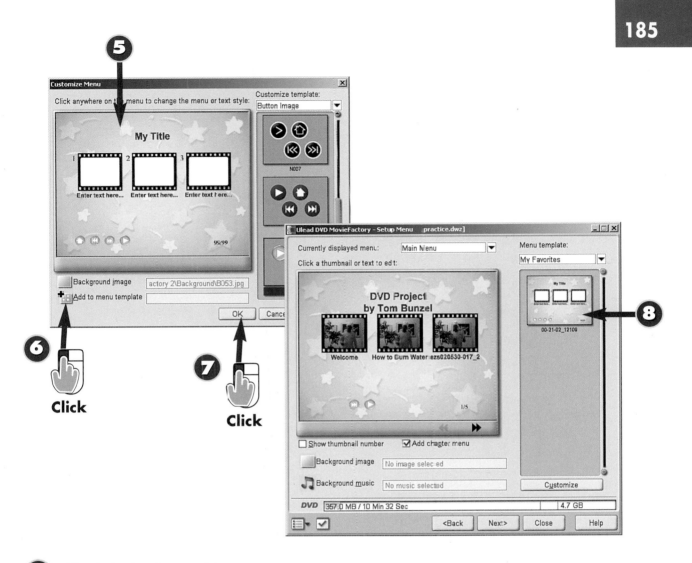

5 Check the background image.

6 Click **Add to Menu Template**.

7 Click **OK** to return to the Add/Edit Video window.

8 Your new customized template is available to be applied to any menu in your My Favorites folder.

End

TIP

To achieve a uniform menu look throughout your project, save your custom menu to the My Favorites folder and reapply it to all the menus that you want to look the same.

Completing Our Interface

Start

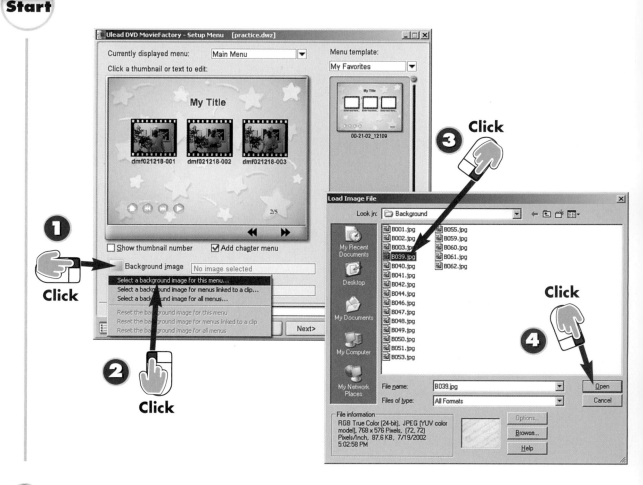

① Click **Background Image**.

② Click **Select a Background Image for This Menu**.

③ Click to locate a nice new image in the MovieFactory Background folder. Notice the preview.

④ Click **Open** to apply and check the background image. (It's applied only to the active menu page.)

INTRODUCTION

Although we added a background image to a template in the Customize area, we can also make some more cool enhancements to the menus themselves back in the main Setup Menu window.

TIP

When you add a background image or background music, you can also add it to all menus or all menus linked to a specific clip. (This affects projects where your titles are set to return to the previous menu.)

5 Click **6** Click

5 Click the **Previous Page** button to see that the other pages remain as they were before.

6 Click **Background Music**.

See next page

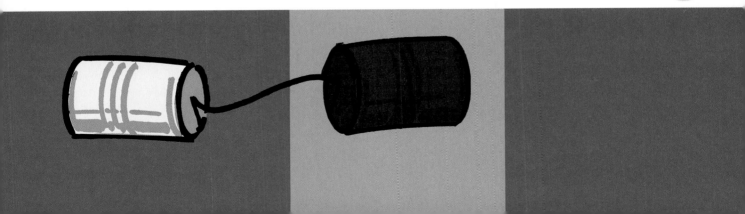

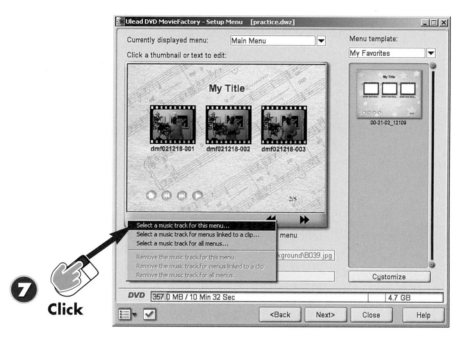

 Click

7 Click **Select a Music Track for This Menu**.

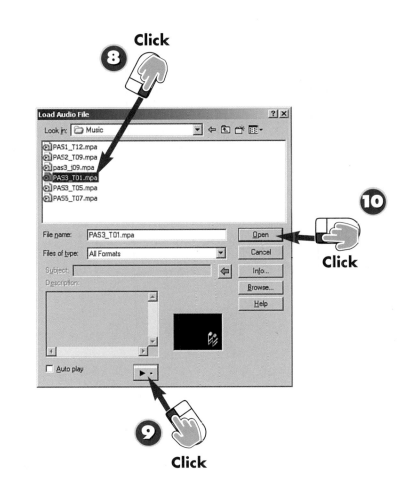

8 Click to select an audio file from the Music folder.

9 Click **Play** to preview it.

10 Click **Open** to apply it.

End

TIP
If you want to use your own background images or audio files, you can browse to folders where they are saved. We will see how to create our own background images in Chapter 9, "Tips and Techniques."

Finishing Our DVD Project

By now, you should be comfortable with reopening your project and clicking Next from the Add/Edit window to go to the Setup window, where you created your menus.

In the next (and final) stages of our project, we will use a remote controller to preview what we have done—and to burn the disc when we are satisfied. We can always use the Back button to return to a previous step to refine our clips (by re-editing or reordering them) and change our menus.

Previewing Your Project

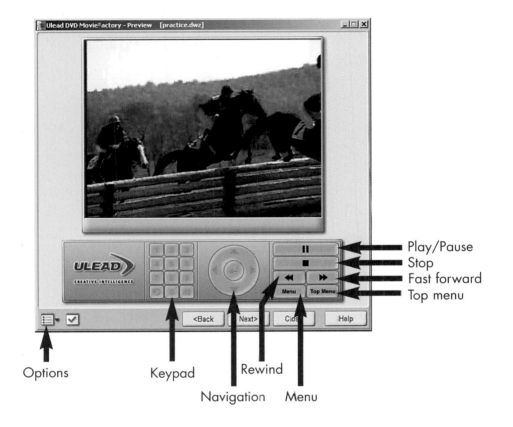

Options   Keypad   Navigation   Rewind   Menu   Play/Pause   Stop   Fast forward   Top menu

Getting to the Finish Line

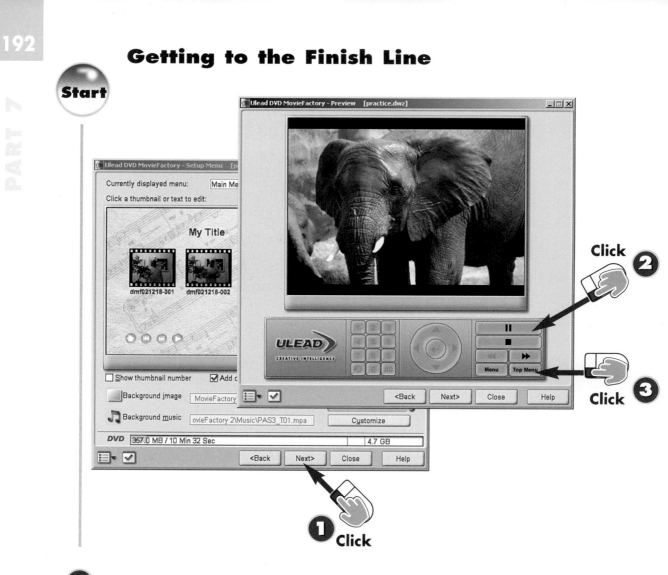

1 From the Setup window, click **Next**.

2 The Preview window opens. Click **Play**. (While it's playing—as shown—the Stop button appears.)

3 Your First Play video begins (if you have chosen one). You can also click **Top Menu** to advance to the Main Menu.

By now, you should be anxious to see how your project will play. Don't get discouraged if you see mistakes during preview—this is generally how you will truly learn the fine points of titles and chapters and learn to distinguish the Main Menu and chapter menus. Finally, think about how an inexperienced viewer might navigate through your project.

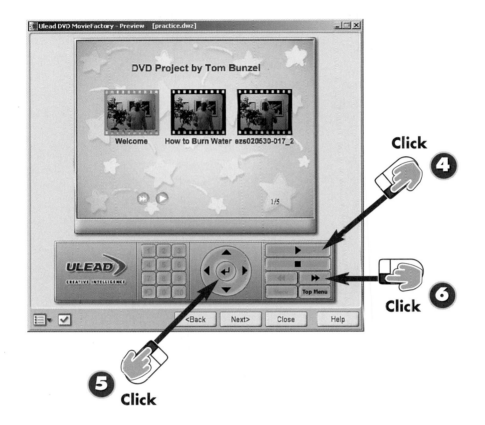

In the Main Menu, you can click **Play** to start the highlighted clip or click the thumb-nail itself. For now, use the remote controller—the viewer of your movie will use the button on the menu.

You also can select which clip to play by clicking the **up** and **down arrows**.

Finally, you can click a **Fast Forward** button to advance to the next menu and check any clips.

Your remote controller will look different for a VCD or SVCD project. Because you select your segments for these formats by number, your menus will have numerical references and the number keypad will be active for you to make your selections.

Checking the Chapter Menus

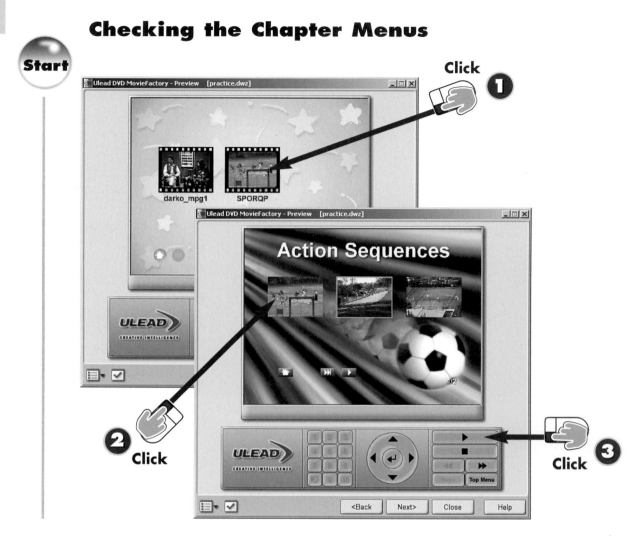

1 Click a thumbnail for a longer clip with chapters. Instead of playing the clip, the chapter menu opens.

2 Click the first thumbnail to select the sequence.

3 Click the **Play** button to begin the sequence. The clips will play consecutively until the final one, and then you return to the chapter menu.

Use the double arrow buttons to advance through the menus and find clips for which you have set chapters.

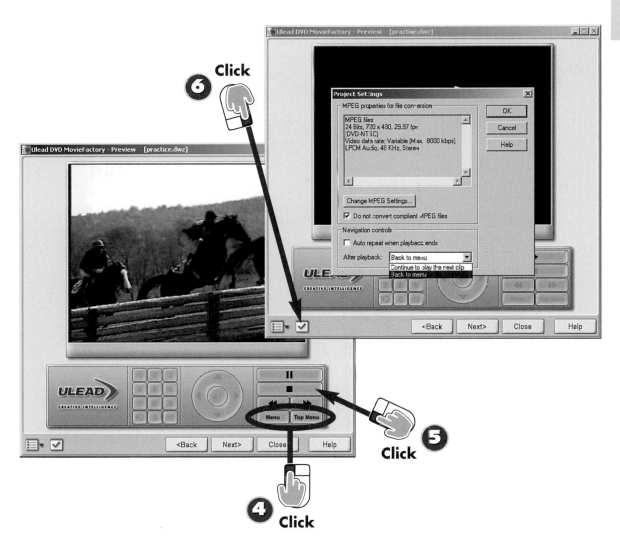

Click 6

Click 5

Click 4

4 To return to the Main (Top) Menu or the previous menu, click the appropriate button during playback.

5 To stop the preview, click **Stop**.

6 You can easily change your sequential playback choice by clicking **Project Settings**.

End

HINT You should also use the preview area to check the look of your headings and captions for errors or to check for clips for which you've forgotten to put a caption. Their filenames will be there instead, which looks a bit odd.

Preparing to Burn Your Disc

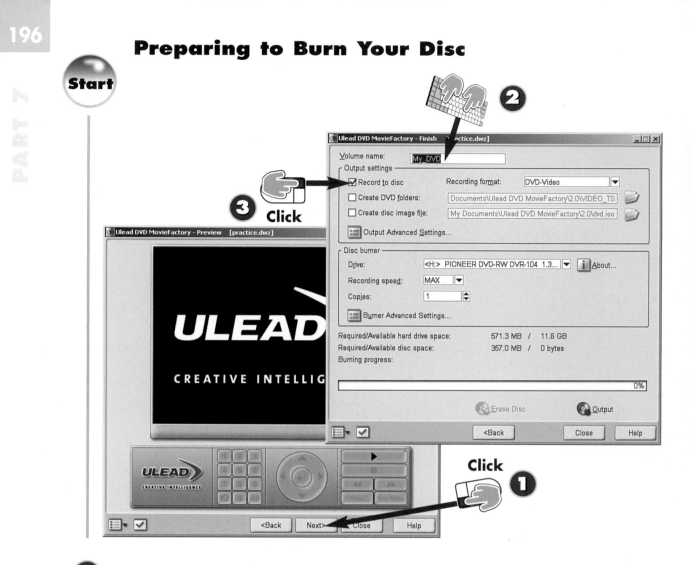

1 Click **Next** to proceed to the Finish screen.

2 Now you're truly at the Finish step. Enter a volume name if you like.

3 Click **Record to Disc** to record the project. Notice that other choices become active.

If everything is okay with the playback, you're ready to proceed to the burning area. Otherwise, you can go back and fix any errors. Be sure to save your project.

Creating DVD folders lets you play the project from your hard drive with a software DVD player program (without a DVD drive).

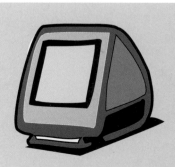

Click ④

Ulead DVD MovieFactory - Finish [practice.dwz]

Volume name: My_DVD
Output settings
☑ Record to disc   Recording format: DVD-Video ▼
☑ Create DVD folders: Documents\Ulead DVD MovieFactory\2.0\VIDEO_TS
☑ Create disc image file: My Documents\Ulead DVD MovieFactory\2.0\dvd.iso
▤ Output Advanced Settings...

Disc burner
Drive: <H:> PIONEER DVD-RW DVR-104 1.3... ▼   ℹ About...
Recording speed: MAX ▼
Copies: 1 ⬍
▤ Burner Advanced Settings...

Required/Available hard drive space:
Required/Available disc space:
Burning progress:

⑤ **Click**

Click ⑥

Ulead DVD MovieFactory - Finish [practice.dwz]

Volume name: My_DVD
Output settings
☑ Record to disc   Recording format: DVD-Video ▼
☑ Create DVD folders: Documents\Ulead DVD MovieFactory\2.0\VIDEO_TS
☑ Create disc image file: My Documents\Ulead DVD MovieFactory\2.0\dvd.iso
▤ Output Advanced Settings...

Disc burner
Drive: <H:> PIONEER DVD-RW DVR-104 1.3... ▼   ℹ About...
                    <H:> PIONEER DVD-RW DVR-104 1.30 (Ulead)
Recording speed: <I:> YAMAHA CRW2200E 1.0D (Ulead)
                    <I:> YAMAHA CRW2200E (NTI)
Copies:
▤ Burner Advanced Settings..

Required/Available hard drive space: 929.2 MB /   11.6 GB
Required/Available disc space: 357.0 MB /   0 bytes
Burning progress:
                                                                    0%

🔴 Erase Disc   🔴 Output

▤▼ ☑   ◁Back   Close   Help

④ Click **Create DVD Folders** to add them to your hard drive.

⑤ Click **Create Disc Image File** to create a file that you can reuse for additional copies.

⑥ Click **Drive** to change the drive (if you have multiple drives), the driver, or the burn speed.

End

Creating a disc image creates a data file you can burn for additional copies.

If you are ready to burn, put a blank CD-RW or DVD into your drive and click **Output**.

At the bottom of the panel is some important information. You will need significant free hard-drive space to burn a DVD. You should also make sure that the data you are burning does not exceed the capacity of a DVD (4.7GB) or a CD-RW (650MB) for a mini DVD.

Checking Advanced Options

Start

Ulead DVD MovieFactory - Finish [practice.dwz]

Volume name: My_DVD

Output settings
☑ Record to disc   Recording format: DVD-Video
☑ Create DVD folders: Documents\Ulead DVD MovieFactory\2.0\VIDEO_TS
☑ Create disc image file: My Documents\Ulead DVD 'MovieFactory\2.0\dvd.iso

▣ Output Advanced Settings...

Output Advanced Settings

Disc burner
Drive: ☑ Include project file to disc   OK   bout...
Recording spe ☐ Include personal folder to disc   Cancel
Copies: [   ] [...]   Help
▣ Burner A   ☐ Archive images of slideshows

Required/Available hard drive space: 929.2 MB / 11.6 GB
Required/Available disc space: 357.0 MB / 0 bytes
Burning progress:

[0%]

Erase Disc   Output

▣▾ ☑   <Back   Close   Help

1 Click

Click

Output Advanced Settings

☑ Include project file to disc   OK
2 ☑ Include personal folder to disc   Cancel
C:\Documents and Settings\Tom\My D [...] Help
☑ Archive images of slideshows

Click 4

3 Click

1 Click **Output Advanced Settings**.

2 Click **Include Personal Folder to Disc** to burn a data folder that a PC can access.

3 Click to archive images of a slideshow to your hard disc.

4 Click **OK.**

The default choices we made in the last section will generally work fine, but there are still some more choices you can make before clicking Output.

HINT

Adding a personal folder can allow you to use the disc as a backup of your files or provide the user with additional information or resources.

5 Click **Burner Advanced Settings**.

6 Click to Enable buffer underrun protection if available. Click to test your burner speed if necessary. Click to keep the disc open or to format a rewritable disc.

7 Click **OK**, and put in a blank disc.

8 Click **Output**.

End

TIP

Be sure to test your disc on as many different machines and platforms as you can. Using the combination DVD players and TV sets at an electronics store will let you know whether it will truly play anywhere.

Editing a Completed Disc

Start

Click ❶ **Click** ❷

Click ❸

Click ❹

❶ Instead of (re)starting a project when you open MovieFactory, click **Edit Disc**.

❷ Click **Show Disc Details** for information on its contents.

❸ Click **Next** to proceed.

❹ Re-edit your titles as you would normally. Drag and drop them in the title list to change the order. Then click **Next**.

PART 7

INTRODUCTION

There are still some other types of projects that you can do with MovieFactory. If you need to re-edit a finished disc, for example, you can restart the program to do it.

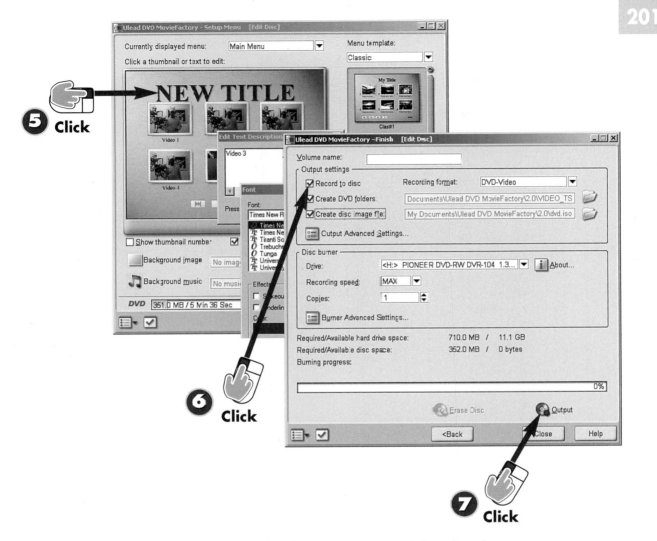

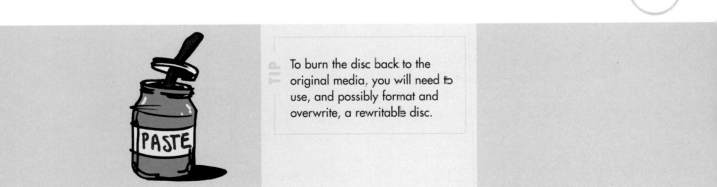

5 Create your menus as you would with a new project. Click in the title or caption areas to change the text and/or the font. Be sure to preview your revised project when done.

6 Click the **Record to Disc** checkbox.

7 Click **Output** to burn your revised project to disc.

End

> **TIP**
>
> To burn the disc back to the original media, you will need to use, and possibly format and overwrite, a rewritable disc.

Copying a Completed Disc

Start

② Click

④ Click

① Click

③ Click

Ulead DVD MovieFactory - Start

DVD MovieFactory 2

- Start Project
- Edit Disc
- Direct to Disc
- Copy Disc

Copy from
- ⦿ Disc
- ○ Disc image file

Copy Disc:
Copy DVD videos or a disc image file from a another disc.

Click Next to proceed.

Next>

Ulead DVD MovieFactory - Copy From Disc/Disc Image File

Volume name: ULEAD_DVD

Copy disc from
DVD drive/folder: I:
☐ Create disc image file first

         <H:> PIONEER DVD-RW DVR-104 1.30
         <I:> YAMAHA CRW2200E 1.0D
         Browse...

Disc burner
Drive: <H:> PIONEER DVD-RW DVR-104 1.30 (...) ▼ **i** About...
Recording speed: MAX ▼
Copies: 1

⊟ Burner Advanced Settings...

Required/Available disc space: 98.0 MB / 0 bytes
Burning progress:

0%

Erase Disc   Output

<Back   Close   Help

---

① Instead of (re)starting a project when you open MovieFactory, click **Copy Disc**.

② Click **Disc** to copy from a disc.

③ Click **Next** to continue.

④ Click the Folder icon in **Copy Disc From** to select your source drive and folder. Click to highlight and select it.

MovieFactory makes it easy to copy a DVD. If you have only one drive (source and destination will be the same), you should first copy the DVD to a disc image.

Click **8**

Ulead DVD MovieFactory - Start

Start Project

Edit Disc

Direct to Disc

Copy Disc

DVD MovieFactory 2

Copy from
- ○ Disc
- ● Disc image file

Copy Disc:
Copy DVD videos or a disc image file from a disc or hard drive to another disc.

Click Next to proceed.

Next> | Close | Help

Ulead DVD MovieFactory - Copy From Disc/Disc

Volume name: ULEAD_DVD

Copy disc from
DVD drive/folder: I:
☑ Create disc image file first

Disc burner
Drive: <H:> PIONEER DVD
Recording speed: MAX
Copies: 1

Burner Advanced Settings...

Required/Available disc space: 98.0 MB / 0 bytes
Burning progress:

[_____]%

Erase Disc | Output

<Back | Close | Help

5 **Click**

7 **Click**   **Click** **6**

---

5 If you want to keep a disc image of the source disc, click **Create Disc Image File First**.

6 If you have a different destination drive, click **Output** to begin copying.

7 If you have only one DVD-recordable drive, click **Output** with **Disc Image File** checked. Then, click **Back**.

8 Select **Disc Image File** instead of DVD (after creating your disc image file).

End

Burning Directly to Disc

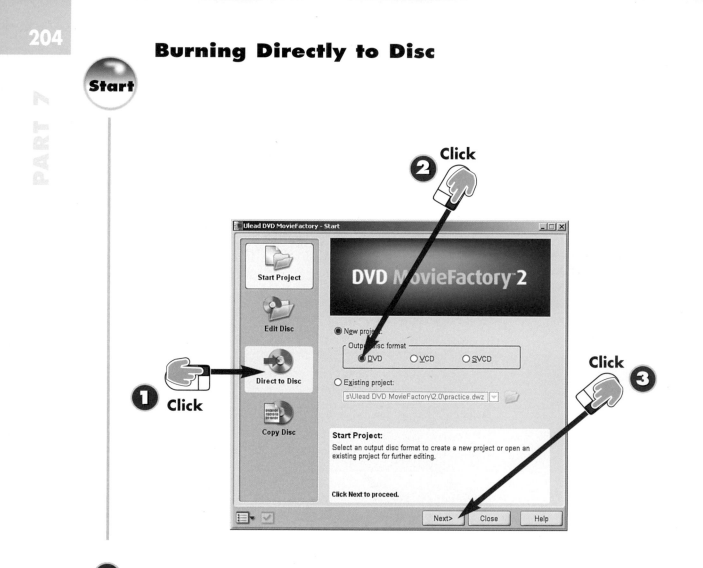

1 Instead of (re)starting a project when you open MovieFactory, click **Direct to Disc**.

2 Click **DVD**.

3 Click **Next** to proceed.

MovieFactory has an amazing feature that works only with DVD-RW or DVD+RW media—these support the Fast Edit feature. With a disc like this in your DVD recorder, you can literally burn on-the-fly directly to the disc.

If you try this with analog capture, you will need to start your camcorder automatically. This process is tricky, so doing it with a DV/FireWire camcorder is more stable.

Click

4

5 **Click**

6 **Click**

Ulead DVD MovieFactory - [Direct to Disc] Output Options   [DVD_021231.dwz]

Volume name: DMF_C2D

Output settings

☑ On-the-fly: DVD-Video (fast editable)

☐ Do not erase existing DVD-Video (fast editable) data

☐ Create menus

Output Advanced Settings...

Disc burner

Drive: <H:> PIONEER DVD-RW DVR-104 1.30... ⓘ About...

Recording speed: MAX

Copies: 1

Burner Advanced Settings...

<Back   Next>   Close   Help

4 Click the **On-the-Fly** option box to make it fast editable.

5 To create menus, click the **Create Menus** check box.

6 To add a personal folder, click the **Output Advanced Settings** box. (You must uncheck **On-the-Fly Fast-Editable** to access these options.)

 See next page

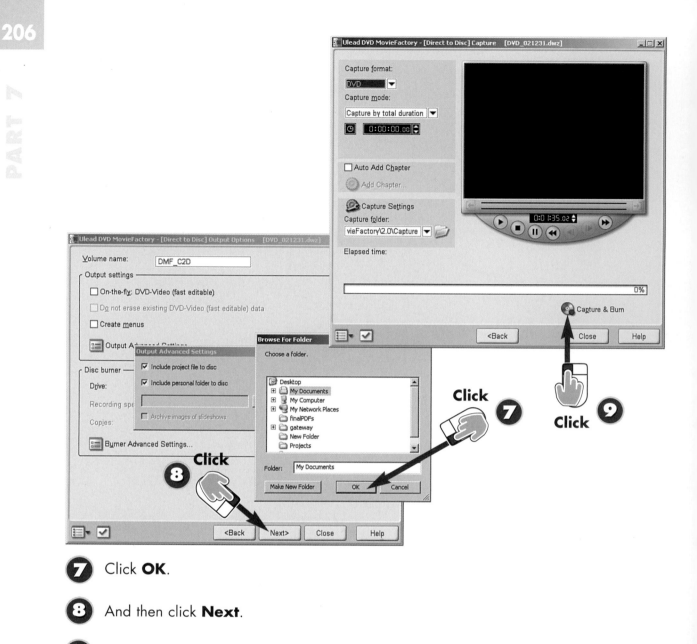

7 Click **OK**.

8 And then click **Next**.

9 In the familiar Capture window, set your options, and then click **Capture & Burn**.

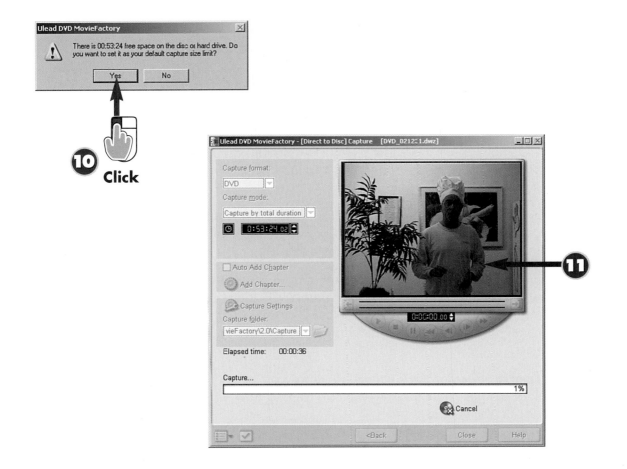

10 Click **Yes** to agree to lose data on the disc (not shown) and to the default length of the video prompt shown in the dialog box.

11 Be patient and watch as your video plays and is captured.

End

Completing Three Simple DVD Projects

In the preceding chapters, we went through Ulead MovieFactory 2.0 in detail for creating DVDs, VCDs, and SVCDs. We have concentrated on the program itself and learned how to use the various features in depth. In this chapter, we're going to de-emphasize the program and think through three representative projects that will get your creative juices flowing.

First, we'll pretend we came back from a vacation with camcorder video and photographs that we want to share with our friends and family. Then we'll do a business presentation that includes still images and video.

Finally, we'll do a VCD project that might be close to your heart. We'll convert VHS taped footage of an older, wiser grandmother, footage that we want to keep and share in digital format, and we'll make it a VCD so that viewers won't need a DVD drive on the computer to watch it and can also watch it on most commercial DVD players.

Remember, these projects aren't meant for you to follow step by step. Instead, try to think about the ideas behind what we do and how you can accomplish something similar at home or at work.

Capturing Your Project Footage

Select capture format

Select capture mode

Select capture duration

Elapsed time

Open capture settings

Select capture folder

Captured videos

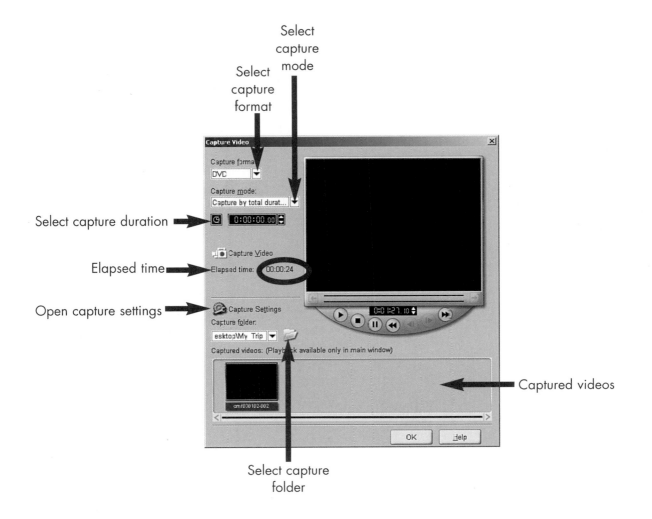

Beginning a Travelogue DVD

Start

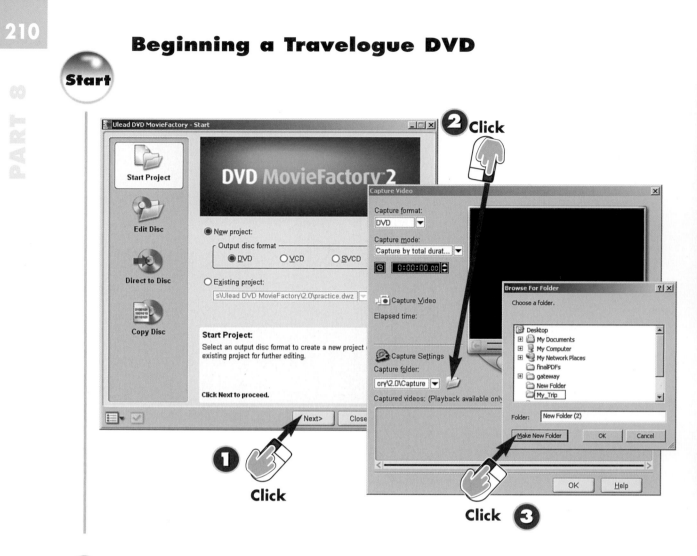

Click

Click

Click

1️⃣ Choose a format and begin my project by clicking **Next**.

2️⃣ For an important project, we want to save all our significant files into a single folder. Click the **Capture Folder** icon to begin.

3️⃣ Click **Make New Folder** and create a new folder (My_Trip) on the desktop.

Probably the two most popular DVD projects for home use are the wedding video and the travelogue. In each you may have both still images and video, and you'll want to organize them so that viewers get a sense of the entire event and can quickly access significant portions or chapters. Let's put together a tavelogue.

TIP

Using the default MovieFactory settings within your My Documents folder can make it easier to find and open recent projects.

HINT

Working with a new folder keeps your captured files and project file together for efficient backups, but you need to remember where they are.

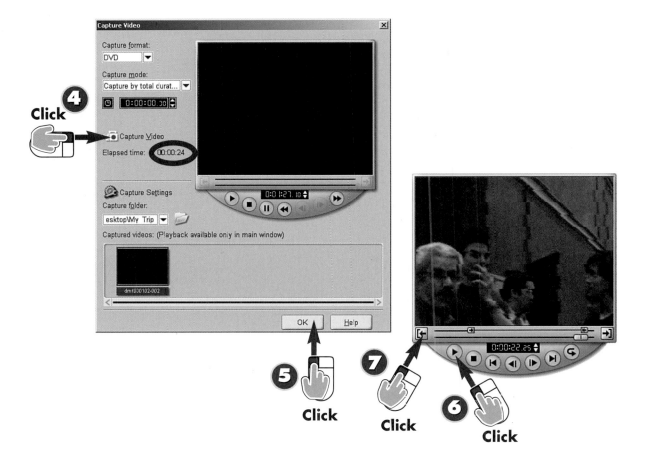

Click

Click

Click

Click

Click

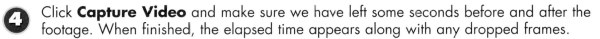

4 Click **Capture Video** and make sure we have left some seconds before and after the footage. When finished, the elapsed time appears along with any dropped frames.

5 When we are finished capturing segments, click **OK** to return to the Add/Edit window.

6 Click to play the video; begin with the people we met at events on our trip.

7 Click to set an in point past the lousy footage.

See next page

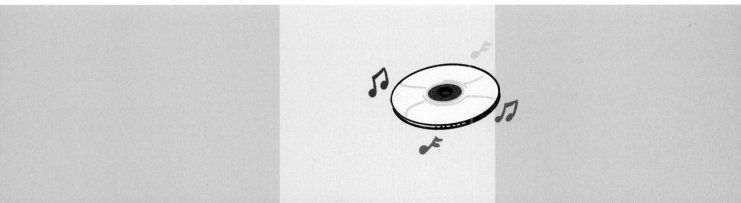

Click **8**

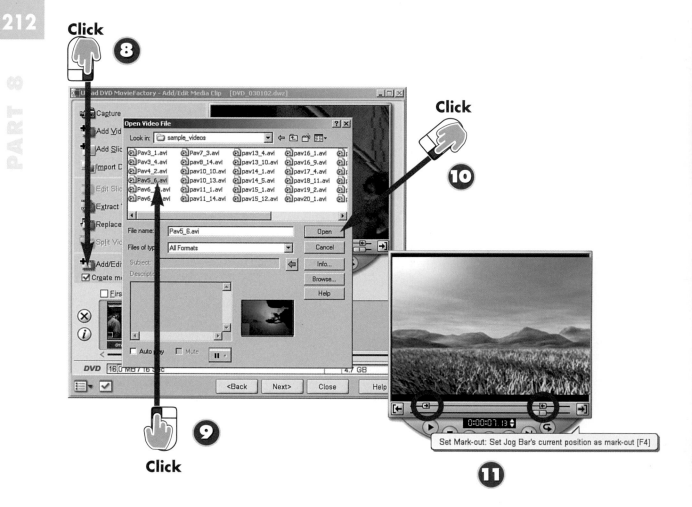

Click **10**

Click **9**

Click

11

8 Click **Add/Edit Video** and import other clips of scuba diving or of places and people from our recent trip—be sure you know the folder location.

9 Click to select a video.

10 Click **Open** to add the clip.

11 Preview any of your clips in the Add/Edit window and create in and out points using the trim features.

End

 Clicking **Preview** lets you see whether you have the right stuff.

Setting new in and out points does not affect the source video, but it gets rid of material that does not fit.

 Save your project file after you have accomplished a fair amount of work, capturing and trimming. It will go into the new folder you created and let you resume working where you left off.

Adding Photos to a Slideshow

Start

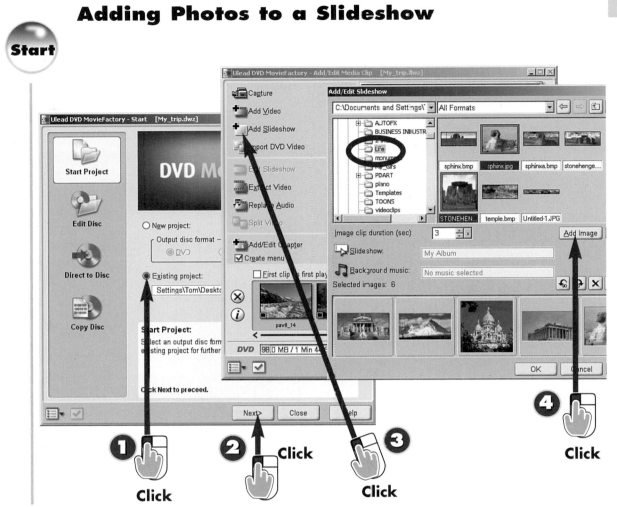

Click ①

Click ② **Click**

Click ③

Click ④

① Reopen the project we began earlier by clicking **Existing Project** and browsing for the file.

② Click **Next** to continue.

③ Click **Add Slideshow** and find the folder with pictures of places we visited.

④ Use **Ctrl+click** to select the images we want, and then click **Add Image**.

See next page

INTRODUCTION

A trip has a lot more than just video; if we used a digital camera we would have downloaded our pictures via USB. If we had prints made, we would scan them into a folder. In either case, we would probably have a set of images in JPG format to add to the DVD. Let's make a slideshow.

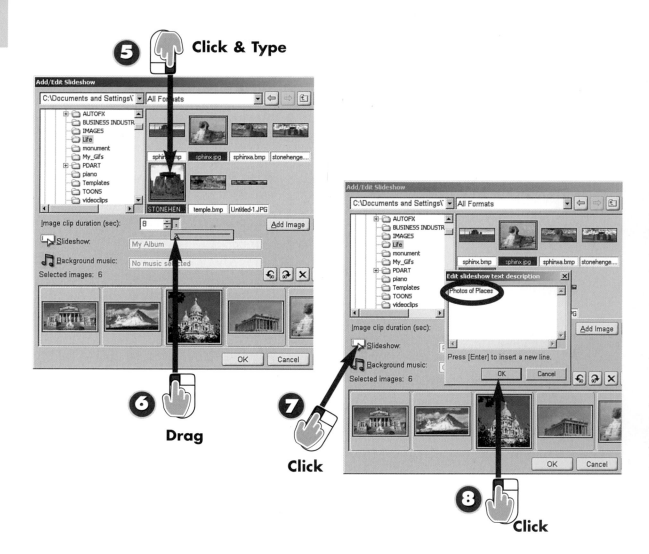

Click & Type

5

Drag

6

Click

7

8

Click

5 Click one of the images, and then press **Ctrl+A** to select them all.

6 Then, drag the slider under **Image Clip Duration** to let each image show for eight seconds.

7 Click the **Slideshow** icon to edit the description.

8 Name this slideshow **Photos of Places**. Then, click **OK**.

TIP
You can also create another album called Photos of People I Met.

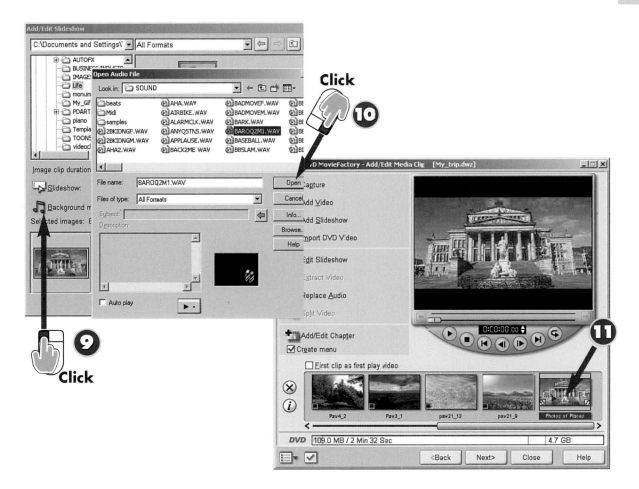

9 Click the **Background Music** icon to bring up the Open Audio File screen.

10 Select a WAV audio file to play with the slideshow, and then click **Open**.

11 When you are finished with the slideshow and click **OK**, the Photos of Places album joins the video clips in the project.

End

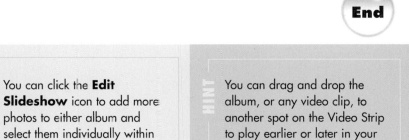

You can click the **Edit Slideshow** icon to add more photos to either album and select them individually within the album to show for longer or shorter durations.

You can drag and drop the album, or any video clip, to another spot on the Video Strip to play earlier or later in your final sequence.

Choosing and Organizing Chapters and Segments

Start

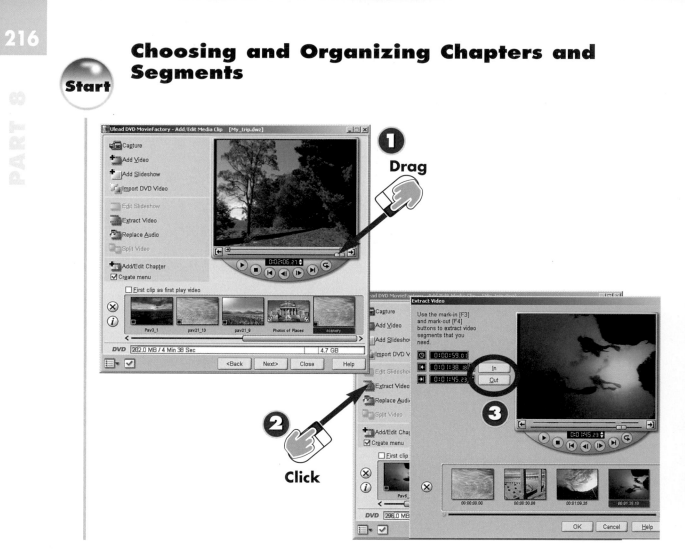

Drag

Click

1 Drag the jog bar to see that this is a two-minute movie with several distinct segments.

2 Choose **Extract Video** to open the Extract Video screen.

3 Define four sections of a clip with separate in and out points.

INTRODUCTION

Although many of our vacation clips are short enough to be titles, one is a compendium of scenic locations for which I want to create chapters and possibly extract some portions.

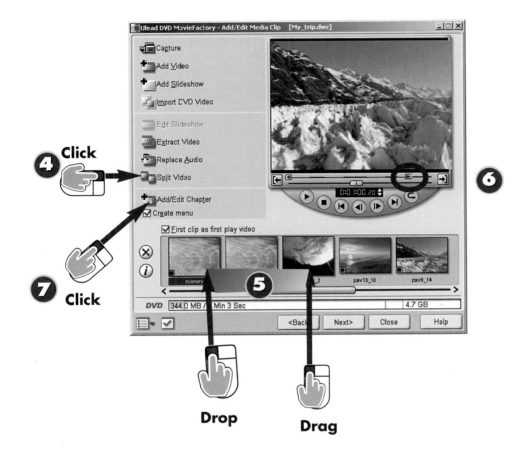

Click 4

Drop

Drag

7 **Click**

4 Back on the Video Strip, move the jog bar between the extracted segments and click **Split Video**. This results in two separate segments in addition to the original.

5 Now you can drag and drop the most breathtaking segment to the first position and make it the First Play video.

6 Remember to adjust the in and out points.

7 For the original clip, click **Add/Edit Chapter**.

See next page

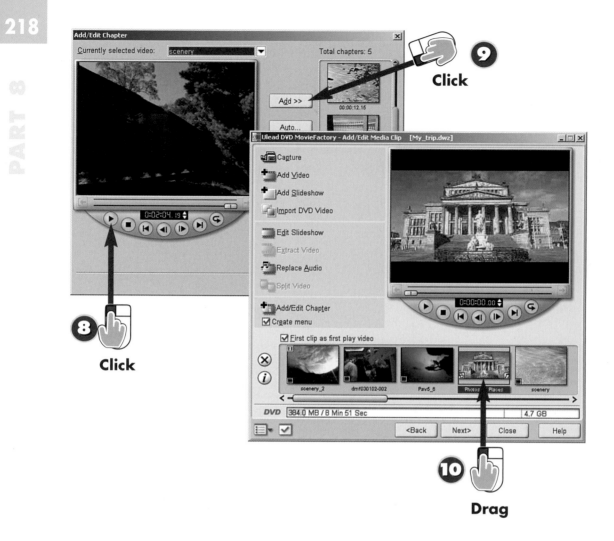

Click 9

Click 8

Drag 10

8 Click to play the clip through its various segments.

9 Click **Add** for five chapters.

10 Finally, reorganize the Video Strip by moving the photo album nearer to the front so that it will appear on the first menu in the final project.

End

Creating the Interface

Start

Click ①

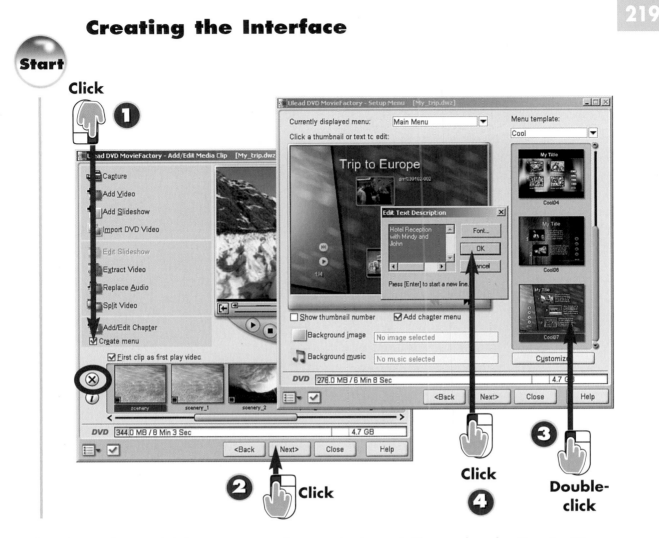

②**Click**

Click ④

Double-click ③

① First, select and delete any extra clips we don't need. Then, select the **Create Menu** option.

② Click **Next** to continue.

③ In the Setup window, double-click a **Cool** template with only three placeholders; the photos are still available in number 3.

④ Use the default fonts to add a main title and captions to the placeholders. Click **OK** when finished.

See next page

INTRODUCTION

We have a lot of different footage in this project, so we need to create some menus.

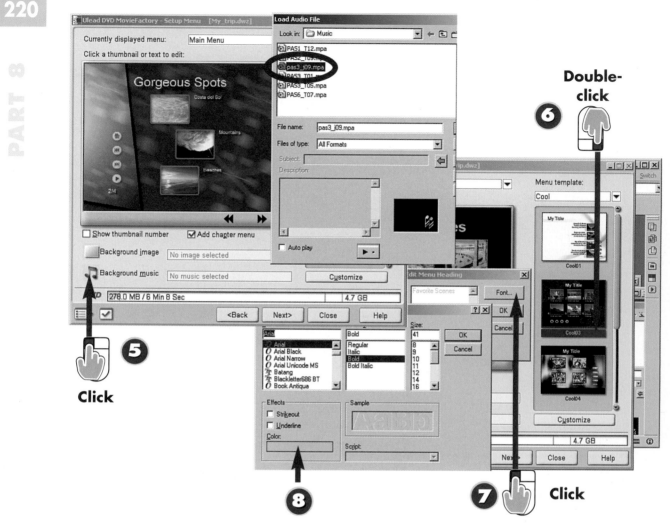

Double-click

6

Click

5

8

7 **Click**

5 The next set of titles get another main heading; click **Background Music** to load an accompanying WAV music file.

6 For the long clip with chapters, select a **Cool** template with enough placeholders.

7 Open the Edit Menu Heading window and click **Font**.

8 Click the color and change it to a nice light blue.

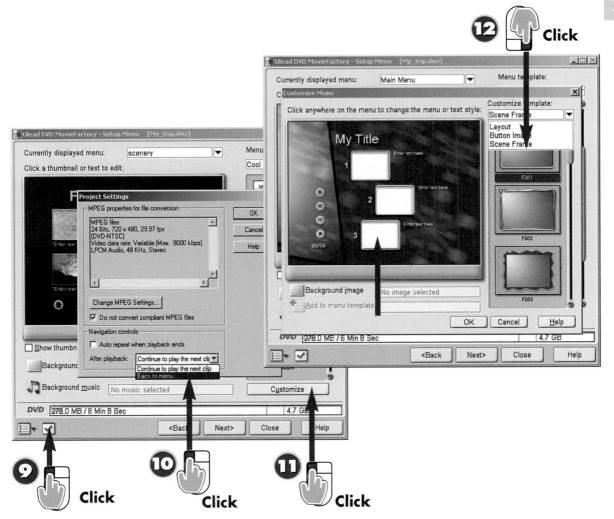

9   Before we forget, open the **Project Settings** box.

10 Click the **After Playback** box to make sure that all the clips actually return to the menus when they finish.

11 For a finishing touch, open the **Customize** panel.

12 Select **Scene Frame** and pick a nice orange outline for the main menus.

End

Completing the Travelogue DVD

 Start

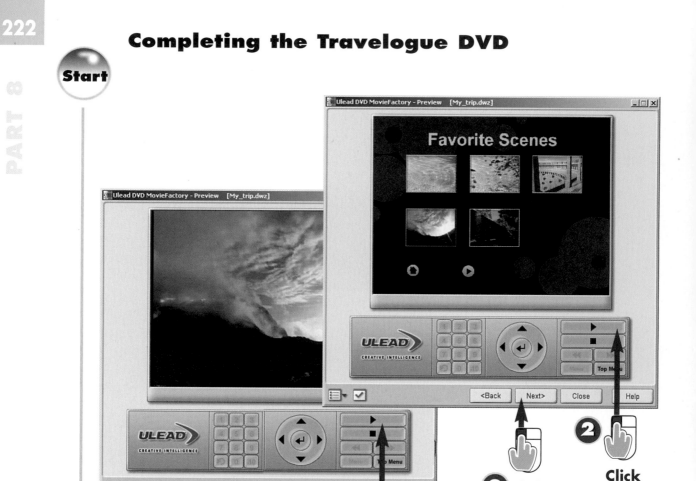

1 Click

2 Click

3 Click

1 Click **Next** out of **Setup** (not shown) and find the remote controller in the **Preview** step. Clicking **Play** brings up that gorgeous opening sequence.

2 The first video concludes with the first menu, and we can test our Photo Album and other clips—especially our chapter menu. Select a scene and click **Play** to play it.

3 We're ready to burn, so click **Next**.

The only thing left to do now is to preview the project to make sure it will play properly; then we'll burn the disc.

TIP

To check the chapter menu, you need to find the longer clip with chapters by clicking the double-arrow button for the next menu.

HINT

The more observant among you may notice some of these clips from the stock video footage available from Ulead.com and other Ulead products.

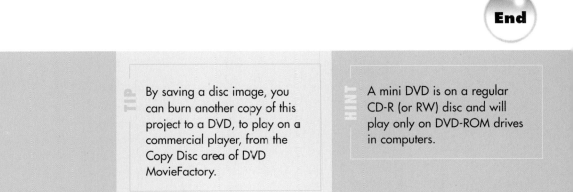

Click

Click

5

4

6

Click

Ulead DVD MovieFactory - Finish [My_trip.dwz]

Volume name: DVD_030102

Output settings

☑ Record to disc

☐ Create DVD folders: Documents\Ulead DVD MovieFactory 2.0\VIDEO_TE

☐ Create disc image file: My Documents\Ulead DVD MovieFactory\2.0\dvd.isc

Recording format: DVD-Video

Output Advanced Settings...

Disc burner

Drive: <H:> PIONEER DVD-RW DVR-104 1.3...   About...

    <H:> PIONEER DVD-RW DVR-104 1.30 (Ulead)
    <I:> YAMAHA CRW2200E 1.0D (Ulead)
    <I:> YAMAHA CRW2200E (NTI)

Recording speed:

Copies:

Burner Advanced Settings...

Required/Available hard drive space: 839.3 MB / 9.4 GB

Required/Available disc space: 278.0 MB / 0 bytes

Burning progress:

0%

Erase Disc   Output

<Back   Close   Help

---

4 Besides recording to disc in the Finish step, we want a disc image that we can reuse and some folders on our hard drive for DVD replays. You make all these selections under **Output Settings**. Note the location of the folders.

5 For this run, let's burn a mini DVD (this is the DVD format burned to CD). Select the NTI driver for your CD-RW drive.

6 Put a blank CD-R disc into the drive and click **Output**.

End

TIP
By saving a disc image, you can burn another copy of this project to a DVD, to play on a commercial player, from the Copy Disc area of DVD MovieFactory.

HINT
A mini DVD is on a regular CD-R (or RW) disc and will play only on DVD-ROM drives in computers.

Beginning a Promotional DVD

Start

1 Open a new DVD project. Then click **Next**.

2 To capture the video footage using FireWire, click **Capture**.

3 Click **Play** to play the source video.

4 Click **Capture Video** to begin the capture.

Now that we've worked with DVD, we can put together a business presentation with MovieFactory 2.0. This is an interactive promotional video project for a medical professional who does public speaking and needs to present images of blood types to his audience.

TIP

For a business DVD, dubbing to DV/FireWire is a great option to get the best possible quality. The first segment should be a nicely scripted introduction that tells the audience what the video is about.

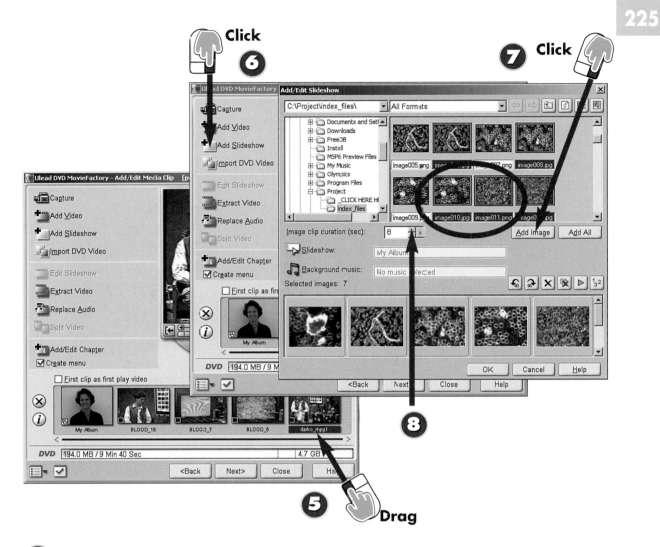

Click 6

Click 7

8

5 **Drag**

5 Drag and drop to assemble and organize your video clips.

6 Click **Add Slideshow** to use a slideshow for still images.

7 Select your images and click **Add Image** to add them to your show.

8 Set duration for the image slides and drag and drop to rearrange them.

See next page

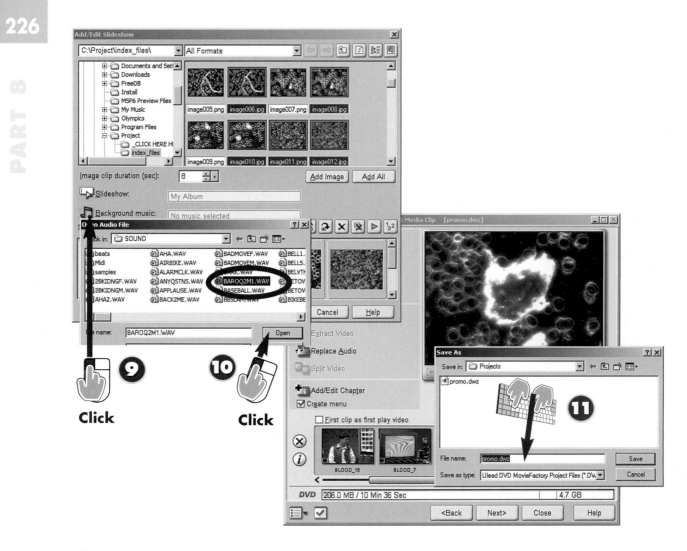

9 To add music to the slideshow, click **Background Music**.

10 Select a music file and click **Open**.

11 Save the project in an appropriate folder.

End

Creating the Promo DVD Interface

Start

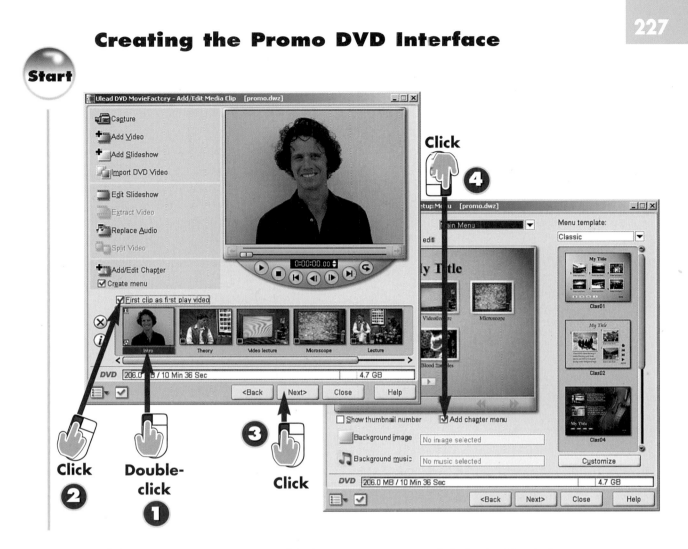

Click ④

Click ②

Double-click ①

Click ③

① To aid the menu creation step and help us stay organized. let's double-click to rename our clips.

② Click to set the introductory video for First Play.

③ Click **Next** to go to the Setup screen for menu creation.

④ Renaming the clips was a great idea—now we have captions under every segment automatically! We can also uncheck **Add Chapter Menu** because there are none.

 See next page

INTRODUCTION

Now we need to think about how to present the material. Although we could divide the clips into chapters or extract portions, as we did for the travelogue, for a promotional video, one simple main menu will be ideal.

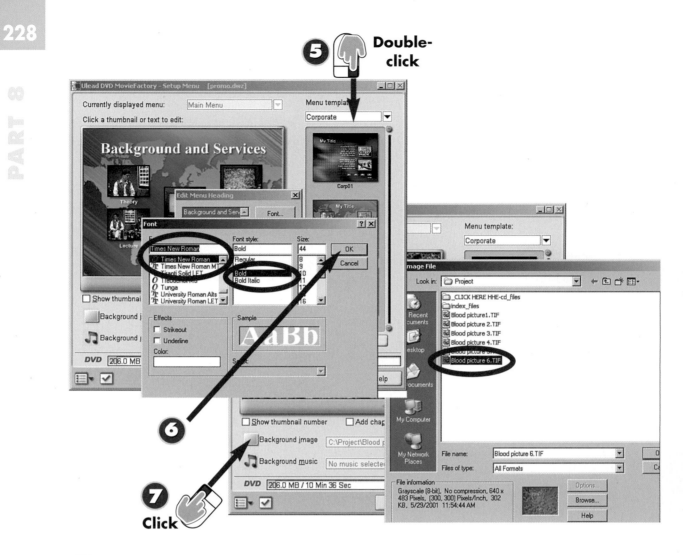

 5 Double-click in the **Template** gallery to apply a Corporate background.

 6 Change the font and title for the main menu.

 7 To set the tone, click **Background Image** to load an image from the slideshow as a full-screen background—showing blood cells!

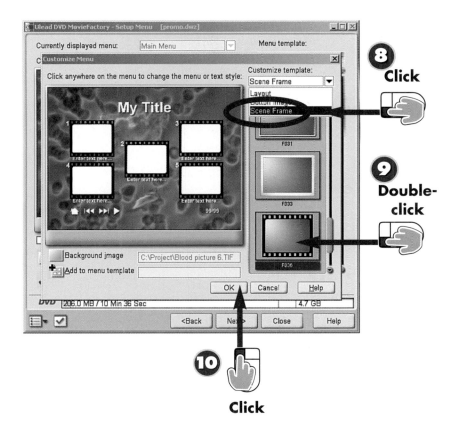

Click

Double-click

Click

8 Applying a more cinematic theme from the Layout panel is a nice final touch. Click to select the **Scene Frame** template.

9 Double-click to select the film template.

10 Click **OK** to apply your changes and continue.

End

TIP Click in the title placeholder and choose a more user-friendly title.

HINT To add our own narration to the slideshow, we can record our own WAV audio files. We'll learn how in Chapter 9, "Tips and Techniques."

Completing a Promotional DVD

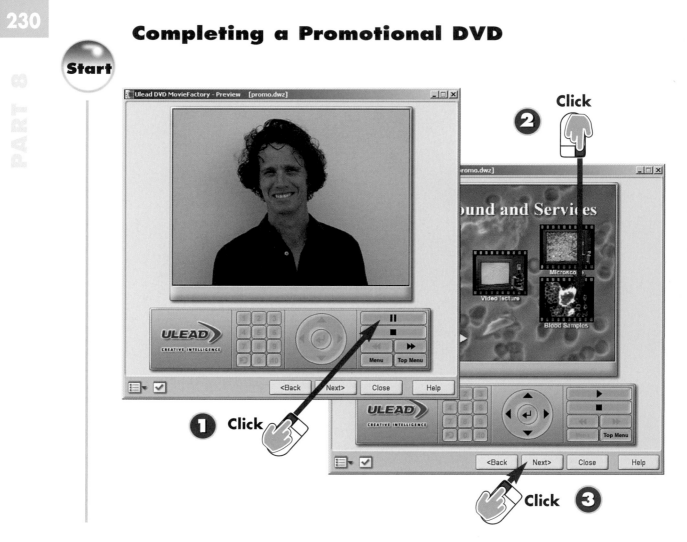

1. Click to play the opening segment to check that it's not too long and to be sure it's interesting enough to involve the viewer. Click **Pause** to stop playback for a moment.

2. Check all the segments to see playback...

3. Click **Next** to go to the Recording panel.

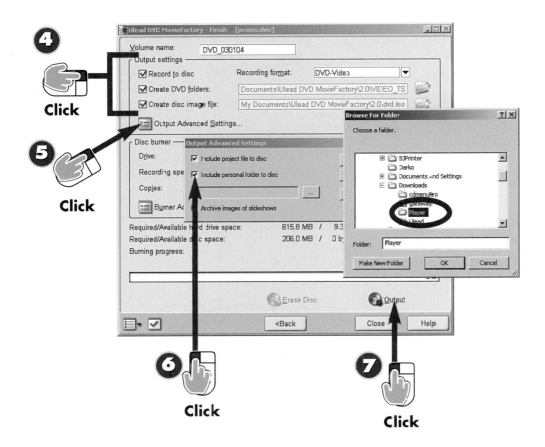

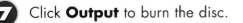

4 Select the **Output Settings** to record to disc and save files to our hard drive.

5 Click **Output Advanced Settings**.

6 Click to add a personal folder and include a DVD Player program that the user can install, if necessary.

7 Click **Output** to burn the disc.

End

TIP
If you want to expand the user base to viewers without DVD drives, you could create and burn this as a VCD—and use CD-R discs.

HINT
In the personal folder, you could include free players for DVD or VCD formatted discs that you can download from the Web. (These players can be found on Download.com, Cnet.com, and ZDNet.com.)

Beginning a Family History VCD

Start

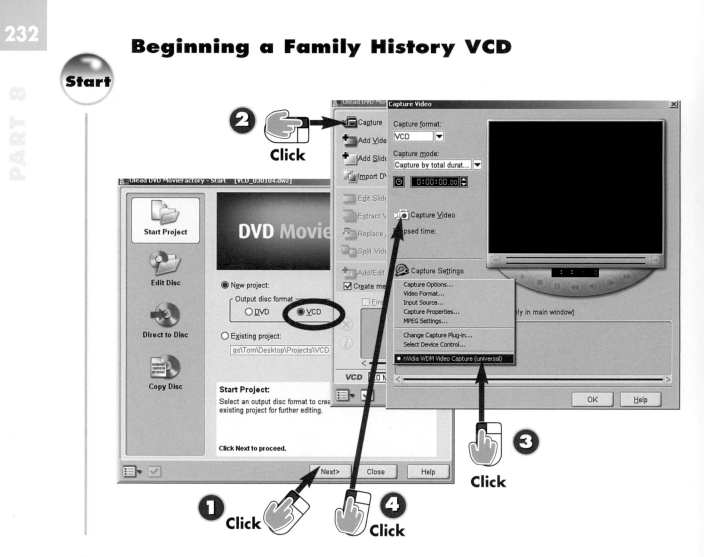

② **Click**

① **Click**

③ **Click**

④ **Click**

① Open a new VCD project. Then click **Next**.

② Click **Capture** to open the Capture Video screen.

③ Click **Capture Settings** to check your analog capture driver. Notice that device control is inactive.

④ To capture your video footage, play your source video and click **Capture Video**.

The VCD option also applies in a family history project, because some family members might not have DVD drives. In addition, it is very likely that some of the source video will be on VHS tape, which you want to preserve digitally. Because VCD is VHS quality, it is an ideal choice for a family history project captured from an analog source.

 TIP

For a family VCD, your source video may be on older VHS tape. You would either use an analog capture device, or dub the video to a DV camcorder.

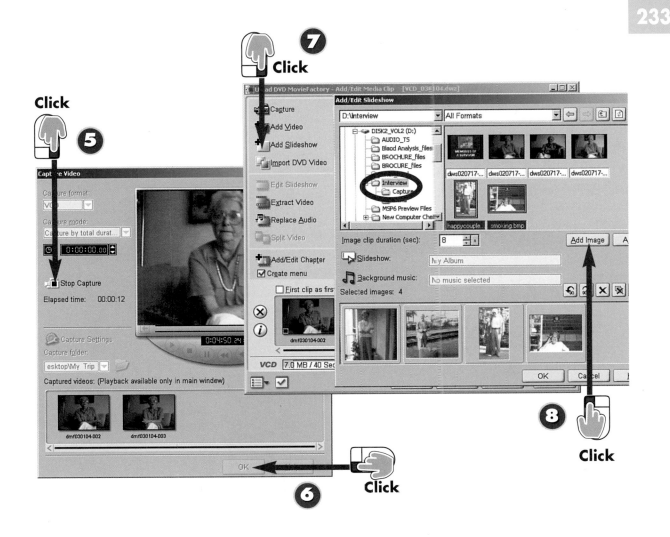

5 With your video captured, click **Stop Capture**.

6 Click **OK** to continue.

7 Click **Add Slideshow** for still images. Find the folder with the images and select the ones you want.

8 Click **Add Image** for each image you want to add.

See next page

 To add your still images, you might need a scanner to import old photographs; some video capture devices also will grab single frames from your video.

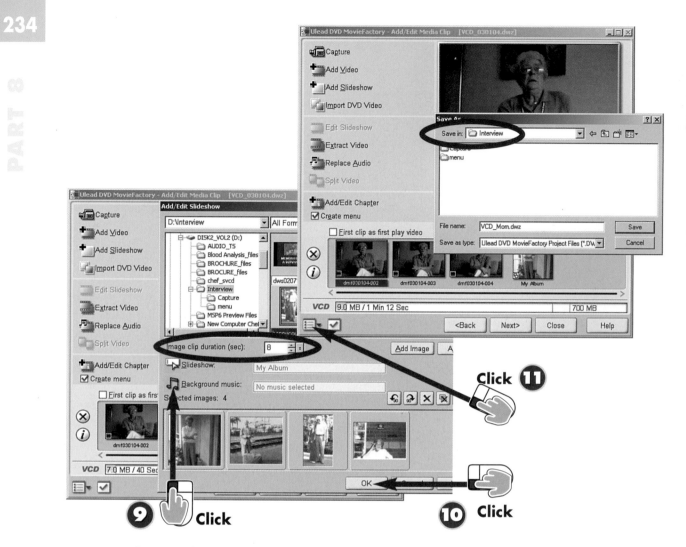

9 Set duration for the image slides, drag and drop to rearrange them, and add background audio as you did with the DVD.

10 Click **OK** to continue.

11 Save the VCD family history project in an appropriate folder.

End

HINT

Remember that if your capture device is analog, the controls under the Preview window won't be active in the Capture window, only during playback.

Creating the Family History Interface

Start

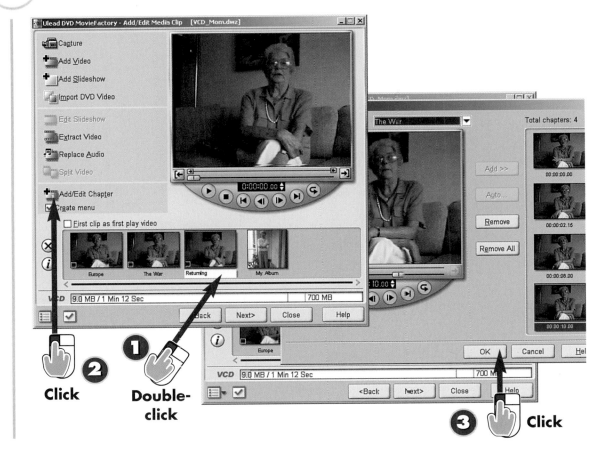

Click

Double-click

Click

1 To aid the menu creation step, let's rename our clips by double-clicking in the **Name** panel.

2 To add some chapters to a longer clip, click **Add/Edit Chapter**.

3 Play the footage, and add the frames that begin important stories. Then click **OK**.

See next page

INTRODUCTION

For a family history video, we might want to create some chapters to find specific stories. But first, let's get organized.

TIP

When you add chapters, you should probably take notes on which frames begin which tales so that you can put captions into your menu.

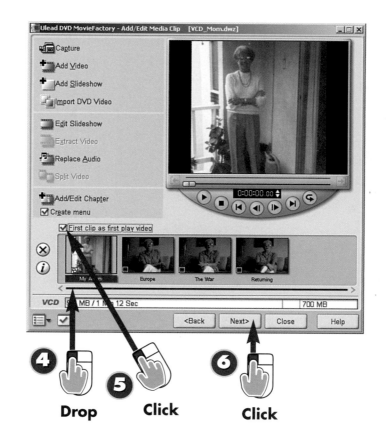

Drop   **Click**   **Click**

4 Drag and drop the photo album to the first slot.

5 Click to set the first clip for First Play.

6 Click **Next** to go to the Setup screen for menu creation.

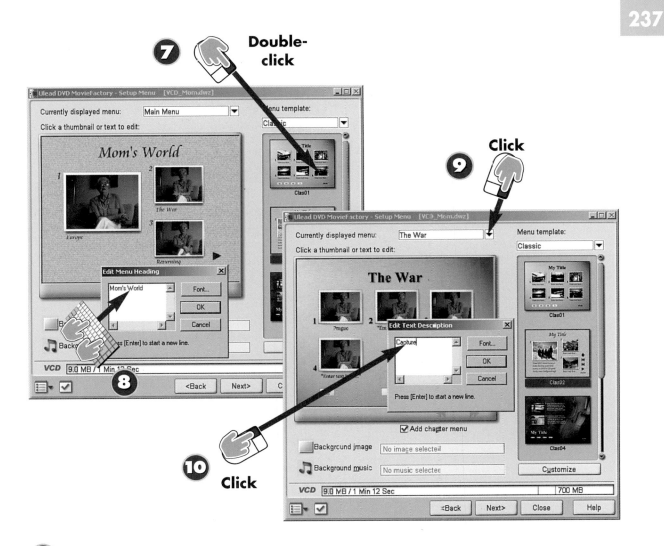

7 Double-click in the **Template** gallery to apply a **Classic** background.

8 Change the font and title for the main menu.

9 Select the video segment within which you've created chapters for a chapter menu.

10 Click to add a title and captions to the individual segments

End

Completing a Family History VCD

Start

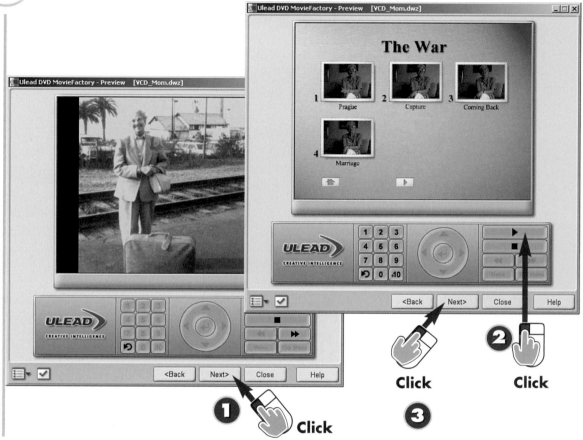

1 Click

2 Click

3 Click

---

1 Continue by clicking **Next** to access the remote controller in the Preview step.

2 The Main Menu of the VCD has numbers, and the keypad is now active. Clicking the number of the chapter video brings up the submenu, which also has automatic numbers. You can select clips and click **Play** to preview them.

3 Click **Next** to go to the Recording panel.

Now it's just a matter of previewing and burning the video project. We want to watch the opening photos. We can always click **Back** to change the slideshow by adding photos or music.

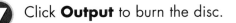

4 In Output Settings, click to record to disc and save files to the hard drive.

5 Click to open the Output Advanced Settings window.

6 Click to add a personal folder, and include a VCD Player program that the user can install, if necessary.

7 Click **Output** to burn the disc.

End

TIP
In the personal folder, you can include a free player that you can download from the Web for VCD format discs. (These players can be found on Download.com, Cnet.com, and ZDNet.com.)

HINT
A great way to make a DVD family history if you have a DVD recorder and one source tape is to use Direct to Disc with a DVD-RW or DVD+RW disc.

Tips and Techniques

Now that we've covered the two programs for CD burning and one program for creating DVDs, let's take a step back and think about some concepts and procedures that can help us work "smarter, not harder" in all these applications.

For example, one of the projects we did with the CD-burning programs was backing up our data files, and we saw how important it is to know which files to back up.

Well, what about our DVD projects? In the travelogue project in the previous chapter, I suggested creating a folder on your desktop for your captured movie files. This has advantages and disadvantages. The disadvantage is that when you reopen MovieFactory and want to locate the project, you will need to remember where you saved it to reopen it.

But the advantage is that if it's an important project, it makes it a breeze to safeguard and back up all your assets. With a CD or DVD recorder, for example, you would just burn the My_Trip folder on your desktop. If something happened, you could restore the project file and the captured video files, along with any other assets.

Let's examine the desktop folder strategy more closely, along with some other tips and techniques.

Using Windows Media Player to Manage Music Playlists

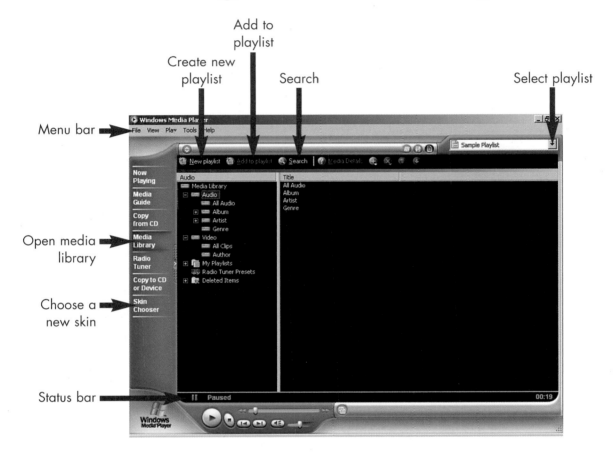

Add to playlist

Create new playlist

Search

Select playlist

Menu bar

Open media library

Choose a new skin

Status bar

Managing Your DVD Projects

Start

1 Open the My_Trip project folder and click to change the view to **Details**.

2 Drag the slider (if necessary) and find the project file. Note some of the image files that went into the slideshow.

3 VIDEO_TS and AUDIO_TS are the saved video and audio folders that can be played with a software DVD player.

4 Restarting the travelogue project is just a matter of browsing to the desktop folder when you open MovieFactory.

End

INTRODUCTION

Along the way, we've stressed the importance of Location, Location, Location—knowing where your files and projects have been saved. If you followed the travelogue project in the previous chapter, we created a folder called My_Trip on the desktop. Let's examine the contents of that folder.

TIP

The desktop folder can also hold scanned images or downloaded shots from a digital camera and any documents or spreadsheets that have to do with the project.

HINT

In some software players, the VIDEO_TS and AUDIO_TS folders need to be in a root directory of a drive. Just move them to the C: drive or another hard drive.

Start

1 Use the **Start** button, **All Programs**, and **Accessories**, **Entertainment** (or a shortcut) to open Windows Media Player.

2 To create a playlist, click **Media Library**.

3 Click **New Playlist**.

See
next
page

INTRODUCTION

When we used both CD Creator and Nero to create audio files in folders that contained collections, we noticed that we could use either of these programs to play one or more albums or tracks. But probably the best way to do this is to create Play Lists in Windows Media Player.

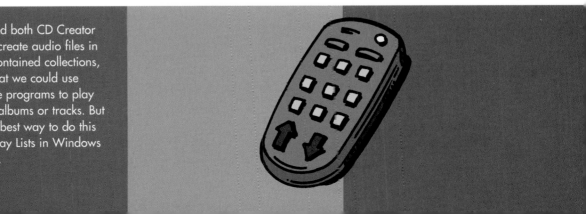

Click

Click

④ Give the playlist a name and click **OK**.

⑤ Click to select the new playlist in Media Player, and then open the **My Music** folder to the location of the files you want to add.

⑥ From the main My Music folder or subfolders (Classical), select and then drag and drop your files into the new playlist.

TIP Now you'll see the value of having your albums organized as WAV or MP3 audio files. You may have to click and resize both Media Player and Windows Explorer to see both windows. To see filenames instead of icons in the folder, click **View**, **Details**.

HINT Your playlist need not be audio files—you can use the source of trimmed MPG or AVI video files from MovieFactory individually or as playlists.

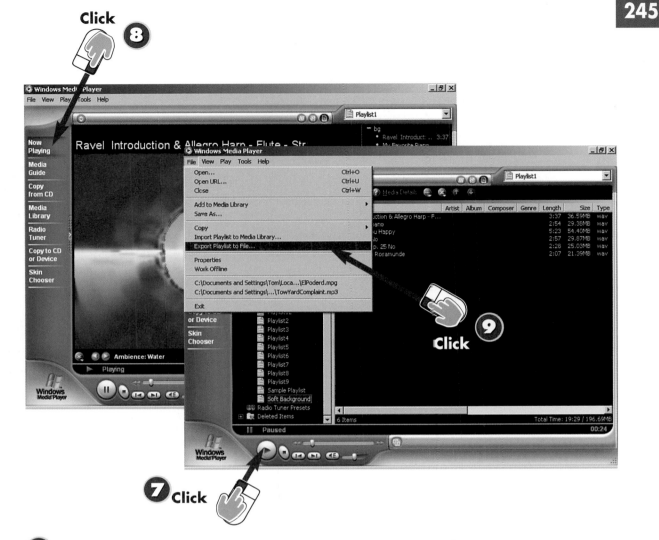

Click **8**

Click **9**

7 Click

7 Select the top (or any song) and click **Play** to hear the cuts from that point on.

8 Click **Now Playing** to view the Skins.

9 Click **File, Export Playlist to File** to create a text file with your selections that you can reuse or import. (Name and save the file as a text file.)

End

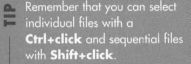

TIP
Remember that you can select individual files with a **Ctrl+click** and sequential files with **Shift+click**.

HINT
You can open Media Player to your playlist instantly by double-clicking the icon for an exported playlist file.

Adding Narration to Your DVD Project

Start

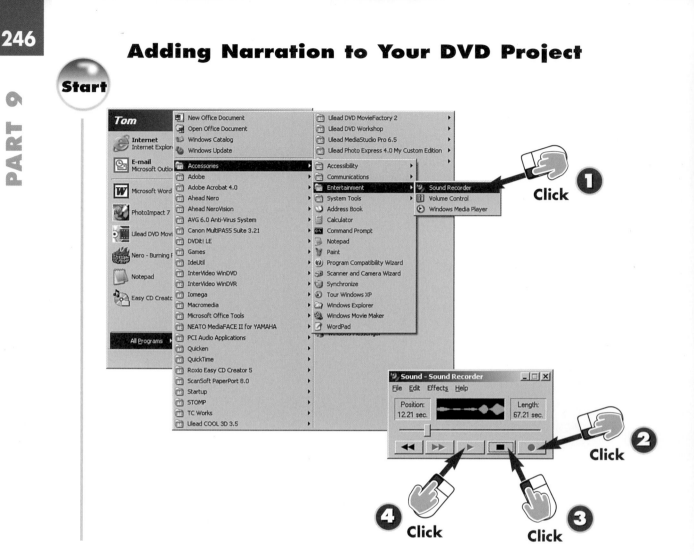

Click ❶

Click ❷

Click ❸

Click ❹

❶ Click to find the Windows Sound Recorder under **All Programs**, **Accessories**, **Entertainment**.

❷ Click the red **Record** button and speak into the microphone to record your voice. (This button is grayed out while recording.)

❸ When you're done, click **Stop** to stop recording.

❹ Click the **Play** button to preview how the clip sounds.

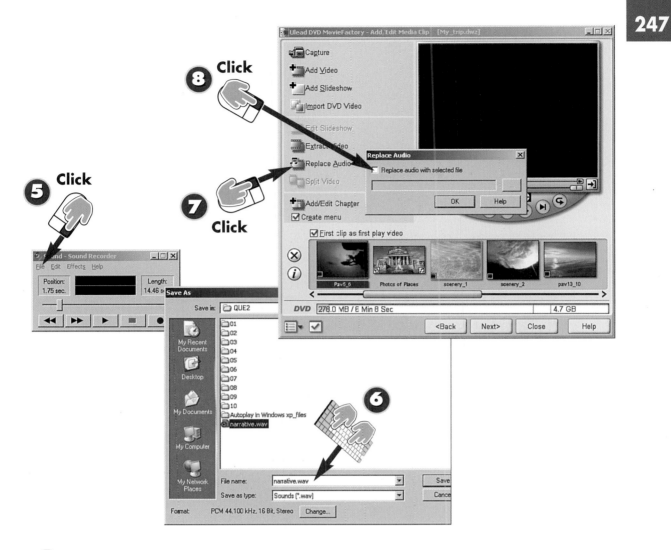

Click ⑤

Click ⑦

Click ⑧

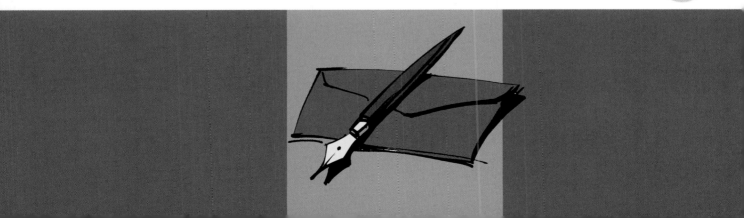

⑤ Click **File** to view your options.

⑥ Click to save the clip as a WAV audio file to a folder you designate.

⑦ To use the file in MovieFactory 2.0, click the video whose audio you want to change, and then click the **Replace Audio** button.

⑧ In the dialog box, click the **Replace Audio with Selected File** check box.

See next page

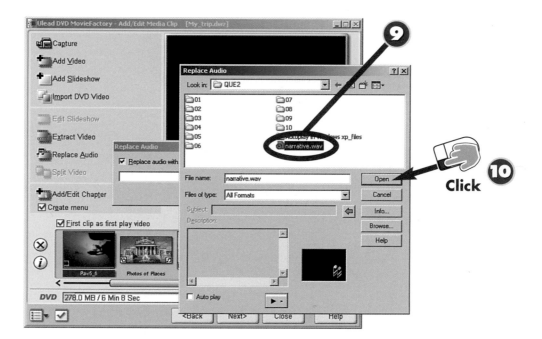

 Locate and select the file you just saved in Sound Recorder.

 Click **Open**.

End

TIP
As you work in Sound Recorder, everything you record is appended to what you recorded before, unless you click **File**, **New**. If you mess up, start a new file before recording again. If you succeed, save the good file and start a new file before continuing with a new clip.

HINT
If your microphone is not active in Sound Recorder, right-click the **Speaker** icon in the taskbar, then select **Options** and **Properties** to get to the Recording Options panel in Windows. Be sure the microphone is clicked as **Active** and the volume is up high.

1 In your Finish step, click **Create DVD Folders**.

2 Click the folder icon to change the location of the files.

3 Click to choose a root directory of a drive—C: or D: for example—and click **OK**. When the conversion is complete, use **My Computer** to see the actual folders that are created. They are called VIDEO_TS and AUDIO_TS.

See
next
page

INTRODUCTION
In your Finish step in DVD MovieFactory 2.0, you have an option in the Output Settings section of the dialog box—Create DVD Folders. Using this option creates a set of files that you can play in most software DVD players.

TIP
Common DVD players are WinDVD or PowerDVD. By default, they will generally open a DVD in your DVD-ROM or DVD-recordable drive.

HINT
Notice that if you open the VIDEO_TS folder, you have some rather large, cryptic files. Although they are video files, they are not standard PC video files.

 Click **5**

Click **6**

Click **4**

4 In WinDVD (or your computer DVD player), click **Toolkit**, **Properties** and change the default drive to the one where you saved your DVD folders.

5 Click **Apply** and **OK**.

6 Click **Play** on the software player to watch your project.

End

TIP If you saved your VIDEO_TS and AUDIO_TS folders to your project folders, just move or copy them to a root folder of a hard drive, if necessary.

HINT Burning the VIDEO_TS and AUDIO_TS folders generally won't result in a DVD that is playable on a standalone (commercial) drive. The possible exception is using the DVD movie disc setting in Nero-Burning ROM.

Using 3D Animation in Your Project

Start

Click

2

1

3 **Click**

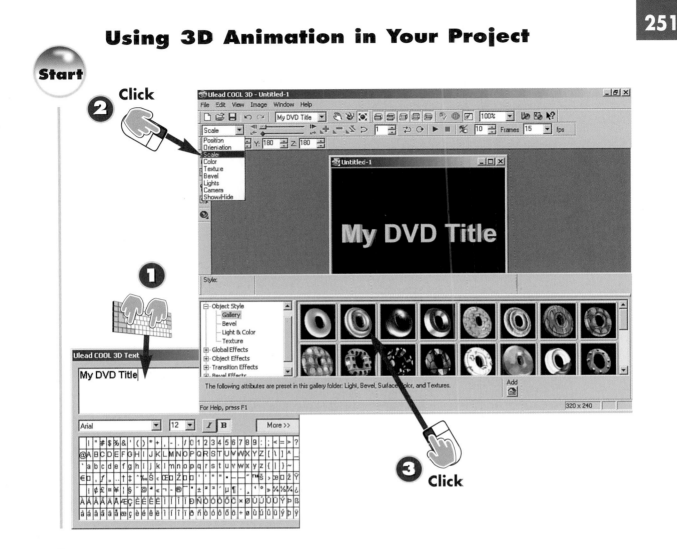

1 Cool 3D makes it easy to insert text—the dialog box welcomes you to the program.

2 By selecting a parameter such as **Scale** or **Position** on the animation toolbar, you can quickly change the text's look.

3 By applying textures and bevels (edges) from the Easy Palette, you can quickly transform the text.

See
next
page

INTRODUCTION

Because we've been working with Ulead products, let's quickly look at Ulead Cool 3D. It's a tool that you can purchase cheaply from the Ulead Web site. Probably one of the neatest things you can do with Cool 3D is an animated logo or title sequence. Here's a "quick and dirty" example.

TIP

Choosing the right resolution and compression can help you later. If you have the patience and the disc space, render your animation at full screen for DVD (720×480) and uncompressed video; that way, DVD MovieFactory 2.0 will convert it without having to recompress it.

HINT

At 30 frames per second, a 5-second animation would be 150 frames.

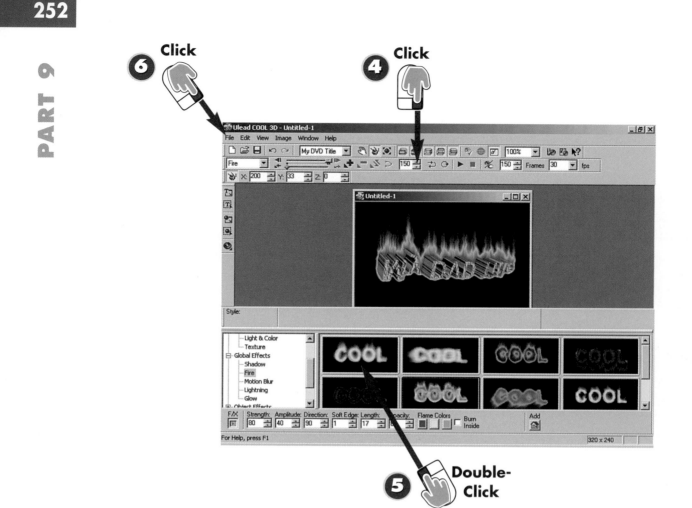

4 By changing the position of the text at key frames over time, you can quickly create an animation.

5 Double-click to add an effect—while your logo is twirling, it can just as easily be flaming.

6 Finally, click **File**, **Export** to export your animation (or render it) as a file (AVI) that DVD MovieFactory accepts.

Click 7

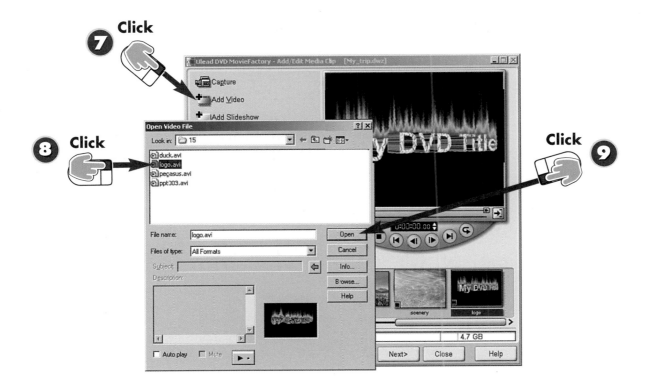

Click 8

Click 9

7 Use the **Add Video** button in MovieFactory to put the special effect into your project.

8 Click to select the file you exported from Cool 3D.

9 Click **Open** to finish.

End

TIP You also apply effects in Cool 3D by double-clicking them from the **Easy Palette**.

HINT You can also add a soundtrack in DVD MovieFactory with **Replace Audio**.

Using Business Graphics in Your Project

Click ①

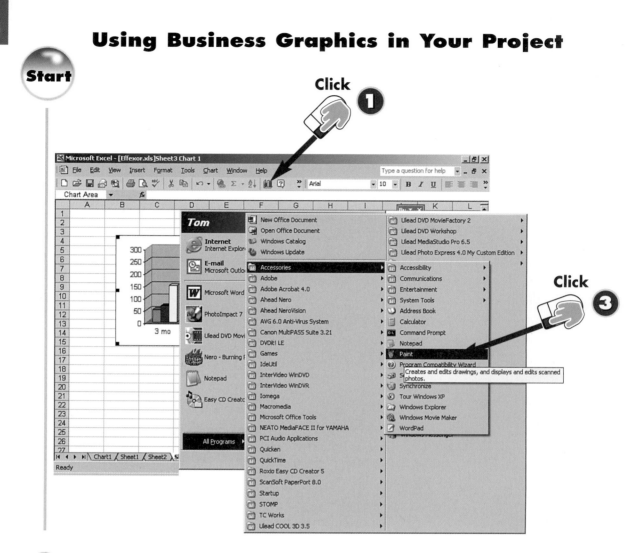

Click ③

① Open Excel and insert a chart using the Chart Wizard.

② With the chart displayed the way you like, press the **Prntscn** key on your keyboard.

③ Click **Start**, **All Programs**, **Accessories**, **Paint** to open the Windows Paint program.

INTRODUCTION

There are a number of ways to export your business graphics as MovieFactory-friendly files. If they are JPG, TIF, or BMP files, you can use them in a slideshow. But what if exporting proves too difficult? Let's use screen capture on an Excel chart.

TIP

MS Paint is the simplest graphics program you can use. In other popular programs (PhotoImpact from Ulead, Paint Shop Pro 8, PhotoDeluxe, or Photoshop from Adobe), you can sometimes crop the image and change its screen size.

HINT

Instead of creating a new slideshow, you can also edit an existing show and import the image.

Click ④

Click ⑤

⑥ **Click**

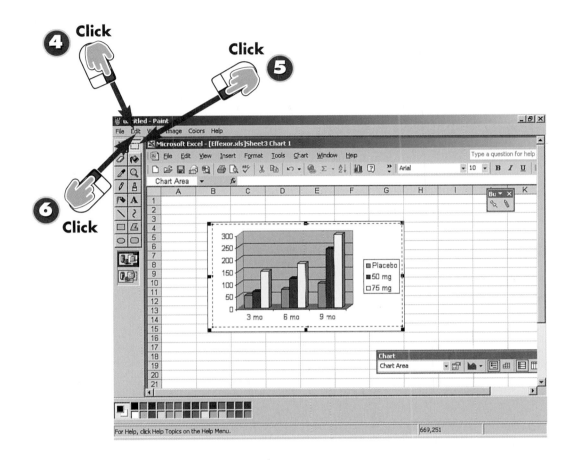

④ Click **Edit**, **Paste (Ctrl+V)** to put the screen capture of the chart into MS Paint.

⑤ Use the **Selection** tool to select just the chart by dragging a box around it.

⑥ Click **Ctrl+C** or **Edit**, **Copy** to copy the chart to the Clipboard.

See next page

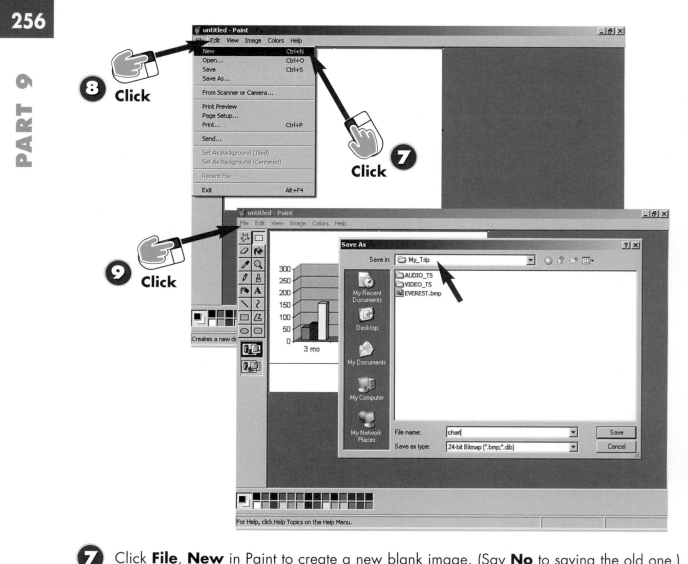

7 Click **File**, **New** in Paint to create a new blank image. (Say **No** to saving the old one.)

8 Click **Edit**, **Paste** to paste the chart into the new image.

9 Click **File**, **Save As** to save the new file as a BMP file in a folder you'll remember.

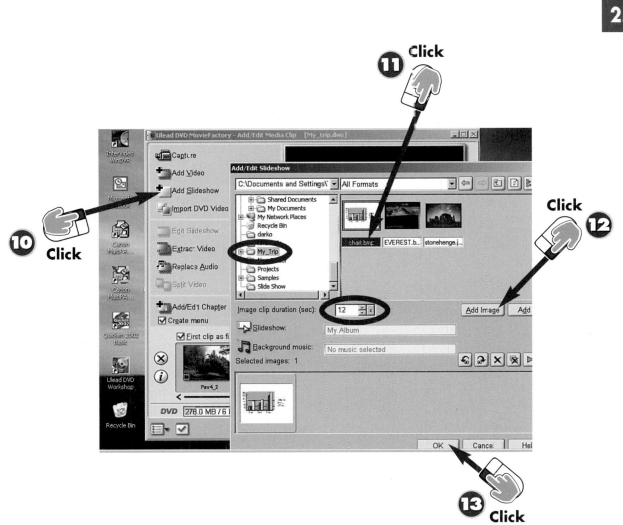

Click (11)

Click

Click (12)

(10) **Click**

(13) **Click**

(10) Click **Add Slideshow** to create a slideshow in MovieFactory.

(11) Select the image from the folder you saved it to.

(12) Click **Add Image** to add it to your slide show; don't forget to set a longer duration for the image to sink in.

(13) Click **OK** to continue.

End

TIP You can use the slideshow as a title in MovieFactory.

TIP Click the **All Formats** drop-down arrow in Slideshow to see the many image formats that it accepts.

Fine-Tuning Your System

Start

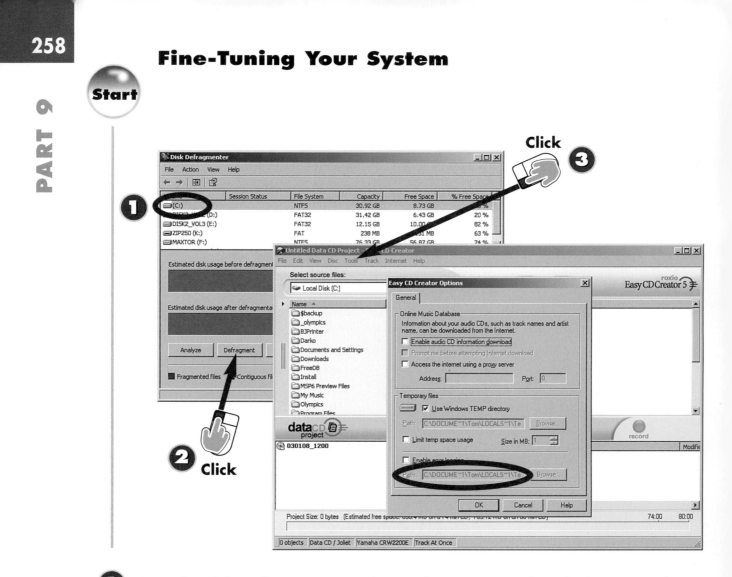

Click ❸

①

② **Click**

1 Open the **Disk Defragmenter** in the Windows System Tools and select your **C** drive.

2 Click **Defragment**.

3 In **CD Creator**, click **Tools**, **Options** to bring up the Preferences window. Note the location of your Temp folder. In **Nero**, click **File**, **Preferences**, and then click **Cache** to locate the Temp folder.

INTRODUCTION

CD recording software has really improved, and with buffer under-run protection now a common feature, burning errors are not as common as they once were. But there are still ways to keep your system in top shape.

TIP

If you use a secondary hard drive, be sure you defragment it regularly as well.

HINT

You can change the location of the temporary directory to make it more accessible, or fine-tune CD Creator in the Options panel.

4 Type the location of your temp folder into your folder or browser.

5 Select the files you'd like to delete.

6 Press the **Delete** key.

See next page

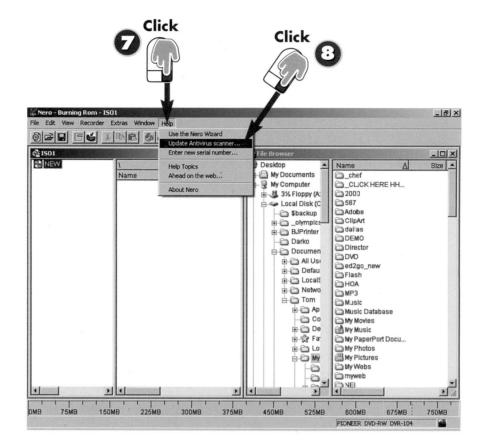

7 Keep your antivirus program up to date. You can use the Nero antivirus prior to burning, or run one regularly to check all your files. In Nero, you can update its virus scanner by clicking **Help**.

8 Make sure you're online, and select **Update Antivirus Scanner**.

End

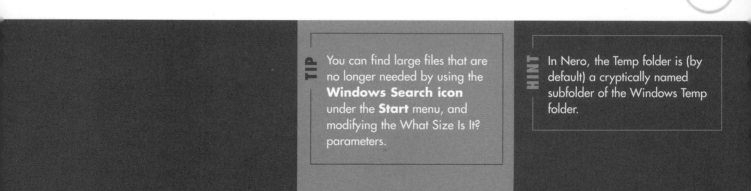

Making an Autoplay CD

Start

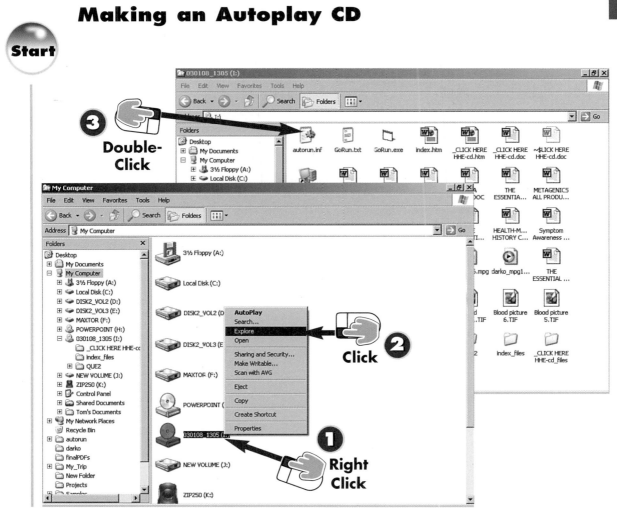

3 Double-Click

2 Click

1 Right Click

1 Open any Autoplay disc to its root folder by right-clicking the disc.

2 Click **Explore**.

3 Locate the **autorun.inf** file, and double-click it to open it in Windows Notepad.

 See next page

INTRODUCTION
You might want to set your project to open automatically when your disc is inserted. This requires a text file in the root directory named autorun.inf. In Windows XP, autorun.inf must access an *executable* file—namely, another program or application. Fortunately, we can download a file of this type from the Web.

TIP
Double-clicking the disc icon activates the Start program—typically, the installer for a software program.

HINT
To create your own autorun.inf file, write the text file and save it under this filename, but make sure you select **All Files**, not TXT under Files of Type.

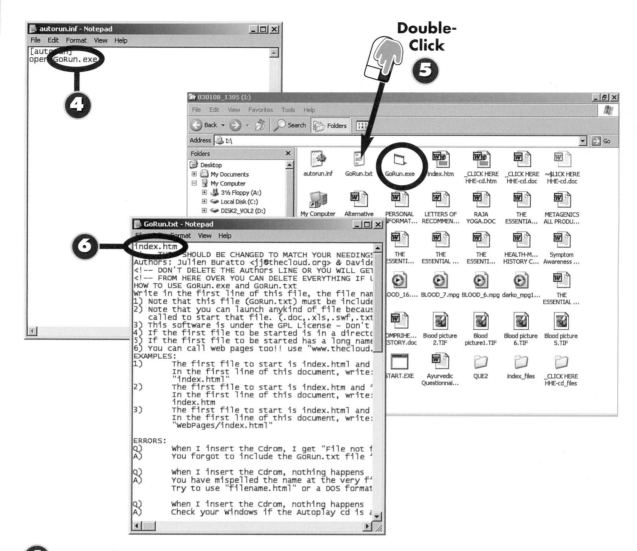

Double-Click **5**

4 Notice that it simply runs an executable program—in this case, GoRun.exe.

5 Back in the CD root folder, notice two other files: **GoRun.exe** (the executable) and **GoRun.txt**. Double-click the **GoRun.txt** file to open it in Notepad.

6 This file is referenced by GoRun.exe to open an htm file in the default browser.

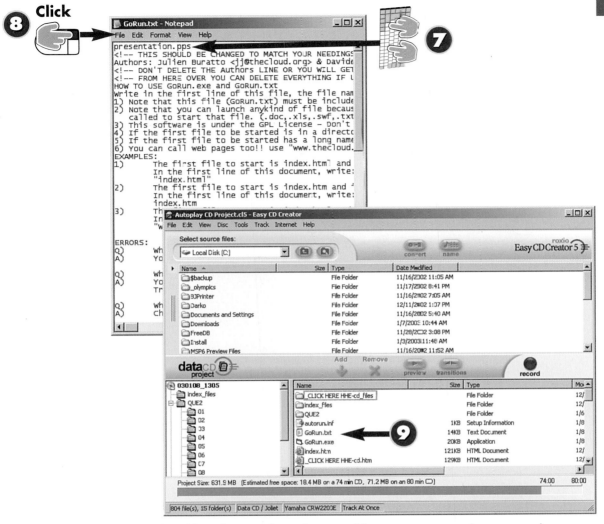

Click 8

7

9

---

7 To open up any other file, change the reference filename to any other name that you've burned to the disc. Type to replace index.htm with **presentation.pps**.

8 Now you can simply click to **Save** this TXT file as GoRun.txt into the same folder as the autorun.inf and GoRun.exe files. Click **File**, **Save**.

9 When you are ready to burn the disc, be sure your software has the four necessary files in the root folder of the CD compilation.

End

TIP
To get the files you need to create an Autorun CD like this, go to http://www.judaweb.com/devs/autorun.html.

TIP
If you did the CD-ROM project for the business presentation, this is the familiar index.htm. It opens automatically on insertion.

HINT
In this case, the file is a PowerPoint Show file. PowerPoint must be available on the destination machine for it to open, although it can be opened in Internet Explorer 5 or later.

Understanding Disc Recording Options

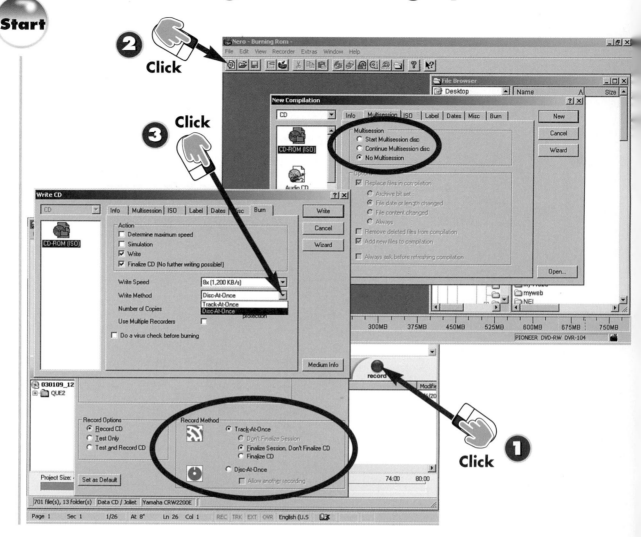

Start

2 **Click**

3 **Click**

Click **1**

 In CD Creator, **Track-at-Once** and **Disk-at-Once** are available after you click the red **Burn** button.

 In Nero, you set your Multisession option in the Multisession tab of a new compilation.

3 In Nero, you can alter the Disc-at-Once or Track-at-Once settings in the Burn tab of the Write CD dialog box.

End

There are two basic ways to burn digital media: Disc-at-Once and Track-at-Once. With Disc-at-Once, the whole disc is written in one pass without stopping the laser. This requires more hard drive space for a temporary disc image file but results in fewer errors. Always burn audio, video, and Super VideoCDs using Disc-at-Once. Use Track-at-Once for multisession discs.

TIP If you select Track-at-Once for an audio CD, it won't read in standard audio CD players.

HINT In Nero, you can still change your Multisession option in the Multisession tab in the Write CD dialog box.

Using Windows XP MovieMaker

Start

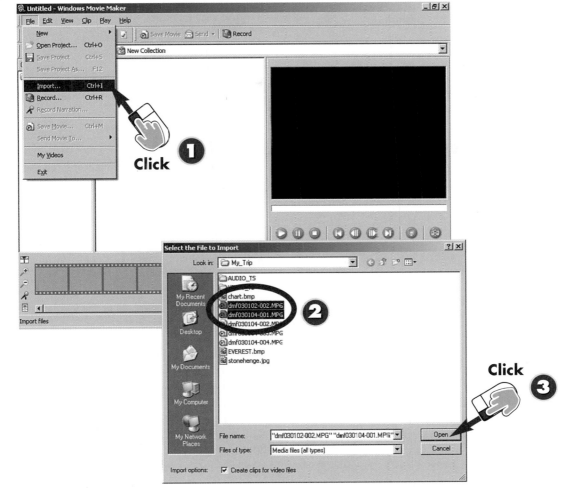

1 Open Windows MovieMaker and click **File**, **Import** to access your captured files.

2 Select one or more files.

3 Click **Open**.

See next page

INTRODUCTION

Although Ulead makes excellent video editing software programs (along with Adobe and others), anyone with Windows XP also has Windows MovieMaker. After you have captured some clips, you can recombine them and edit them in MovieMaker to burn to CD or add to DVD MovieFactory's Title List.

TIP

You can also capture directly into Microsoft MovieMaker, but to ensure the right file quality for DVD, VCD, and SVCD, choosing the project and capturing into MovieFactory 2.0 is probably a better idea.

HINT

The first version of MovieMaker has no special effects, but a much more robust version of MovieMaker with effects and more options is now available for free as a download at Microsoft.com.

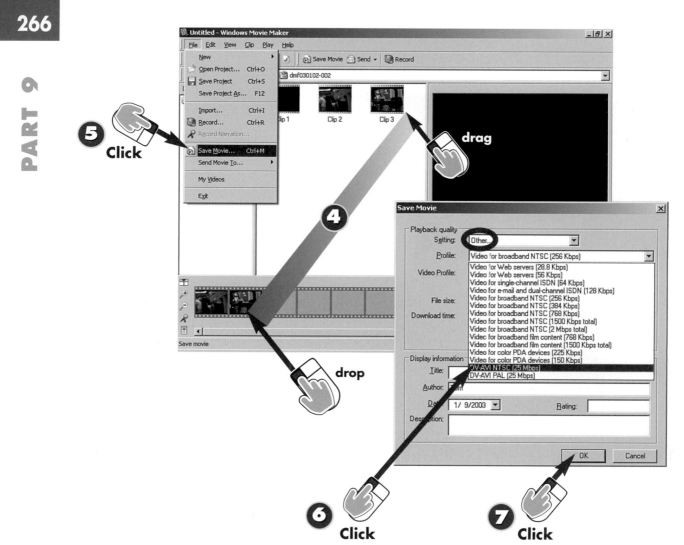

4 You can drag and drop your clips to create a new storyboard; you also can play to preview them, or split a clip in two parts.

5 When you're satisfied with the storyboard, click **File**, **Save Movie**.

6 Click **Other** for Setting if you want DVD quality, and then select **DV-AVI NTSC**.

7 Click **OK**.

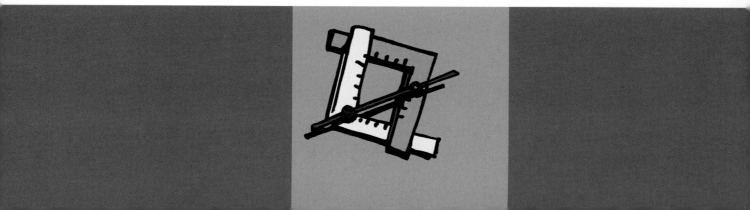

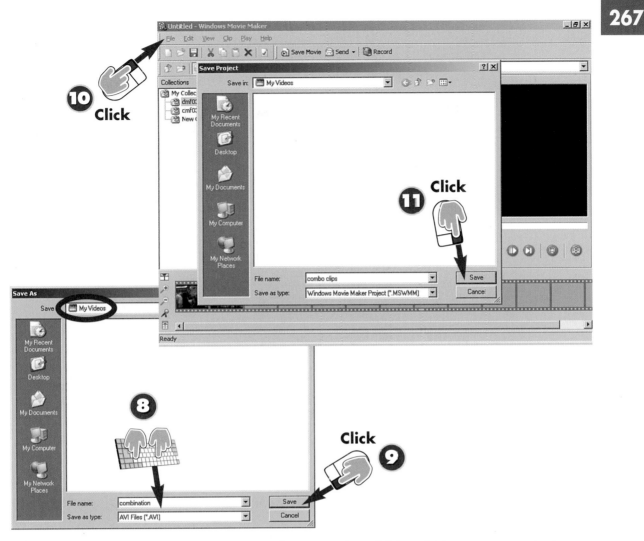

 By default, this file will be saved in the My Videos folder of My Documents (unless you change it). Name it **combination**.

 Click **Save**.

10 It will take a few minutes to render the file. Click **File** and save your project in the same folder.

11 Click **Save**.

 See next page

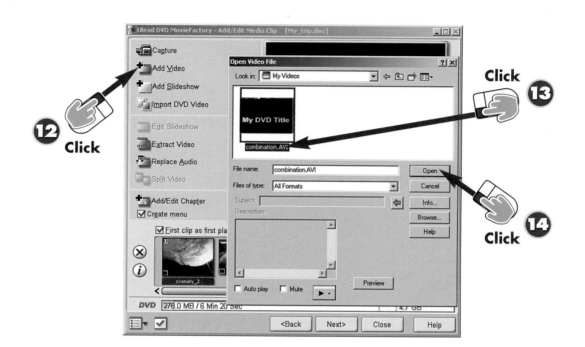

 Now you can click to add this new combination clip directly into a MovieFactory 2.0 project by clicking **Add Video**.

 Click to select **combination.avi**.

 Click **Open**. The added file joins the others in the Add/Edit Media Clip window.

End

TIP Don't confuse your movie files with the project file. Just as in MovieFactory, the project file saves your editing choices and clip library. Your movie files are separate.

HINT Be sure to choose the highest possible output options so that you don't degrade your video files before adding them to MovieFactory.

Reusing a Captured Clip in MovieFactory

See next page

Start

Click ➊

Click ➋

Right-Click ➌

Click ➍

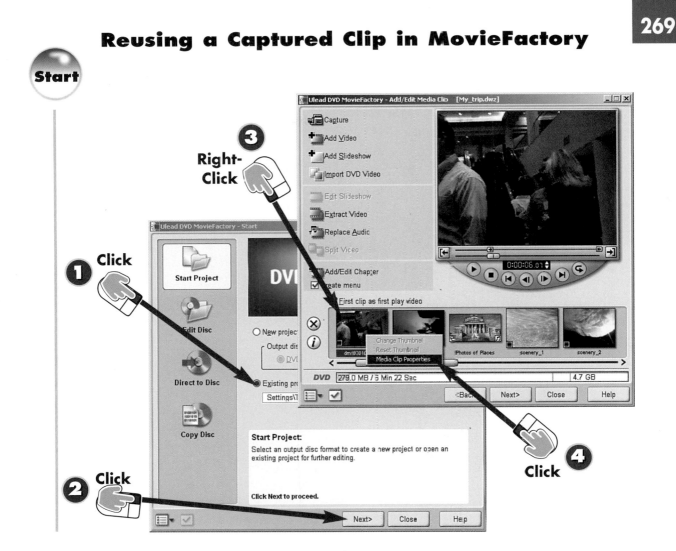

➊ Open **MovieFactory**, and click **Existing Project** to open your project.

➋ Click **Next** to continue.

➌ Right-click the file you have captured.

➍ Select **Media Clip Properties**.

INTRODUCTION

When we went through the MovieFactory steps, we learned how to extract portions of a captured clip and then split the clip. Another way to work with different portions of a single clip is to add it to the title list more than once.

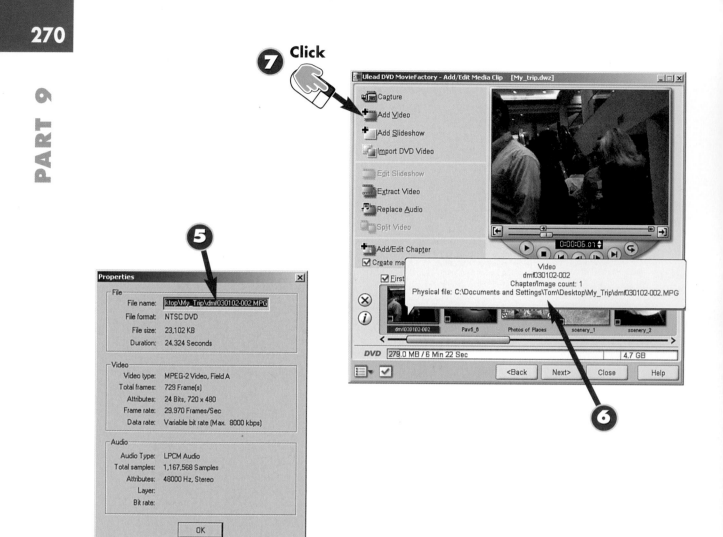

7 **Click**

5

6

5 Note the location of the clip on your hard drive.

6 You can also hover your mouse over the clip to find out where it's located.

7 Next, click **Add Video** and locate the clip.

Ulead DVD MovieFactory - Add/Edit Media Clip   [My_trip.dwz]

Capture

Add Video

Add Slideshow

Import DVD Vid

Edit Slideshow

Extract Video

Replace Audio

Split Video

Add/Edit Chapte

☑ Create menu

☑ First clip as

Open Video File

Look in: My_Trip

AUDIO_TS   dmf030104-004.MPG
VIDEO_TS
dmf030102-002.MPG
dmf030104-001.MPG
dmf030104-002.MPG
dmf030104-003.MPG

File name: dmf030102-002.MPG   Open

Files of type: All Formats   Cancel

Subject: Info...

Description: Browse...

Help

☐ Auto play   ☐ Mute   ▶

dmf030102-0

DVD 279.0 MB / 6 Min 22 Sec   4.7 GB

<Back   Next>   Close   Help

Click 8

Click 9

8 Click to select your clip.

9 Click **Open**. Now a second reference to that clip is available for you to trim differently in the title list.

End

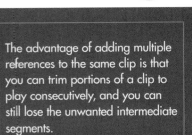

HINT

The advantage of adding multiple references to the same clip is that you can trim portions of a clip to play consecutively, and you can still lose the unwanted intermediate segments.

Index

E

F

Q – R

recovering deleted files (DirectCD), 35

remote controllers, 190, 193, 222

Remove button (Add/Edit Video window), 146

removing
DirectCD files (CD Creator), 36
video, 146
Video Strip thumbnails, 139

renaming video clips, 227, 235

reopening slideshows, 148

repairing DirectCD file structures (CD Creator), 35

replacing audio in video clips, 166-167, 247

resizing images (CD Creator)
case inserts, 56
disc labels, 56

restarting DVD projects, 242

restoring disc space (DirectCD), 36

reusing
audio CD tracks (Nero), 66
video captures in MovieFactory, 269-270

reviewing
capture device settings, 137
video project settings, 168-169

rewriteable DVDs, erasing (DirectCD), 36

ripping audio CD tracks to MP3s (CD Creator), 29-30

S

Save My Settings wizard, 120
saving
audio CD tracks (Nero), 69, 75
CDs to hard drives (CD Creator), 9
customized menus, 185

DVD projects in Windows MovieMaker, 267
Firewire/DV video captures, 143
narration for DVD projects (Windows Sound Recorder), 247

ScanDisc utility (DirectCD), 35

security
antivirus programs, updating, 260
virus scanners, updating, 260

Select Destination CD icon (SoundStream), 11

selecting
audio CD tracks (Nero), 63
desktop files in File Browser (Project Selector), 123
DVD quality in Windows MovieMaker, 266
files (Nero), 62
music database pop-up windows (Nero), 72
Output Disc Formats, 136
slideshow background music, 215
source CDs in CD Copy (Nero), 88
track file formats, 75
video capture drives, 137
video capture folders, 137

Set Mark-In button (DVD MovieFactory), 157

Set Mark-Out button (DVD MovieFactory), 158

setting
Firewire/DV video capture durations, 142
slideshow image clip duration, 214
transition durations (CD Creator), 27
video chapter points, 165
video edit points, 157-158

settings
capture device settings, reviewing, 137
Office (MS) settings backups, 120-121

Setup menu (Add/Edit Video window), 172-173